PRODUCING COUNTRY

Music:Interview

A SERIES FROM WESLEYAN UNIVERSITY PRESS
Edited by Daniel Cavicchi

Yip Harburg: Legendary Lyricist and Human Rights Activist
by Harriet Hyman Alonso

Reel History:
The Lost Archive of Juma Sultan and the Aboriginal Music Society
by Stephen Farina

Producing Country:
The Inside Story of the Great Recordings
by Michael Jarrett

Always in Trouble:
An Oral History of ESP-Disk,' the Most Outrageous Record Label in America
by Jason Weiss

The Music/Interview series features conversations with musicians, producers, and other significant figures in the world of music, past and present. The focus is on people who have not only made good music but also have insightful and profound things to say about creativity, politics, and culture. Each Music/Interview book presents an original approach to music-making, showing music as a vehicle for inspiration, identity, comment, and engagement. The interview format provides conversations between knowledgeable insiders. By foregrounding individual voices, the series gives readers the opportunity to better appreciate the sounds and music around us, through the voices of those who have experienced music most directly.

publication of this book is funded by the

BEATRICE FOX AUERBACH FOUNDATION FUND

at the Hartford Foundation for Public Giving

PRODUCING

MICHAEL JARRETT

COUNTRY

THE INSIDE STORY OF THE GREAT RECORDINGS

WESLEYAN UNIVERSITY PRESS

Middletown, Connecticut

WESLEYAN UNIVERSITY PRESS
Middletown CT 06459
www.wesleyan.edu/wespress
© 2014 by Michael Jarrett
Manufactured in the United States of America
Designed by Richard Hendel
Typeset in Chaparral, TheSerif and Champion
by Tseng Information Systems, Inc.

Wesleyan University Press is a member of the Green Press Initiative. The paper
used in this book meets their minimum requirement for recycled paper.

publication of this book is funded by the
Beatrice Fox Auerbach Foundation Fund
at the Hartford Foundation for Public Giving

Steve Cropper's comments on Otis Redding, "Dock of the Bay," first appeared
in Michael Jarrett, "Mystery and Manners: Steve Cropper and the Sound of Stax,"
The Fretboard Journal, 4 (Winter 2006): 44–59. Reprinted by permission. Portions of
Tom Dowd's comments on Dusty Springfield, *Dusty in Memphis*, and Willie Mitchell's
comments on Al Green appeared in Michael Jarrett, *Sound Tracks: A Musical ABC*,
Vols. 1–3, Philadelphia: Temple University Press, 1998. Reprinted by permission.
Portions of comments by several producers appeared in Michael Jarrett, "The Self-
Effacing Producer: Absence Summons Presence," in *The Art of Record Production: An
Introductory Reader for a New Academic Field*, eds. Simon Frith and Simon Zagorski-
Thomas, Burlington, VT: Ashgate Publishing, 2012, pp. 129–148. Reprinted by
permission.

Library of Congress Cataloging-in-Publication Data
Producing country : the inside story of the great recordings /
[interviews by] Michael Jarrett.
    pages cm. — (Music/interview)
ISBN 978-0-8195-7463-3 (cloth : alk. paper) — ISBN 978-0-8195-7464-0
(pbk. : alk. paper) — ISBN 978-0-8195-7465-7 (ebook)
1. Country music—Production and direction—History. 2. Sound recording
executives and producers—United States—Interviews. I. Jarrett, Michael,
1953–, interviewer.
ML3524.P76 2014
781.642′149—dc23   2013048875

5 4 3 2 1

For all y'all but, mostly, for Pamela

CONTENTS

INTERLUDE: STUDIO MATTERS

3. MULTITRACKING:
CONSTRUCTING THE PERFORMANCE, 1967–1991

**INTERLUDE: THE WRITER AS PRODUCER—
AN INTERVIEW WITH BOBBY BRADDOCK**

4. ENCODING TRACKS: COMPOSITING THE PERFORMANCE, 1992–PRESENT

Photographs follow pages 102 and 206.

ILLUSTRATIONS

ACKNOWLEDGMENTS

One of my iPods holds the fifty-something recorded interviews that, excerpted, compose this book. These interviews form an oral history of country record production that is actually oral—actually audible. I conducted all of them. I spoke with every single person featured in this book (spoke with all but one by telephone). I recorded and transcribed every word they said.

Consequently, I'm familiar with the voices of the people I interviewed. I hear them as I read the words of this book. And that is a singular pleasure. I enjoyed talking with every producer I interviewed. I am, however, realistic enough to understand that a few of the guys who match up with the voices I hear are master manipulators: they're powerful and, probably, ruthless; rich and, therefore, given respect for their rides on fortune's wheel; influential (the unacknowledged architects of our aesthetics); and famous, though nearly as often infamous. The others, for any number of admirable reasons, never gave a shit about creating any sort of legacy. Or to paraphrase Porter Wagoner, with them what was to be just never happened, and what wasn't to be, most of the time, did. Be that as it may, all of the voices I hear while reading evoke one simple and indelible impression: as a species, country producers are really, really nice. I owe them an enormous debt of gratitude, not only for making this book possible; they made it fun to make. I also owe a thank you to those record producers who never responded to my letters, emails, and phone messages. Without them, I never would have finished this project.

I first started writing about record producers twenty years ago when *Pulse!*, Tower Records' magazine, ran a feature I wrote on jazz guys. Marc Weidenbaum edited it. One day, he told me, "You're not just a contributing writer; you're our 'free-range chicken.'" (That was, far and away, the most flattering tag ever clipped to my collar.) Peter Melton gave me the go-ahead to write about producing country records. Instead of chopping up a long piece I wrote, he serialized it. Ned Hammad gave me more great assignments than I can now recollect. A phone call from Jackson Griffith was always a pleasure. From him, I learned to revere Nashville's great visionary artist—the Prophet Omega. And so I want to send out

ACKNOWLEDGMENTS

a loud thank you to the many people, now scattered, that I worked with at *Pulse!*—before the deluge. What skills I possess as a writer are largely attributable to the many opportunities they gave me. They indulged me, repeatedly. As an editor at *Pulse!* and at Amazon.com and, especially, as the publisher of *The Fretboard Journal*, Jason Verlinde gave me work that contributed to the making of this book. He gave me the chance to write about producer and legendary guitarist Steve Cropper.

I pitched the idea of an oral history of country-record production first to Parker Smathers at Wesleyan University Press. He was supportive from the get-go, as was Daniel Cavicchi, editor of the Music/Interview series. Lauren Seidman, Bronwyn Becker, Richard Hendel, and Leslie Starr turned my manuscript into a book, and they made every step of that process a joy. Other people helped me indirectly but significantly. A conversation with Robert Ray leaves me full of ideas and thoroughly energized. We spoke about possible structures for this book, and his suggestions moved me to clarity. Greg Seigworth is my best friend. We've talked about record production many, many times; it's difficult to assess the nature and depth of his contributions to most everything I write. The best stuff in this book is almost always the end result of good questions that he and a few other friends prompted me to formulate. Finally, I want to thank Pam for being in my life. She's not that big on Tammy Wynette or Merle Haggard, which is kinda-sorta okay, I suppose. She's crazy about Wynonna and the Dixie Chicks; I'm fine with that—to a degree. We both love Lucinda Williams, Shelby Lynne, and Buddy Miller. We both think Otis Redding is country, just like Carla Thomas said he was. And we both liked banana sandwiches long before we knew Elvis did too. "Ain't we got love?"

INTRODUCTION

Cowboy Jack Clement knew a thing or two about record production. He made the first recordings of Jerry Lee Lewis, while his boss, Sun Records' Sam Phillips, was away at a music-industry event. Here's something Clement told me:

> I was the guy in there running the board, but I was also in charge of the session, telling the musicians what to do. That made me a producer, but the word "producer" wasn't even extant at that time, as I recall. Sam would be doing the same things. But they didn't put producer credits on records at that time. I think RCA is the first one that did that with Chet Atkins. That's the first I ever heard of putting "produced by" on a record. That wasn't going on in 1956. I think that started happening in 1957 or '8, something like that.

We won't get a better clue for understanding early record production. Clement makes two points: first, there was record production before there were "record producers"; second, the term "record producer" refers to an awareness, a recognition of record production. On the one hand, there are the duties of production (the tasks). They've been around for a long time, ever since recordings were first marketed in the 1890s. On the other hand, there is the designation "producer" (the term).

Chet Atkins clarified the designation for me. He said his boss, Steve Sholes, head of RCA Victor's country-and-western division, was the one who "started listing personnel." He added, "That was his [Sholes's] doing. He wanted to put the producer. He wanted to list the engineer, too, on each single, but they wouldn't do it. The record company claimed there wasn't enough room on the record [label] to print all that stuff," but soon enough, most of "that stuff"—the recording credits—appeared on record sleeves and jackets. Who had brokered the 1955 deal that brought Elvis Presley to RCA Victor? Who was performing the tasks of production, even if he didn't hold the title of "producer"? Why, it was Steve Sholes. Atkins, again:

Steve used me on most everything he did. He'd call me and tell me to record a certain song with a certain artist. I just did it like he did it. I'd already been hiring the musicians for him. I was kind of his assistant for quite a while. So I'd imitate Steve. I owe everything to Steve.

To this comment add a series of events that answers why and, perhaps, how the title "producer"—and not "director"—came into general use. In August 1956, Presley headed out to Hollywood to work on his first movie, *Love Me Tender*. He'd already released his first album, *Elvis Presley* (March 1956). Its jacket listed no personnel, though anyone who cared to know would've understood Sholes's role in its making. He was the all-important head of A&R (artists and repertoire). Working with recording engineer Bob Ferris, Chet Atkins might have fulfilled duties that now look like production (e.g., he assembled the band), but Sholes was the executive tasked with making all of the big decisions. For example, at his first session for RCA (January 10, 1956), Presley recorded three songs he had routinely performed: "I Got a Woman," "Heartbreak Hotel," and "Money Honey." Sholes allowed Presley to record this familiar material, but he'd already planned a follow-up session for the very next night. At that session Presley sang two songs—"I'm Counting on You" and "I Was the One"—from a list created by Sholes. Significantly, both of these numbers were published by a subsidiary of Hill & Range, the firm that had helped underwrite the deal that brought Presley to RCA. From the five songs recorded during these two sessions, Sholes selected "Heartbreak Hotel" backed with "I Was the One" as the first single. To calculate the revenue the single generated, one has to enter the morass of RIAA certification. Suffice it to say, it vindicated Sholes's high-stakes wager. Immediately, the $35,000 RCA had paid for Presley's Sun contract—at that time the most money ever spent on a pop singer—seemed like a bargain. Notice, then, Sholes's tasks make him resemble a "producer" more than a "director" in the Hollywood sense of those titles.

Getting back to *Love Me Tender*, I want to speculate. In the movie Presley sings four songs written by Ken Darby, the film's "musical director." In *Elvis Presley: A Life in Music—The Complete Recording Sessions*, Ernst Jorgensen describes the soundtrack recording sessions and lists the following technical credits: Lionel Newman (producer), Ken Darby (arranger), and Bob Mayer/Ken Runyon (engineers). Thus, while movie credits read "music by" Lionel Newman—David Weisbart had produced the actual movie for Twentieth Century-Fox—credits on the soundtrack album designate Newman as "producer." He *composed* the soundtrack to *Love Me Tender*; he *produced* the original soundtrack album (the OST). If you will, the engineer, who actually compiled the soundtrack album by cobbling together musical selections from the film, directed the OST. Hence, Newman's designation as "producer" makes complicated but perfect sense.

In 1957, RCA named Sholes pop singles manager and, in 1958, pop singles and albums manager. Perhaps Sholes appropriated the term "producer" from its use on OST recordings. If not, he simply recognized that his role in making records was directly analogous to that of Pandro Berman and Hal Wallis in making movies, and he decided to formalize this arrangement (no doubt for financial reasons). Therefore, when Atkins moved into Sholes's old position in Nashville, he became a producer and not, perhaps more logically, a "director of recording."

• • •

That enigma solved, let me describe the organization of this oral history of country music production. The book's chapters identify four distinct eras—four paradigms, really—that structure the story of recording. Each era is characterized by an emergent technology that redefined production, effectively remaking the role of producer. There is, however, one constant that unifies this history. Musicians make music. Producers make recordings. In a nutshell, that's their job.

Thus, I've organized chapters around recordings—songs and albums—arranged chronologically by original release dates. In most cases, producers provide commentary on their own recordings or on their own working methods. Occasionally, people intimately acquainted with the productions of others provide commentary. For example, Don Law Jr. remembers his father's story. Don Pierce points to A&R pioneer Ralph Peer's understanding of publishing as production. Harold Bradley, who has played sessions with pretty near everybody, speaks especially of his brother, Owen. Another guitar great, Reggie Young, focuses on sessions with producers Chips Moman and Jimmy Bowen. Bobby Braddock describes writing songs—"He Stopped Loving Her Today" and "Golden Ring"—for Billy Sherrill. Several producers, especially of the earliest recordings referenced, speak from their experiences preparing classic material for reissue.

All quotations in this oral history derive from interviews that I conducted, recorded, and transcribed (over a period of twenty years). I begin the story of country production with an overture. In it a panel of experts defines the role of record producer. (The experts are real; the panel is simulated.) This topic is expanded in the interludes that preface chapters 2 and 3. Introducing chapter 4 is a conversation with producer and Country Music Hall of Fame songwriter Bobby Braddock.

This book's focus on country records ought to prompt any number of observations in readers, but for now, I'll anticipate two. First, you'll see that producers have their hot streaks, as does country music as a whole. For example, speaking of Nashville in 1962, Jerry Kennedy declared, "This whole town exploded." His claim is substantiated in the text. Moments, cycles, and trends—all manner of patterns—should materialize in the reading of this history. Second, you'll see that every paradigm of production contains within it all past paradigms. New ways of working never completely supplant old ways: methods accrue; they don't replace previous methods. Thus, during an era when digital editing enables producers to comp (composite) vocals, some producers use the newest technology, for all intents and purposes, as if the tools for cutting vocals direct to discs made of wax had finally been perfected. Then again, any given technology can always do more than a culture will allow; as a corollary to this rule, new technology is always employed to realize fully the potential of—to prop up the ideology that supported— the old technology.

Chapter 1 (1927–1949) opens with a recollection of Ralph Peer, the famed A&R man who superintended country music's big bang—the 1927 recordings of Jimmie Rodgers, the Carter Family, and other musicians at the Bristol Sessions. Thus, it refers back to a time that also witnessed the adoption of electrical recording. This chapter ends as magnetic tape replaces acetate discs as the recording medium of choice. Chapter 2 (1950–1966) sees the A&R man become the producer. His overarching ideal is to create conditions that evoke perfect performances. Chapter 3 (1967–1991) marks the era of multitrack recording, a full realization of what tape can do. Chapter 4 (1992–present) could be labeled "the digital era." My late start date calls attention to the near-ubiquitous use of multitrack digital recording that followed the release of ADAT recorders in 1992.

• • •

Several recording artists discussed in these pages do not readily fit prevailing notions of country music. The Dinning Sisters, Robert Johnson,

Otis Redding, Joe Tex, and Al Green will never be inducted into the Country Music Hall of Fame. That's fine. To admit them would weaken or efface a border crossing that country music, as an institution, actively guards. It would prompt us to ask, not the commonplace question, "What counts as country?" but rather, "What doesn't?"

Nevertheless, I've included a few nonconventional artists and recordings in this history. I've done so for four reasons. First, I want readers to notice that producers often don't see (or that they simply ignore) borderlines, or that—as was the case of Don Law and Robert Johnson—the genre distinctions listeners now regard as commonsense hadn't been created, or that, at the very least, when Willie Mitchell had Al Green interpret a country song, there was some wisdom (money to be made) in blurring accepted boundaries. Second, country producers take no oaths of genre fidelity. Readers ought to notice that the same guy who produced Robert Johnson also gave us classic recordings from Lefty Frizzell and Johnny Cash. Or that to Buddy Killen and Joe Tex, countrified funk wasn't an oxymoron. Third, there are lessons to be learned about country production when, for example, Ken Nelson narrates a story about recording the Dinning Sisters, a pop group. Fourth, I want readers to push definitions—if only a little bit. I'm aware that *Dusty in Memphis* flies under the banner of "blue-eyed soul," but give it half a chance, and it will play like one of the greatest country records ever made.

• • •

I really enjoy reading *Heartaches by the Number: Country Music's 500 Greatest Singles*, by David Cantwell and Bill Friskics-Warren. Unlike almost every other book devoted to country, it lists producers and frequently acknowledges their importance to the process of creating records. The list of recordings it compiles is subjective, but it's rarely quirky. Though one might argue that it emphasizes older recordings, the book supplies a handy canon of country. Count the producers who worked on those 500 recordings, and the length of that list is astonishing. It's so short. Of the songs listed, 36 credit no producer. For their work on the remaining 464 songs, a little more than 170 people earned production credit. That number is, however, slightly inflated because it includes co-productions. Jerry Wexler, Tom Dowd, and Arif Mardin produced Dusty Springfield's "Son of a Preacher Man." That's three producers, one recording. Drop names that appear only once, and the list shrinks from 170 producers to 58; drop names that appear only twice, and the list goes to 37; drop names that appear only three times, and we're left with 24 producers. But here's the kicker: these 24 producers worked on 313 of the 464 credited recordings! That's close to 70 percent.

As you might expect, the 51 people I recorded for this oral history represent a big chunk of history and a whole lot of great music. As many of the names won't be familiar even to avid country fans, I've provided brief biographical sketches of the producers and others I interviewed for easy reference.

BIOGRAPHICAL SKETCHES

Producing Country was built from my interviews with
the following people:

DAVE ALVIN (1955)
 In his playing (with the Blasters, X, and solo) and in his productions
 (for the Derailers and Big Sandy & His Fly-Rite Boys), Alvin
 manifests a vision of country that's two thousand scorched miles
 west of Nashville.

ERIC "ROSCOE" AMBEL (1957)
 Ambel's guitar playing with the Del-Lords and the Yayhoos is more
 rock than country, while his production work with the Bottle
 Rockets is more country than rock.

PETE ANDERSON (1948)
 For many years, Anderson, a guitarist of distinction, was Dwight
 Yoakam's go-to producer.

CHET ATKINS (1924–2001)
 After Steve Sholes moved up the corporate ladder in 1957, Atkins
 became RCA's man in Nashville. He and Decca's Owen Bradley are
 widely regarded as the chief architects of the Nashville sound, the
 urbane style of country that found a mass audience.

JAMES AUSTIN (1946)
 In his former position as vice-president of A&R at Rhino Records
 (whose parent company is the Warner Music Group), Austin
 produced many historical reissues.

JIMMY BOWEN (1937)
 Before Bowen, Nashville producers cut songs that, with luck,
 became hits. Taking his cue (and his budgets) from pop, Bowen
 produced albums that generated hits and changed Nashville forever.

BOBBY BRADDOCK (1940)
 Braddock produced Blake Shelton's first five albums. In 2011, he was
 elected, as a songwriter, to the Country Music Hall of Fame.

HAROLD BRADLEY (1926)

Owen Bradley's kid brother is the most recorded session guitarist in the history of American music, a constant presence on Nashville's music scene for more than fifty years.

THOM BRESH (1948)

Merle Travis's son is also a producer, writer, actor, and guitarist.

TONY BROWN (1946)

Someone once summarized the historical eras of Nashville production in the following manner: Bradley, Bowen, and Brown. While at MCA, Brown produced George Strait, Wynonna Judd, Lyle Lovett, Steve Earle, and Vince Gill.

STEPHEN BRUTON (1948–2009)

The brief on this Texas producer says that he was the model for Jeff Bridges's character in the movie *Crazy Heart*.

BLAKE CHANCEY (1962)

While working A&R for Sony Music in the 1990s, Chancey signed genre-defining musicians: the Dixie Chicks, Montgomery Gentry, and Mary Chapin Carpenter.

JACK CLEMENT (1931–2013)

Sizable chunks of country music's history have been made in Nashville studios built by Clement. Before taking up residence in Music City, Clement was a mainstay at Sun Studios in Memphis.

MARSHALL CRENSHAW (1953)

Best known as a musician, Crenshaw has also readied several historical recordings for reissue, most notably a Louvin Brothers collection.

LAWRENCE COHN (1942)

Cohn directly impacted country music as a reissue producer for Sony Music's Legacy Recordings; he created the Roots 'n' Blues series for the label.

DON COOK (1949)

Cook's strength as a songwriter—he's a top executive at Sony/ATV Tree Publishing—has powered much of his success as a producer.

STEVE CROPPER (1941)

More or less the manager of Stax Studio in Memphis, Cropper worked shoulder-to-shoulder writing songs with Otis Redding, the most countrified of legendary soul singers.

TOM DOWD (1925–2002)

One of the most admired recording engineers of all time, Dowd was also a producer of note, devoting most of his professional life to Atlantic Records.

SID FELLER (1916–2006)

Feller produced Ray Charles, including the game-changing album *Modern Sounds in Country and Western Music.*

BOB FERGUSON (1927–2001)

At RCA and in the genealogy of country production, Steve Sholes begat Chet Atkins who begat Bob Ferguson.

TOMPALL GLASER (1933–2013)

Glaser built a Nashville studio commonly known as Hillbilly Central. In it a group of insurgents initiated country's Outlaw movement.

SCOTT HENDRICKS (1956)

A Nashville producer and record-company executive, Hendricks has held leadership positions at Capitol Nashville, Virgin, and Warner Bros./Reprise Records. He has produced recordings by Brooks & Dunn, Alan Jackson, Faith Hill, and Trace Adkins.

BOB IRWIN (1957)

As a reissue producer for Sony/Legacy, Irwin's country credits include Lefty Frizzell, Buck Owens, Bob Wills, Johnny Cash, and the Byrds. In 1989 Irwin started Sundazed Records.

ROLAND JANES (1933)

That's Janes's guitar on Billy Lee Riley's "Flyin' Saucers Rock and Roll" and Jerry Lee Lewis's "Whole Lotta Shakin' Goin' On." He also engineered a number of the hits that tumbled out the doors of Sun Records.

BOB JOHNSTON (1932)

Most famous as Bob Dylan's producer, Johnston followed Don Law Sr. as head of Columbia's country-music division.

JOHN KEANE (1959)

In his Athens, GA, studio, Keane has produced R.E.M., the Cowboy Junkies, 10,000 Maniacs, and Nanci Griffith.

JERRY KENNEDY (1940)

From his post at Mercury Records, Kennedy produced, among others, Jerry Lee Lewis, Tom T. Hall, and Roger Miller. That's his guitar on any number of hits.

BUDDY KILLEN (1932–2006)

Perhaps, country music's greatest song hunter, Killen signed hundreds of writers to Tree Publishing Company. He produced the countrified soul singer Joe Tex.

JON LANGFORD (1957)

Langford's sensibilities as an artist (drawing, painting, and making music) come from punk, and they are discernable in the music he's recorded solo or with the Mekons, the Waco Brothers, and the Pine Valley Cosmonauts.

DON LAW JR.

Law is one of music's most successful concert promoters; his father (1902–1982) was a legendary producer for Columbia Records.

WILLIAM MCEUEN

A producer of both film and music, McEuen made his mark on country when he brought his brother John's group, the Nitty Gritty Dirt Band, to Nashville and recorded *Will the Circle Be Unbroken*.

BLAKE MEVIS

Standout items on Mevis's resume include production work with George Strait, Vern Gosdin, Keith Whitley, and Mila Mason.

BUDDY MILLER (1952)

Singer, songwriter, and guitarist, Miller has production credits that include Emmylou Harris, Robert Plant, Allison Moorer, Solomon Burke, and Richard Thompson.

WILLIE MITCHELL (1928–2010)

At Royal Studios in Memphis, Mitchell created a patented brand of soul music that Al Green took to the world.

GURF MORLIX (1951)

An Austin-based guitarist and producer, Morlix's work is heard to great effect on albums by Lucinda Williams and Robert Earl Keen Jr.

KEN NELSON (1911–2008)

For Capitol Records, Nelson produced the Louvin Brothers in Nashville, but it was his Hollywood-based production work with Merle Haggard and Buck Owens that defined a genre: the Bakersfield Sound.

JIM ED NORMAN (1948)

Before moving from California to Nashville in the early 1980s, Norman worked with the Eagles, Jennifer Warnes, and Anne Murray. Their sound anticipated country's subsequent musical direction.

JOHN PALLADINO (1920)

Palladino was a pioneering recording engineer for Capitol Records in Hollywood.

DON PIERCE (1915–2005)

More than anyone in Nashville, Pierce knew how to market country music. Along the way, he produced a few records.

ALLEN REYNOLDS (1938)

Reynolds produced Garth Brooks (all of the defining albums), which is fame enough, but he also produced hits for Crystal Gayle, Don Williams, Kathy Mattea, and Kenny Rogers.

JIM ROONEY (1938)

Albums produced with Iris Dement, Nanci Griffith, and John Prine made Rooney an alt-country luminary.

SHELBY SINGLETON (1931–2009)

With money he earned from sales of Jeannie C. Riley's "Harper Valley P.T.A.," Singleton bought Sun Records (1969). Before that, he produced records for Mercury.

CRAIG STREET

Street crosses all musical boundaries and has produced k. d. lang and Norah Jones.

JAMES STROUD (1949)

The key to much of Stroud's success as a producer (with Clint Black, Toby Keith, Tracy Lawrence, and Tim McGraw) is his ear for a groove. He started out as an R&B drummer.

MARTY STUART (1958)

Stuart's production work with gospel group Jerry and Tammy Sullivan is a labor of love, reflecting his zeal for country traditions.

JEREMY TEPPER (1963)

Tepper's Diesel Only Records has issued several compilations of truck-driving ("rig-rock") songs.

BOB THIELE (1922–1996)

Though he is best known as a jazz producer at Impulse! Records, Thiele played a pivotal role in the career of Buddy Holly.

MICHAEL TIMMINS (1959)

A songwriter and guitarist, Timmins has produced albums by the Cowboy Junkies, the band he helped found in the mid-1980s.

JERRY WEXLER (1917–2008)

Legendary as an R&B producer, Wexler made few forays into country music, but he did notable work with Willie Nelson.

PAUL WORLEY (1950)

The Dixie Chicks, Lady Antebellum, and Big & Rich earned hits with the production assistance of Worley.

REGGIE YOUNG (1936)

In the 1960s, as house guitarist at Chips Moman's American Studio, Young contributed his signature sound to chart-topping pop and R&B singles. After he moved to Nashville in the 1970s, he continued to play as he always had, but on chart-topping country hits.

PRODUCING COUNTRY

OVERTURE
WHAT IS A RECORD PRODUCER?

BOB THIELE (produced Buddy Holly, "Rave On")
It was all left up to the A&R [artists and repertoire] guy in those days as to who to record, when to record, how much to spend. Then you worked closely with the sales department. But the A&R guy was the important guy. Everyone relied on the A&R man to have hit records.

Producers were in those days actually looking for the talent. They'd bring the artists to the attention of the executives at the company. The producers were pretty much on their own. As long as records were selling, the producer had it his way all the way through.

SCOTT HENDRICKS (produced Faith Hill, *It Matters to Me*)
A producer in country is different than a producer in other genres of music. A large part of our artists are not necessarily writers. One of the most important roles of producing in this format or genre is finding the songs and developing the direction for the artist that you're going to be recording. That's pretty different than other genres. We rely more on the songwriting community in Nashville than probably other communities do. It's a very time-consuming process.

ROLAND JANES
(produced Travis Wammack, *That Scratchy Guitar from Memphis*)
If you're in the studio and you're participating in sessions, then you gradually go from one type of participation into another. Every musician on the session is really a producer, but they don't have the final say. They kick in with their ideas. In essence they're helping produce the record. I went from being a musician to being a recording engineer, working with producers in the booth with me. It's a matter of educating yourself. You gain experience with every session you do. You learn what works and what doesn't. The reason for going into production is because you have a better chance to make a little more money in different ways.

CHET ATKINS (produced Don Gibson, *A Legend in My Time*)
You just let the musicians play what they want to play, and you use whatever you hear when you run it down. Somebody will do something, and you'll think, "Goddamn, we could expand on that. That might be good for this record." That's the way I did it. I don't know how other people did it.

If you hear a mistake, you correct it. Later on in my career, we could do that, but at first we recorded in mono and, then, eventually went to stereo two-track. Then we went to three-track. Then we went to four, eight and sixteen and twenty-four and so forth. I used to record a lot of artists, about twenty-five people. Les [Paul] came up with that eight-track machine and, then, with the sixteen and so on. Ampex did. I told Les I was going to kick his ass for that. It caused me to have to do a lot more work and hire a lot more people.

BOB FERGUSON (produced Dolly Parton, *Coat of Many Colors*)
It reached the point where the company meant the artist. There were production people and vice-presidents and everything else, but somebody had to work directly with the artists. That is the role of the producer, to represent the company to the artist, and, conversely, to represent the artist back to the company. I don't know how many I produced (one of the guys told me he counted fifty-one), but each artist comes with a different set of needs. My role, the role I assumed, was to find out the needs of each artist and try to fill them.

> *In your autobiography you mention three producers — Leonard Chess, John Hammond, and Phil Spector — who represent different modes of production. Spector is the auteur or producer-as-star. . . .*

JERRY WEXLER (produced Willie Nelson, *Phases and Stages*)
And Leonard Chess was a documentarian. A documentarian is somebody who goes out, hears or sees a performance, and takes that into the studio and replicates it. He saw Muddy Waters at a bar and recorded what he'd heard. John Hammond was the same kind of producer that I believe myself to be. He served the project. He tried to perceive the essence of the artist and then provided him with the most comfortable and fruitful setting to elicit what that essence might be. That has to do not only with attitude in the control room and the talk-back, it has to do with — once you've established the parameters — letting the musicians

and the singer, if there is one, bring out the best in themselves. What you do is try to find the studio, the players, the arranger, the time, and the venue that will be most comfortable for them. And if they're interested in your view of their material, to see whatever they may have self-written and to try to agree with them, reach an agreement about what will be the most appropriate for a particular session. If they don't have material, then part of my job is to bring them a smorgasbord of songs for them to select from.

TOMPALL GLASER (produced Waylon Jennings, *Honky Tonk Heroes*) I've pretty much made all the mistakes that there ever was. If a producer gets too involved in someone else's work, he winds up overproducing it, and it ruins the soul in it. What really works the best, as far as drawing the artist out, is to just suck them dry, get every piece of input they've got, and then enhance it, make sure the music's right. That's what Owen Bradley always used to say, "If you get the music right, let the singer sing the song." I think that's probably the best.

But then, there're other types of music to do. If a singer wants to get a certain type of a situation, and he doesn't know how to get it and you do, then you kind of take the reins and lead him down the road a way until he gets the feel of it. You watch the [session] musicians that they don't shuck him or you, either one. They get pretty slick in that studio. They'll use the same licks over and over again. You think you're getting the original 'cause you didn't see them when they did it just yesterday.

STEVE CROPPER (produced Otis Redding, "Dock of the Bay") There are different types of producers. I refer to myself as a hands-on producer. I get involved with the music, with the songs, with the direction, with the musicians who are going to be on the session, and I'm usually on the session myself. I decide on the studio and the engineer. I call that a hands-on thing. I'm doing more than talking on the telephone, trying to make a deal and talking to the record executives. I talk to them very little, as little possible. I like to make the artist happy, and I like to make the manager of the artist happy. Unless you really know what you're doing, it's not worth making them unhappy. You can get a hit on them and say, "Well, I told you so," but where does that get you? It gets you one hit record, and that's all you get. If you make them happy and get a hit record, then you get them again and again and again, until you run out.

JERRY KENNEDY (produced Jerry Lee Lewis, *Killer Country*)
The approach I took was one I've seen the most or one any producer who's been a musician usually takes: the approach that that's a real team effort going on in there [in the studio]. If you've ever been on the other side of that glass with the guys, that's where I came from. Maybe it's true only here in Nashville, but I always felt that this is a great, creative bunch of musicians. I think it's kind of neat to have sat back and let them inject things into what was going on. Anybody who didn't, back when I was playing, usually had to pull teeth to get something to come off. Boy, I'll tell you what, working with those guys was so great! It was hard to make a bad record in this town. There were bad songs. There weren't very many bad records.

ALLEN REYNOLDS (produced Garth Brooks, *No Fences*)
The job varies according to what's needed for an artist in a given situation. But my bias as a producer is and has always been toward performance. Two things are important. One is great material for the artist in question. So it may be a great song, but if it's not great in the hands of the artist you're working with, it doesn't mean anything. Record labels never seem to understand that you have to find a song that's a great song for the artist that you're working with. Record companies tend to think, "Well, this is a great song. Paste it on Charlie over there, and it'll be a hit for him." You can't do that. It has to be a song that the artist handles well—handles magically—and that they feel some enthusiasm for at least by the time you get through. As I'm saying that, I'm remembering Kenny Rogers doing "Lucille," which was a huge record for him, and Larry Butler, the producer, told me Kenny didn't really want to cut it. They did it in about the last fifteen minutes of the session. So I don't want to generalize overmuch.

My handshake deal with the artist has always been this. First, we both look for songs. We meet and talk and listen together lots, and our hard work is basically done before we go to the studio. The studio is where you have fun. The deal is this: neither of us has to go into the studio and work with a song that either of us has serious problems with. If there's a problem, we just keep looking until we find material that we both feel great about. We may not feel equally great, but we both feel great about it. And then you can go in there and do wonderful things.

The second thing that's important is a great performance from the artist and the band, whatever the size, whether it's a band or an orchestra. I like live. I don't like quantizing.* I don't like metronomes, click tracks. I like everybody there as much as I can—because to me the job is to catch that moment when a performance is given for the record that's good enough to stand up to repeated listening. That's where my bias is. I'm not heavy on technology. I'm heavy on the human aspect, and I always have been.

BLAKE MEVIS (produced George Strait, *Strait from the Heart*)
I've always looked at music as something that there is no right or wrong. It's almost like fashion: what's in or out. There're some sounds that are in; some are out. They change from time to time. But I always think that the job of a producer is to make sure that it sounds different, that it stands out on the radio, that people reach over and, maybe, turn the knob up.

JIMMY BOWEN (produced Reba McEntire, *My Kind of Country*)
You have one type of producer who is heavy, heavy-handed. Heavy-handed sounds negative. It's not meant that way. I use Burt Bacharach as an example. He and his lyricist, Hal David, wrote the song; he selected the musicians, he did the arrangement, and he told Dionne Warwick how he wanted her to do the song. He was very definite. That's one kind of producer. I did that a lot in the '60s in California with pop artists.

When I started working with Kenny Rogers, it started to dawn on me that there was another way. That was to help an artist to do their music, and to do everything you can to make it better. Fill in only when needed, and try never to insert your own thing. One thing I did learn from working with Sinatra: it was his music, not mine, even though with Frank I had to find the songs, get the arrangements and the musicians and all that. There was never any question about whose record it was when it was finished. With Phil Spector, those were his records. He was the artist and the producer. It didn't really matter who sang the songs.

BLAKE MEVIS
A producer should help artists get their music on tape—and really stay out of the coloring process as much as possible, in the sense that it's the artist's music that has to be on tape, not the producer's music. Every

---

* Quantizing is a means of achieving absolute precision through digital music technology.

artist that you do should sound different. If you can accomplish that, then I think, hopefully, you're doing the job of being invisible, yet you're making sure that the quality of music is there. The technical part of the process is there, but at the same time you know it's impossible to totally stay out of the process because you're in it. If a producer's music starts sounding alike and he's got five different artists, then he's being too intrusive.

PAUL WORLEY (produced Lady Antebellum, *Need You Now*)
I think it's impossible for a producer to be invisible, but I think a producer should try to maximize the creativity and the point of view and the musical vision of the artist they're working with. So in my view the role of the producer is a facilitator and a translator, someone who communicates the artist's musical vision and direction to the engineers and the musicians and, ultimately, to the record company involved. He tries to give any specific project its own identity.

CRAIG STREET (produced k.d. lang, *Drag*)
Production in that way is what I'd call translucent. That is, it's not transparent. It's not *not* there. But it's not completely apparent. It could be very much like the air that you breathe. If it weren't there, you'd definitely know it.

PETE ANDERSON (produced Dwight Yoakam, *This Time*)
I think it's important to be invisible. If the [film] director was a writer, you're going to see influence. He's directing his script, his writing. The producer's never the songwriter. I mean sometimes he is, but it's more in things that would be understood as technical that he appears. Things that you like to do technically in film are visible; in music they're audible. So you've got to be a little bit more sophisticated or educated in it to pick up audible things that a producer would do—that he likes to do. I don't think those are negatives. I always have sonic concepts for records and songs and artists that I work with. People that really, really knew the business would be able to go, "It sounds like you did that" or "That's something you would do." But it's not anything that would in any way cloud the artist. If you start to have a formula, and people pick up that you have a formula, I think it's really dangerous.

STEPHEN BRUTON (produced Alejandro Escovedo, *Thirteen Years*)
The production should be such that everyone wants to hear the recording again and again. I don't think that you should have this [sounds a grand entry]: Stephen Bruton Productions. You might get in there and the song that they've been playing as a band—it's their anthem—you listen to it and go, "This song would be best with you and a piano instead of a guitar." If that's what gets the song out, then that's the way I go.

GURF MORLIX (produced Lucinda Williams, *Lucinda Williams*)
I've always felt like the producer's job is to make the artist happy and to enable them to come out with the record they want. Maybe they don't have the ability to get that done. That's not their job. Their job is to come up with the concept. I figure the artist writes the songs; the artist has the vision. The producer's role is to bring that to fruition. The artist should be satisfied with the work.

TONY BROWN (produced Steve Earle, *Guitar Town*)
I played with Elvis during the last year and a half of his life. To be able to play in that band with Ronnie Tutt, Jerry Scheff, David Briggs, James Burton, and Joe Guercio, who conducted orchestras for Streisand, Diana Ross, and you name it! If you get great musicians together, you have to find a way where they become one. Otherwise you don't get to experience great music from great musicians. If they're fighting and bickering, and it's not harmonious, it's just a bunch of shit.

Every night, there was so much chaos on that tour. Elvis would walk out on stage, and he was out of it. You could see some of the musicians going, "Oh, great." They weren't into it. And there I was, proud to be part of such a stellar band. We'd play. It was not together. We wouldn't end together. We wouldn't play together. There was a lot of bickering. Then, on one night or two nights of one of the tours, it was just magic. You'd feel like you had to hang on for dear life to play with Tutt and Burton and those guys.

I learned that when you cut records one person in a room can screw up the whole groove of everything. The best thing that you can learn for producing records is human psychology: how to get rid of that problem. If it's a musician, let's say, who's messing things up 'cause he's not playing right, he's got a bad attitude, you need to know how to pull him out without causing a scene. Or if the artist is in a place where they're causing the problem, best thing you can do is just shut it down. Without them, you're screwed anyway. It's like the old weak-link-in-the-chain proverb. You get all these great, talented people together, and if you can't make them all communicate with each other, you're not going to get something great. You'll get something okay, because they're good. But it won't be great. You get something great when you've got everybody communicating with each other.

JIM ED NORMAN
(produced Kenny Rogers, *Something Inside So Strong*)
I had the conviction that a producer's responsibility was to create a great work environment for the artist. You had to have great material, and you then had to bring people together. You had a creative management job: how you deal with the moment and the opportunity that everyone has when you're collected together in the studio to work and to create. A producer has to give guidance and direction, but as much as anything, he has to create an environment in which the creative energies that are already inherent in the people that are there—who have come together that day—can flourish.

JIM ROONEY (produced Iris DeMent, *Infamous Angel*)
One of the things I think a producer needs to be, temperamentally, is a person able to make a lot of little, tiny decisions pretty quickly. In my own case I basically rely on my instincts. Because I also play and sing, I want the musicians or the artists to be as comfortable as possible and to forget about the fact that we're making a record. In other words, I want them to focus on playing and singing and doing what they do. I want those conditions to be right for them. I don't want the earphones to be nonfunctioning. I want them to be able to communicate easily. That means positioning them in the room so that they're comfortable—things like that. It's all kind of mundane in certain ways, but I think it's extremely important to pay attention to those things.

I figured this out myself by watching other people and by being in circumstances that I found uncomfortable. One thing I never liked, as a musician or as an artist, was if I was ready to sing or ready to play, and the engineer or producer wasn't ready to record. I found that very frustrating. I've seen the wind go out of the sails of a recording session for the simplest reasons.

PETE ANDERSON

I am a musician-producer as opposed to an engineer-producer. To be very broad and general, there are probably three ways you can get into this producing thing. One, you're a producer like, let's say, a Phil Ramone—who was an engineer and, then, crossed the line and became more musical. I come from a musical background: from playing guitar on sessions, being on the other side of the glass, being on the floor as a musician, and then having some concept of what I wanted to do technically with music—learning enough technical dialogue to communicate. [I wanted] to learn the language but not necessarily plug things in, EQ stuff, or do anything technical with my hands. And then there's the kind of music collector, the musicologist. The greatest one is probably John Hammond Sr. He didn't play an instrument that I know of, and he wasn't a musician or an engineer. He was intelligent, astute, and had great taste. He signed countless great people throughout history. More and more, that particular style doesn't exist.

CRAIG STREET

There was a record not long ago that I fired myself from because the artist wanted to do something that I absolutely did not agree with. What I was told coming into the record and did and delivered dutifully, the artist decided to do something different. It wasn't just something different, it was like taking a circle made out of titanium and saying we want this to be a rubber square. "I am not an alchemist. I can't do that. And I won't do it. It's boring." I think the label was stunned that I just walked away—and walked away from back-end [earnings]. I think the artist couldn't quite figure it out. But you have to do that sometime.

That's one of the great lessons that I learned from T-Bone [Burnett], who has always been helpful and a champion. I remember seeing him walking away with his golf clubs.

"What's going on?"

"We are not quite agreeing in there anymore. So I fired myself. I'm going to play golf."

I'm like, "Cool, man, I like that! I'm going to remember that one. I'm going to use that someday."

1

CUTTING TRACKS
CAPTURING THE PERFORMANCE,
1927-1949

Very soon after 1877, the invention that Edison called a phonograph articulated in such a way as to serve the interests of corporate capital; which is to say, technologies for recording and reproducing sound worked to the distinct advantage of newly formed record companies — not musicians. Entertainment companies, in the guise of their designees, artists and repertoire (A&R) men, managed musical production by controlling all facets of preproduction.

Cutting tracks to disc allowed A&R men only limited control of the production phase of record-making. Hence, they don't talk much about time spent in studios, because production happened outside that space. Early producers were tasked with choosing who (artists) and what (repertoire) to record. They crafted deals more than they crafted sounds. They functioned as agents of "artificial selection," in a Darwinian sense of the term. However invisible (or inaudible) the manifestations of their control may have been, in seeking to ensure the survival and profitability of corporate interests, A&R men profoundly shaped, even defined, country music. They were mediating figures, standing between artist and record company, artist and technology, and artist and public.

• • •

Interviewed in his Hollywood office in 1959, Ralph Peer (1892–1960) informed Lillian Borgeson that the recording sessions he supervised back in the 1920s yielded nothing more than movable pieces in a complex financial game. Records weren't end products, packaged goods, or software necessary for newfangled hardware. And they sure weren't timeless treasures. They were a means to accruing copyright royalties. That's where the real money lay.

As a young man hired to produce "race records," Peer had learned this lesson well. The money he made for the General Phonograph Company's OKeh label could have filled a caravan of red wheelbarrows. In 1923, when Peer and Atlanta businessman Polk Brockman scored a hit recording with Fiddlin' John Carson, they initiated what would later become known as "country music." Peer called it "hillbilly" music. Years later, when Borgeson pressed him to recall the "hillbillies" he'd recorded, Peer responded, "Oh, I tried so hard to forget them."

Presumably, Peer wasn't referring to Jimmie Rodgers or to the Carter Family—unforgettable "discoveries" of his 1927 recording expedition to Bristol, Tennessee. But it's a safe bet he didn't want to talk about country music's patriarchs. His fondest memories undoubtedly revolved around the deal he struck with the Victor Talking Machine Company and any number of talented hillbillies. Compared to the strip-mining techniques favored by other A&R men, where songs were bought outright for measly sums of cash, Peer employed an approach to American song that country scholar Richard Peterson, in *Creating Country Music* (1997), labeled "deep-shaft mining." At OKeh Records Peer's salary was sixteen thousand dollars a year; not bad for the mid-1920s. At Victor he managed to strike an even better deal. He agreed to work for free! In return, the company allowed Peer to copyright—technically, to hold the "mechanical rights" on—all the music he recorded. Victor obviously knew the Copyright Law of 1909. Every record manufactured earned its copyright owner two cents. Victor reasonably assumed that sales of hillbilly records wouldn't amount to much. They didn't figure on a paradigm shift: Peer using his deal to institute a new regime (Southern Music), one that would forever change American music.

Peer paid musicians a fifty-dollar performance fee for each side recorded, and he offered two contracts. The first guaranteed "royalties." Artists received a half-cent for every record sold (while Peer pocketed a cent and a half). The second contract appointed Peer as the artist's exclusive manager. In no time Peer was a wealthy man and gatekeeper to an industry.

VARIOUS, *RCA COUNTRY LEGENDS: THE BRISTOL SESSIONS, VOL. 1* (ORIGINAL RECORDINGS, 1927; COMPILATION, 2002, RCA) AND "A SATISFIED MIND" (1954)

JEREMY TEPPER

Even before there was a term "producer," the producer was the A&R guy who brought the material to the session. There'd be an engineer, but the producer was sort of an executive scout who selected the material, unlike in rock where the producer is, generally, coming from more of an engineering direction; he creates sounds. The term "to produce" in Nashville is more to select the material and match it with the artist.

DON PIERCE

He was a genius, that Ralph Peer, and he was an angel to me. For some reason, he liked me because I would get in my car and go coast to coast and work with distributers and listen to disc jockeys and get to the one-stops. That reminded him of when he was on the road for RCA and how he picked up Jimmie Rodgers and the Carter Family and others. He deplored the people in his office in New York. He wouldn't even go into the office, didn't even have an office where he had his headquarters in the Brill Building. He said, "Got all these people in there, and nothing's happening. You're the only guy I know of that's out there on the road scratching the way I used to. Come on up and have lunch with me at my house."

He had a place on about 59th, off of Hollywood Boulevard. I went up there. A butler came to the door. I couldn't understand why Peer was interested in me, except he says, "I would like to have my people in New York learn something from you, about what you're doing and how you're able to operate when you don't have any money."

Eventually, he offered me a hundred dollars a week to be a song scout. I said, "Mr. Peer, I appreciate that, but I'm your competitor. I have my own publishing company. If I find a song, I'm not going to give it to you."

"No, here's what I have in mind," he said. "I want my people to see how you function. When you get a song that's a hit, I want you to give me the sheet-music selling rights, and I want you to give me the rights to the song for publishing outside the United States and Canada. I'll take it for the rest of the world. I've got twenty-six branches around the world."

I said, "That sounds like a gift on the ground to me." At that time, when we were starting Starday [Records], that was a lot of damn money. I took him up on it. When I'd go to New York, I'd kind of headquarter in his offices, and tell his people what I was doing.

We came up with a song called "A Satisfied Mind" [written by Joe "Red" Hayes and Jack Rhodes]. Peer was quick—got about five or six pop records out there in New York. Any record that he got from it, he got half the money on it. He sold about twenty-two thousand sheet-music copies on it, and then he had the rights for the rest of the world. He was real happy with his association with me. We did well with that song.

It got recorded by Red Hayes down in Texas. I was traveling through . . . I got to Midland City in Texas on my way back to California, and I saw Red there. He played that song for me, and I said, "I've got to have it."

He said, "Well, you can't have it unless I make the first record on it." I sent him down to Pappy [Daily] in Houston, and Red made the first record on it. We didn't sell very many, but it got up to that station in Springfield, Missouri [KWTO]. Porter Wagoner heard it, and Red Foley heard it, and Jean Shepard heard it, and all three of them cut it in one week. We had mailed out copies, and they had heard the copy of our record on Starday. They loved the song, and so they all jumped in and recorded it.

Peer could see when [performing-rights organization] ASCAP [the American Society of Composers, Authors and Publishers] almost committed suicide by taking everything off the air [in the 1942–1944 musicians' strike, protesting radio broadcasting recorded music]. That gave rise to BMI [Broadcast Music, Inc.]. And even though he was probably on the board for ASCAP, he became one of the early founders of BMI. He was that kind of an entrepreneur. He knew what had to be done. For a guy like him to go down and tie up those tunes from Cuba and from Mexico, "Amapola" and "Green Eyes" and all that stuff. That Kansas City, red-headed Swede was one smart dude. Ralph Peer was a music man.

Later on, I discontinued it [the publishing arrangement with Peer] when I started doing business with the Hill and Range people. But we were always on a friendly basis, and I always considered Ralph Peer an angel to me.

CHET ATKINS

Peer made a speech down here [in Nashville] to the Country Music Association. It must have been about '51 or '52. He worked for RCA, you know. He ran their publishing company, and he signed songwriters. He saw potential where they didn't.

I remember one article I read. He said, "I started the race business. I started the hillbilly business." And he was right. He did. He told how he did it. It's interesting. Up to when he came along, people would just record the same songs over and over. Well, he had a publishing company. So he'd ask the artist, "What songs do you want to do?" They'd come in and sing "Ol' Joe Clark" again and all that stuff. He'd say, "Now, you've got to write some songs. Maybe you've got to change. You've got to give me something fresh and different." He did that. He was at Columbia [OKeh], while he did that over there too. He's responsible for country and for rhythm and blues, maybe, because of that.

All music mentioned in this chapter on pre-tape production was originally recorded direct to discs that were, typically, made of lacquer (also referred to as "acetate"). Then, through a multistep process that derived metal parts from the lacquer or master recording, 78-rpm discs were stamped or pressed. That means all historical albums that include tracks recorded before 1950 are compilations. To create these albums, reissue producers work from materials that are as close to the master disc as possible.

**VARIOUS, *ROOTS N' BLUES:
THE RETROSPECTIVE 1925–1950*
(COMPILATION, 1992, COLUMBIA/
LEGACY)**

LAWRENCE COHN

From the late '20s to the late '40s, the recording process was a direct-to-disc process. They [engineers] cut acetates; there were no tapes. Once the acetates were cut, they made impressions, and they got metal parts from the impressions, because the metal parts are much more durable. It was a more simplistic way of recording. There was just one microphone. Even Benny Goodman and the big bands in the '30s recorded with only one microphone, an overhead mike. Someone came in here last year, and they turned down working in the studio because it didn't have a ninety-six-track capability! I was reduced to hysterics. That's all really bullshit. My God, we used to record the New York Philharmonic, Leonard Bernstein, with one mike.

Those guys in the '20s and '30s were out there. They were documentarians. They had an ear for talent. They would set up the equipment, they would cut the tracks, and then onto the next person. Some guys were tremendously musical as producers.

Art Satherley went back and forth between country music and blues, and so did Tommy Rockwell, Don Law, and Frank Walker. It seems that none of them had a real specialization. In other words, they were all expected to record and to find rural gospel artists and blues artists, on the one hand, and white string bands on the other hand. They were very selective, and the selectivity was really occasioned by what they thought would sell. To my mind that's the way producers are supposed to be.

When you acquire acetates, where do you get them?

We [Columbia/Legacy] have a huge archive back east at a place called Iron Mountain, which is about a hundred miles north of New York City. That's where all the assets of this company are: metal parts that were recorded in the '20s and '30s; acetates from the late '30s up to 1948, when we started to use tape; and all the tapes. They're stored at this huge facility that looks like something out of James Bond. It's the most incredible thing you've ever seen in your life. That's where they were. They have a whole storage system.

There's a regular procedure that producers go through. Once we decide that we're going to do a project, then I do the research for the sides that I want or, generally, everything the guy recorded. We put in a request. There's a whole methodology that we employ. It goes to the studio in New York. Then it goes up to the facility, Iron Mountain. They search it, and they get the stuff. And then I have it.

I did a thing called *The Retrospective*, which is a four-CD set. All the '20s, '30s stuff that we found—except for some of the very late '30s blues stuff, around '39, which were on acetate—everything was on metal parts. So the metal parts varied in quality. Some of them looked magnificent and hadn't been played since 1926 or '7. You put them on, and they were terrible. Others looked awful. They were stained, looked like they were ready to be thrown out. You'd play them, and they would be absolutely perfect. There was no rhyme or reason. We had no formula. We had to take every single track individually and set up for each track individually. In other words, we couldn't make a setup that would work for all the things that we were doing. It was just impossible. Obviously, that compounded our work.

BILL MONROE, *THE ESSENTIAL BILL MONROE AND HIS BLUEGRASS BOYS 1945-1949* (COMPILATION, 1992, COLUMBIA/LEGACY)

LAWRENCE COHN

The project was my idea. Luckily, I found the original acetates that were recorded at the sessions in the '40s. They were in dreadful shape. There were a lot of tapes that had been done over the years, rechanneled stereo and all kinds of crappy endeavors. I destroyed those things and threw them away. As I said, we'd found the original acetates. They were beat up and scratched. We worked hard to clean them up and get them to where I felt they were really proper.

I remastered the thing three different times, because it was not quite right till the end, and then, of course, it was right. My engineer said I was hallucinating. I was hearing things. He locked me out of the studio at a point. He claimed I was giving him a nervous breakdown.

I said, "Well, I don't know what to tell you. All I know is that it just does not sound the way I want it to."

In the end it came out very well. I found so many unissued alternate takes. I know Bill was very happy. He went on Nashville television, TNN, with the box and said that he felt it was the nicest thing that anyone had ever done for him, for his career. Unsolicited, he sent me an autographed picture saying, "Dear Larry, thanks for a great job." I understand, from a friend of mine, who was his manager for many years, that he saw Monroe do that maybe four or five times in twenty-five years. So I was very proud. I was very happy that I could give it to him before he passed away.

BOB WILLS, *THE ESSENTIAL BOB WILLS 1935-1947* (COMPILATION, 1992, COLUMBIA LEGACY)

BOB IRWIN

That's the thing that's most intriguing to me about country performers as opposed to rock 'n' roll performers. And I don't mean this to be disparaging at all toward rock 'n' roll performers, but country guys were nailing this stuff in one to three takes. You listen to Bob Wills lacquers from the '30s and '40s [supervised by Don Law]. It's pretty much—for all intents and purposes—the band producing themselves. When [guitarist] Eldon Shamblin blows a solo, the whole band stops. You hear them laugh, and then they kick up the next take. And like [Wills's band] the Texas Playboys, many country musicians were, number one, in essence producing themselves and, number two, nailing stuff in two or three takes.

In the earlier days, when people were recording to lacquer or to full-track mono tape, I really do believe that, not just in Don Law's case, but with most producers, it was much more in an A&R capacity than in a producer's capacity. They let the groups be themselves more. Outside of certain miking techniques, which I'm sure was more the engineer's responsibility than the producer's, I can't hear the producer. I could be wrong about that. Maybe Don Law was sitting there saying, "No, no, no, I don't want that to sound like that. I want the mike over there." But I'm going to bet that most of the time the engineer was doing that. Certainly, once you start hitting the mid-to-late '50s and, especially, the early '60s, you can hear producers' trademarks all over the place. That's not so much the case in the '30s and '40s. People weren't picking producers. Producers were pretty much assigned, or the producers were picking which artists they were going to work with.

Could be his name, but Don Law (1902–1982) illustrates early record production—as a rule. He recalls any number of film directors from Hollywood's studio era: professionals not considered auteurs.

Law immigrated to the States in 1924. By the end of the Depression, he was supervising recording sessions for the American Record Corporation, working with another pioneering A&R man, "Uncle" Art Satherley. When Satherley retired in 1952, Law was appointed head of Columbia's country division. During the '50s and '60s, he produced a full roster of country legends: Lefty Frizzell, Johnny Cash, Flatt & Scruggs, Jimmy Dean, Ray Price, Johnny Horton, Marty Robbins, and the Statler Brothers.

GENE AUTRY, *THE ESSENTIAL GENE AUTRY (1933-1946)* (COMPILATION, 1992, COLUMBIA/LEGACY)

DON LAW JR.

My father came from a formal English background. He was a member of the London Choral Society. He had two uncles who had been knighted. He came over [in 1924], and through family connections, he was given a job in the import-export steel business. He worked in New York. After the steel market collapsed, he decided, "I'm going to go south."

He went down to Georgia, and he hooked up with a White Russian friend of the family. With backing, they started a large sheep ranch. The sheep got hit by some disease. My father described riding from dawn till dusk, doing an operation on these sheep—trying to save them and being unable to. He said it was catastrophic. So the White Russian friend went down to Brazil.

My father said, "I'm going to go see what cowboys are about." He got on the bus and went to Dallas. He really had no idea what he was going to do. He went to work for Brunswick, who made bowling balls and phonograph records. They were bought by the American Record Corporation [in 1931]. There, he started working with another Englishman named Art Satherley, and he worked his way into doing field recordings. Then ARC took over Columbia [1934], whose home base was Bridgeport, Connecticut. That was before they were bought by CBS [in 1938]. My father and Satherley did the early recordings of Gene Autry—"Back in the Saddle Again" and the first recording of "Rudolph, the Red-Nosed Reindeer"—and a lot of the early Carter Family stuff.

ROBERT JOHNSON, THE COMPLETE RECORDINGS (1936–1937) (COMPILATION, 1990, COLUMBIA/LEGACY)

LAWRENCE COHN

Don Law made all of the Robert Johnson recordings; he was Robert Johnson's producer. He had nothing to do with the LPs [issued 1961, 1970]. The guy responsible for the LPs was a guy who was a staff producer at Columbia Records in the '60s, named Frank Driggs. He was one of the premier jazz reissue guys. It was his idea to reissue the Robert Johnson stuff. He did the two LPs, and of course he worked for John Hammond Sr. Hammond was the consummate Robert Johnson freak. So he had Hammond's full support. By that time, Law was strictly doing country music and nothing else.

DON LAW JR.

I always imagine my father as an oddity early on; it certainly wasn't what he was used to in England. It was very different than anything he had been exposed to, and it fascinated him. It was kind of like what happened later in the '60s with the British blues musicians who picked up on American blues and then changed the blues form and changed popular music forever. There was a little bit of that same fascination for him, I'm sure, as an Englishman.

But I think who he signed and what he recorded was a function of if he really liked what he heard. In the beginning, he did a lot of blues. A lot of those field recordings were both country-and-western artists.

I talked with my father about the sessions he did with Robert Johnson [in San Antonio, 1936, and Dallas, 1937]. They had to do those recordings in un-air-conditioned venues; they made the record on-site. You had an engineer, and as they recorded, they were actually cutting the record—the final record. It was the engineer, Robert Johnson, my father, and a bottle of whiskey. They would all drink.

At the session in San Antonio, they had a bathtub filled with ice and a fan blowing the air across the ice to keep the records from melting. Field recordings were really pretty crude and primitive.

My father was a quasi-salesman. He had to go try to sell it; he had to get the record distributed, get it out into the marketplace, around to stores and so forth. It wasn't a very big business back in the '30s, particularly in the South.

My mother talked about walking down the street with Robert Johnson and my father. She described this really bizarre circumstance, where my father was determined to walk alongside Robert, and Robert was determined not to let him. My father kept stopping, and Robert kept walking farther back. My mother, who was from Texas, said, "Don, he can't walk with you because he'd be seen as 'uppity.' He'd get beaten up." My father didn't get it. It wasn't like where he'd come from, but he had wanted no part of the environment that he left.

When I think of my father, I think of that Jack London passage where he talks about "a sailor on horseback" — a man totally out of his environment. I think of my father as this wrecked English gentlemen in the Deep South, trying to walk along the road with Robert Johnson. It must've been the strangest thing in the world: this guy with an English accent recording this Delta blues singer. A "sailor on horseback" — I love that image of cultural dichotomy: the two of them walking down the street; my father bailing Johnson out of jail; that whole nonsense of "I'm lonesome, and there's a lady here. She wants fifty cents, and I lacks a nickel."

In 1942, Glenn Wallichs, Johnny Mercer, and Buddy DeSylva formed Capitol Records in Hollywood. The first country recording issued by the new company was Tex Ritter's "Jingle, Jangle, Jingle."

TEX RITTER, "JINGLE, JANGLE, JINGLE" (1942), *CAPITOL COLLECTORS SERIES* (COMPILATION, 1992, CAPITOL)

KEN NELSON

One day, Glenn came to Chicago and asked Lee [Gillette] what he was doing. He told him, "I'm musical director of [radio station] WJJD."

Glenn said, "You're just the guy I'm looking for." So Lee and his wife moved out to California, and I went back to my old job at JJD. We had live country music at that time. We had Uncle Henry's Kentucky Mountaineers, Bob Atcher, and several other artists [including Les Paul as "Rubarb Red"]. The program was called the *Suppertime Frolic*, and it was tremendously popular. Then, the station decided they were going to drop the live musicians, and I had to buy records by the umpteen millions. It was all country records. I bought records from Canada and, even, from England.

Are you familiar with transcriptions [recordings cut to sixteen-inch discs for radio broadcasts]? There was Standard. There was World, which was owned by Decca. There was Lang-Worth and Capitol. When Lee went with Capitol, he started out in the transcription department. He wasn't producing any records at all. Finally, they decided that they were going to go into the country field. At that time it was called "hillbilly." So Lee took over the country department of Capitol. Then, they decided he couldn't do both jobs, and Lee went strictly into country.

Lee went to Glenn Wallichs, who was president of Capitol. He said, "Hey, get Ken Nelson out here." I had a fairly good knowledge of songs. So Capitol brought me out to take over the transcription department [in 1946].

With the help of Cliffie Stone, Lee really got into the country department.* He brought Tex Williams to Capitol. He brought Hank Thompson, Tennessee Ernie Ford, and Merle Travis. Next, Capitol decided that they wanted Lee over in the pop department, and I took over the country department. Lee was probably the greatest producer of that era. He did all of Nat King Cole. He did Kay Starr, Stan Kenton, and Jan Garber. He did Guy Lombardo.

Oh, and Capitol put transcriptions out of business. They started to give away promotion records, started to send them to radio stations. Lee had recorded a song on transcription called "Twelfth Street Rag" with Pee Wee Hunt. The demand for it as a record was tremendous. There weren't any records [only transcriptions were available]. So they [Capitol] decided to put out a record and to give them away [to radio stations for promotional purposes]. Before that, the radio stations had to buy their records. I know because I was buying them. All the other [transcription] companies said, "Hey what's going on here?" So record labels started to give out promotion records. The radio stations said, "What the

---

*A musician, producer, and A&R man par excellence, Cliffie Stone (1927–1998) was largely responsible for Capitol's exceptional roster of country musicians. He was inducted into the Country Music Hall of Fame in 1989.

hell? We're getting all these records free. Why should we pay for transcriptions?" Every transcription company went out of business. Capitol Transcriptions shut down, and I took over the country department.

THE MADDOX BROTHERS AND ROSE, AMERICA'S MOST COLORFUL HILLBILLY BAND: THEIR ORIGINAL RECORDINGS, VOL. 2, 1946-1951 (COMPILATION, 1995, ARHOOLIE)

DON PIERCE

At that time following the war, if you were in an Army uniform and went to Bel Air, which is a very exclusive club, they'd let you play golf. So a buddy and I had both gotten our discharge, and we went to California. We had a lot of fun and played a lot of golf. While we were at Bel Air, they asked if a person could join us for nine holes, and it turned out to be Hoagy Carmichael [actor, musician, and composer of "Stardust" and "Georgia on My Mind"]. He was a charming person, and we had a real good time. Later on, I met him at the Melrose Grotto. We talked shortly, and I told him that I was in the music business. He made one remark to me. "When you're making stuff," he said, "keep your eye on the dollar. Don't get swept away by something that you happen to like." In other words, don't be overly artistic.

I first worked in the studio probably in 1946 and '47. There was a little studio called Crystal down at the Riverside Drive in Los Angeles. Eddie Dean did "I Dreamed of a Hillbilly Heaven" in that studio and "One Has My Name and One Has My Heart." We were doing business with them, and I produced the Maddox Brothers and Rose there, a number of things. I produced T. Texas Tyler there, and later on, I produced "Deck of Cards" by T. Texas Tyler. But we did that at Radio Recorders up on Hollywood Boulevard.

We did sound checks, and we'd experiment until we got the right balance. I was always a stickler for getting the vocalist isolated to the point where the feed in music didn't make the lyrics hard to understand. That was always frustrating to me, not being able to understand the lyrics to a song. But other than that I was more concerned with song selection and getting an acceptable recording and getting the maximum number of tunes in during the amount of time given us by the union so that we could avoid the time-and-a-half cost of overruns.

T. TEXAS TYLER, "DECK OF CARDS" (1946, 4 STAR)

DON PIERCE

It's a funny thing how I came across that song. Tex Tyler had made it into a transcription [disc, formatted for radio play]. I think he was in West Virginia at the time working with Little Jimmy Dickens. When he came out West and formed a Western swing band, he brought the transcriptions that he had, which were just for radio airplay at that time.

He took them down to ["border blaster"] XERB, the Mexican radio station right across from San Diego, in Tijuana. Matter of fact, it was out on Rosarito Beach. They had 150,000 watts that they aimed right up the coast of the U.S. They could sell products by mail order with that powerful signal. So he left those transcriptions down there, and they played them.

I'd go out and sell records on the road. I'd go up in the San Joachim Valley and go all through Bakersfield and Fresno and Stockton and Sacramento, go all the way up to Washington. People started asking for "Deck of Cards."

I said, "There is no such record. I control T. Texas Tyler, so that's it."

But when I got ahold of Tex, I said, "Tex, I've got people wanting to get this record 'Deck of Cards.' What is it?"

He said, "That's no good for a phonograph record. That's just a spoken recitation. I've got it on a transcription."

"It doesn't make any difference," I said. "We've got to make that record." And so we did.

We recorded on acetates. We were very concerned that . . . On a 78-speed record, we could just barely get three minutes of sound on a side. The song was running long. We didn't want to eliminate any of the story; it was all important. We had to speed up the recitation, to get it down to three minutes and ten seconds. We had Tex Tyler say it just a little faster.

But we were afraid that, when the pressings came out, needles wouldn't track. They'd get kicked out of the groove. We had to be careful not to have too much bass sound in there because there were wide swings down at the bottom of the groove. You could see them with a magnifier. We had to limit the bass and concentrate on the higher sounds so that we could get that much music, that much recording, on the disc.

That was typical of what we did when we recorded on acetates. Then, we made the metal master [or "matrix," created by electrocoating or plating the original lacquer or acetate] and, then, the metal mother and, then, from it the stampers to press records on shellac. We had a plant there in Pasadena where we made the [shellac and, later, vinyl] biscuits that records were made of. We went from the raw material to the finished product right there. Except for the plating. We got the plating done over in Culver City. But we would record there and make the pressings there and warehouse it there and ship from there. We did the whole ball of wax.

I think we shipped about seven-, eight-hundred-thousand copies of "Deck of Cards" on 78-speed. We just worried about production, production, production.

TEX WILLIAMS AND HIS WESTERN CARAVAN, "SMOKE! SMOKE! SMOKE! (THAT CIGARETTE)" (1947), *SMOKE SMOKE SMOKE* (ALBUM, 1960, CAPITOL)

JOHN PALLADINO

The lady who became my wife was the engineer on "Smoke! Smoke! Smoke! (That Cigarette)" [a song written by Merle Travis for Tex Williams]. At that time there was a scarcity of guys. We were coming out of the war, and women had started to do a lot more stuff. She and my sister did what the Army called "deletion work." They took radio checks [live broadcasts recorded on acetate], maybe recorded at Radio Recorders, and deleted the commercials. Then, those records were sent overseas to the Armed Forces.

The theory of the echo-chamber is not that new, but here's how it worked. We were forced to get into small studios. As a commercial recording company, we had to have flexibility. You couldn't have a studio that was big and had a very roomy sound to it. You wouldn't have enough control. For example, we wouldn't be able to do country music.

Country music depends on close miking and, usually, on a lot of individual mikes. Using as many mikes as you had, you would try to get an individual good sound for all the principal guys in a band with mikes of their own. As soon as you did that, the sound became very close. But it wasn't a very exciting sound. It kind of fell flat in the studio.

We knew that the only way you could extend that sound was through the use of echo-chambers. They could be as dumb as a stairwell in a big building. Sometimes, especially when you had to go on remotes, you could put up an echo-chamber, or you would try to find a little room—maybe, a tiled restroom—with very live walls. You had to put a mike in there, and you had to put a speaker in there. Then, you fed a portion of what you were picking up on your microphones into that chamber [through the speaker], and you balanced the amount of reverberation against the quality of sound that you were attempting. The echo-chambers were on the roof at Radio Recorders and on the roof at [Capitol Records Studio on] Melrose. At the [Capitol Records] Tower, they were underground. You'll notice there's a great deal of difference between recordings by various companies because of the sounds of their chambers. Some of them got very distinctive sounds. They might try for more high-end, more delay, and other little tricks.

If a record producer hears a sound done by an independent recording studio, he pretty well knows what's coming out of that place. He's not going to go in there and start telling the engineer how to make a recording. He's going to go in there and sit down. His job is to judge the recording musically. That's the way the good producers did it. All of the Capitol guys used that system. In the early days, it was interesting to see guys like Lee Gillette and, later, Ken Nelson learn the business as we were learning too. Everybody was in the same boat. We knew we were dependent on each other to make the right kinds of recordings.

THE DINNING SISTERS, "BUTTONS AND BOWS" (1947), *BEST OF THE DINNING SISTERS* (COMPILATION, 1998, COLLECTOR'S CHOICE)

JOHN PALLADINO

Sometime in 1942, I came to Radio Recorders [in Los Angeles] and began working as an engineer. It was a very progressive studio. When tape came [in 1948, though it wasn't fully adopted until the early 1950s], editing became part of the recording process. We did editing for two reasons. You either had errors that you are trying to dodge, or you were fighting time. Doing a session, you might not have the leisure of saying, "Another take; another take; another take." Right away, during a take, the producer might say [to the engineer], "Let's use the first half of the last take, and the second half of this one." Usually, it was one edit, and not something that changed the feel of the record. Also, in those days we had a lot of time restrictions on records — singles, ten-inch LPs, twelve-inch LPs. We were restricted by the sheer physical properties of the formats.

BOB IRWIN

The earlier edits to analog tape that I've seen were not necessarily fix-oriented. I think the audience, the producers, the artists, and the music in general were much more forgiving back then and, ultimately, much more interesting. Rather than being fix-oriented, edits had to do with things like adding a solo from another take that was particularly fiery, or a vocal phrase or a chorus that was particularly touching, as opposed to so-and-so sang flat there. Let's pick up "but love" from this take and put it in another. Which is what a lot of analog editing seemed to be based upon as time went on.

Although I'm sure that they exist, I can't off the top of my head give you an example of a country recording that I've worked on from the early '50s where something went wrong and they fixed it with an edit, as opposed to calling for another take. I can remember — not song by song — but specific instances where I go, "My God, look at this. They took the solo from this one and put it into here. And listen why!"

You start to see the big change occurring in the latter half of the '50s. It took analog tape literally a good four, five, six years before it differed significantly from cutting to an acetate. I'd probably date it to the advent of multitracking, when Nashville got its first half-inch, three-track recorders in 1958. That's when the whole arena pretty much changed. Up till that time they were still recording to full-track mono tape. It was just a different medium than the lacquer.

KEN NELSON

The first hit record I made was in Chicago with the Dinning Sisters—"Buttons and Bows." During that period, Jimmy Petrillo, who was the president of the Musicians' Union, had threatened to strike, and in fact they were going to strike. All the record companies got panicky, and that's how I actually got started with Capitol [Records]. They were all trying to get in as many [recording] sessions as possible before the strike. The Dinning Sisters were in Chicago, so I recorded them.

Later, when tape first came in, the Dinnings came out to Hollywood. Lee [Gillette] did the session. I did the one in Chicago because they had no choice. They were booked with me. But after the Dinnings recorded with Lee, they left to go to the airport to catch a plane back to Chicago. Lee listened to the tape, and there was a mistake in it. So he grabbed a cab and ran out to the airport and got the Sisters back. They didn't do the whole thing, only the part where the mistake was made. It saved them a barrel of money.

MERLE TRAVIS, *FOLK SONGS OF THE HILLS* (ORIGINAL RECORDINGS, 1947, CAPITOL; COMPILATION, 1993, BEAR FAMILY)

THOM BRESH (guitarist/producer/Travis's son)
Lee Gillette [producer at Capitol Records] was asking him to write more folk songs. Travis was irritated by that. "You don't write a folk song," he said. "People write folk songs. They come out of the ground—the hills. That's why they're called folk songs."

Lee Gillette said, "Well, just write something that sounds like a folk song."

"That's why I sarcastically wrote 'Sixteen Tons,'" he said. "First of all, you can't load"—and he was serious—"you just can't load sixteen tons of number-nine coal. No man can do that. It's like John Henry." He says, "I just gave it ['Sixteen Tons'] to Lee Gillette, and Tennessee Ernie Ford sold it." Travis used to use this line. He said, "Never did like that tune till Tennessee Ernie Ford sold about 5 million copies. Then, I got to where I loved it."

You could not get him to say that he wrote "Dark as a Dungeon." "It's a tune I made up." He would not use the word "write," "write a song." He'd say, "Well, I didn't write it. I just made it up. That's why they're not folk songs, because I made them up. I just put into rhyme and story what I saw around the coal mine."

They inducted him into the Smithsonian Institution as a great American folk song writer. He wouldn't go to the ceremony. They put him in, but he wouldn't go.

When he got the letter, he said, "When is this induction?"

I'm using a fictitious date. "It's going to be June 3."

"Write on the calendar over there, 'Sick.'" He said there was no way he could go in there and take credit for folk songs when he made them up. And that's just the way it was, period, the end.

He said he wrote "Dark as a Dungeon" after making love to a pretty girl in Redondo Beach. "I came out of her apartment. I got on a motorcycle. It was dark, and I looked up. There was a lone street lamp up there."

He said, "I was going to go back out to the San Fernando Valley, and I thought, 'Oh no, I'm supposed to be writing some of those folk songs.' I sat there on a Harley-Davidson underneath that street lamp that looked like a lone miner's lamp in the darkness. That's what it looked like as far as what I thought—the image. I sat there and said, 'Okay, folk songs usually come from the Irish. How do they write?'

"I wrote on a piece of paper, 'Now listen ye children so young and so fine, and seek not your fortune in the dark, dreary mine.'"

"I sat there," he said, "and I wrote that verse in Redondo Beach on a Harley-Davidson"—or an Indian, I don't remember which it was—"looking at a lone street lamp after making love to a pretty girl. That's not a folk song."

But of course "Dark as a Dungeon"—if you look at it—is considered one of the great folk songs of that era. That whole coal-mining era was documented in music by Merle Travis. And that's just the way it is, but to him that's not the way it was at all. It's just something that he knew something about.

He could write about anything. He had a brilliant mind. He wrote all of those train segments for the old Johnny Cash TV show. If they did "Come On, Ride This Train," he'd write the train segments. That was his job. They would say, "Travis, we need a four- or five-song medley on the B&O Railroad."

"That's like taking candy from a baby," he said. "I don't do nothin' except go to the library, read about the B&O, and tell different stories in rhyme. Any idiot could do that."

You try it. Go read a book and write five songs. "Oh, here's a good chapter. That would make a good song." To him, that was like getting paid for doing nothing.

He wouldn't take credit for anything. Grandpa Jones said one time, "He was too humble." If you came up to him and said, "I sure enjoyed your picking Merle," he'd say, "I don't pick like Thom Bresh here," and he'd point at me.

Don't compliment him. Boy, if someone said, "Ladies and Gentlemen, here he is—a legend in his own time," he'd say, "I could just walk out right now and leave. Why do they have to say stuff like that?" It upset him, and he'd go onstage shaking. He never grasped what he'd done. He was a real interesting character.

DALE EVANS, "DON'T EVER FALL IN LOVE WITH A COWBOY" (1949), *HAPPY TRAILS: THE ROY ROGERS COLLECTION 1937-1990* (COMPILATION, 1999, RHINO)

JAMES AUSTIN

In our *Roy Rogers Collection* we put out a song—Dale Evans singing "Don't Ever Fall in Love with a Cowboy"—which is really great. I found out about it through the family. They said, "Maybe you can help us find this song." Actually, Cheryl Rogers Barnett, who is Roy and Dale's daughter, said, "I'm trying to find this." Some of the relatives of Roy, the granddaughters sing in a group called the Rogers Legacy. They wanted the granddaughters to sing that song: "We know about it. My mom's talked about it, but I have nothing on it. I can't find any publishing on it, no lyrics, nothing. But my mom says she did sing that song."

I called the Country Music Foundation, and they were kind enough to help us out. To put it in the [Rhino Records] collection, I needed a letter from the Rogers's family saying that they, indeed, authorized the duplication of the recorded song. We found out that it was a great record, definitely worthy of inclusion in the collection. And it's something that most people didn't even know existed, and it was released as a single. It just fell through the cracks.

INTERLUDE
THE PRODUCER AS DIRECTOR

STEVE CROPPER

The jobs of movie producer and record producer are totally different. The movie producer is the guy that goes around, gets the financing, does all that sort of stuff. That doesn't mean he isn't on set and he isn't around. That doesn't mean he isn't giving suggestions to the director. But the director is the hands-on guy. So actually I'm a musical director rather than a record producer, but producer is what they coin it, so that's what we go with. But there is a definite difference in the job.

PETE ANDERSON

You wear a multitude of hats, but basically it's two jobs. One, you're very much like the director of a film. You work on the script or the songs. You choose the cinematographer or the engineer. You get the locations or the studio. You help cast the actors or the musicians. You work with their performances. Everything that a director would do in a film is very much what a record producer does. Then, you're also like a general contractor. A guy comes to you and says, "I want you to build a swimming pool in my backyard." You go, "Okay, here are the drawings. Here's what it's going to look like. Here's what it's going to cost, and here's how long it's going to take. Give me half the money up front. When I'm done and you're happy, give me the back half." So those are the two broadest terms, I think, in trying to explain to people what a record producer does.

CRAIG STREET

It's a weird, floaty, bizarre kind of a job. It's a really ambiguous job. There's such a wide range of what producers do that it's hard for people to pin down. I think a contractor in construction or an architect or a film director is the easiest way to pin it down. And so, for example, that gives you the realm, the range of possibilities that opens up.

The thing that has always been the most interesting to me is when you have a group of people together in a room with the goal of doing one thing. The artist is always the boss, but people are always looking to the producer and going, "What do we do now?" Some producers lead with an iron fist, just like some film directors—Hitchcock. "This is how it goes. This is how it is storyboarded. This is exactly what we do." Some architects—Frank Lloyd Wright—"this is how it is. This is the furniture you're going to have. These are the curtains you're going to have."

Others, an architect like [John] Lautner or directors like Cassavetes and Fellini: "Let's see what happens. Let's invent another scene, right now. I know it's not written down, but let's do it." You start to rely on the relationship with everybody in the room, the understanding that everybody has something to offer.

If there's a method—and I say if, because I'm trying like mad for there not to be—then it's a bit of a Tom Sawyer thing. I'm getting other people to paint the fence. I'm identifying who those people are. It's a bit of being like a voyeur. I really get off on what happens when people get in a room together. Now the trick is to control who gets into the room. I know that if I put certain thinking, breathing, feeling musicians in a room with certain other musicians—in a room that's a wonderful environment with some great songs—good stuff is going to happen. So those are the control factors, rather than coming in and telling somebody precisely what to play. Once people know that you're trusting them to be them, you get a lot more out of musicians. That's part of it. The other part of it is that I draw really heavily from sources that are nonmusical.

DON LAW JR.

My father was successful in being able to carve out his piece. He existed somewhat autonomously down there [in Nashville]. He had to deal with New York, but for a lot of that time, for a lot of his career, he was his own fiefdom. Back when everything was under one roof, you had the artists, and you were in your own studios with your own engineers. It was pretty much all in-house in a way, kind of like the movie studios were. I always got the sense that he was pretty much left alone most of the time.

It took some effort on my father's part to get Columbia to buy the Quonset Hut [Owen and Harold Bradley's Music Row recording studio], but it was one of the early studios to get that music going. Then, all of a sudden, other companies started doing the same thing. Nashville became more of a central location.

The interesting thing about that market and those artists is that they did well consistently. If you looked at the popular-music market, there was a lot of variability in it, whereas the country market was pretty stable. My father was able to keep that fairly successful. At times he would outsell the popular music division. I remember he and Mitch Miller occasionally had their issues. But the Columbia division in Nashville did quite well for quite a long time. I think his track record spoke for itself.

JIM ED NORMAN

I guess it's a pendulum that swings all the time. It starts off. There're some good things that come from the system, but if you're not careful, the pendulum swings too far. The system becomes more powerful. It begins to take over. If the artists aren't careful, their art can begin to suffer. It declines because people serve the system rather than the muses, if you will. If there's anything that a system like that [Nashville's] has to do, it's to be vigilant and not to create demands on people that are unrealistic.

I say we have to be vigilant and not let that happen, but I guess, to some extent, it's a market-driven system. It takes care of itself. When the artistic community begins to complain about the quality of the music coming out of a particular system, it doesn't take long for the energies that persist to revive the system, so that great music comes out of it. If the system has begun to take over, then, typically, something comes along that busts out of that situation.

When the creative people come to me, their frustration and their ire begin to rise to a level of out-and-out rancor—they're just, "I hate what's going on here! This stinks. This is terrible. How could this happen?"—I always tell them that it's at these times that I have my greatest optimism because I know that out of that frustration will come someone challenging the system, the status quo, and that some fabulous music will come out of it.

A unique system and process developed in Nashville. There are times when that system serves the process extraordinarily well, and then there are times when the process maybe even impedes artistry, but then the frustration gets so high that the cork blows off, and once again in a cyclical sense a new kind of dynamic comes to the music and to the art.

MARSHALL CRENSHAW

Billy Sherrill is a good example of a super auteur-type country producer, somebody with an identifiable sound and a tremendous amount of style. Those Tammy Wynette records, I always compare them to Alfred Hitchcock productions. You can tell that he was really calculating about getting [the listener's] attention and, then, exploding at certain moments. The records rise and fall and have so much drama in them. You get the sense that everybody playing on the records is of one mind. They're spellbinding records; they're effectively done. My guess is that Sherrill was very, very autocratic and, also, really focused. He knew what the hell he was trying to do.

BOBBY BRADDOCK

I always tell people, if they want to know the job of a music producer, I say, "Think of it this way: a director is to film as a producer is to recording."

I'll tell a little anecdote about a lesson that I learned from a master producer, something that I never forgot. Back in the mid-1970s, guitar guru Chet Atkins was producing his own album—co-producing it with Buddy Killen—and decided to record a song of mine, "West Memphis Serenade." He liked the organ on my home demo, and wanted me to play the same thing on his session, and rented an organ just like the one I had at home. Toward the conclusion of the instrumental piece, I was using the organ drawbars to make a steel guitar sound.

The other musicians were hanging around the studio while Chet sat in the control room with Buddy as I was overdubbing an organ part. There was something that Chet wanted me to do differently, but rather than tell me over the talk-back, where everyone would hear it, he walked out into the studio and sat down next to me and said, almost in a whisper, "Why don't you do that thing just half as much? Maybe do it every other time. What do you think?" I wasn't about to argue with Chet Atkins and said, "Absolutely." Then he went back into the control room, and I played it again, exactly as Chet had suggested.

"Hey, I like that," he said over the talk-back; "let's do it that way." It was *his* idea but he was making it sound as if it were *my* idea. In the future, when I was a producer, I would always remember that kind gesture. Always leave musicians feeling good about themselves, and never do anything that might embarrass a musician in front of his or her peers.

2

TAPING TRACKS
CREATING THE PERFORMANCE,
1950-1966

At first, in the early '50s, magnetic tape was used as simply a new medium to do an old job: to capture musical performances. But a quick look at the recordings discussed in this chapter suggests an ensuing paradigm shift. Tape—mono, three-, and four-track—enabled the emergence of the record producer as a fully formed, recognizable figure. He distinguishes himself, less by what he captures (artists and repertoire: Don Law recording Lefty Frizzell singing "If You've Got the Money I've Got the Time"), than by the performances he artfully creates—stages in order to capture (production: Don Law enabling Johnny Cash's 1963 version of "Ring of Fire"). When Owen Bradley produces Patsy Cline's massive hits, he records a sonic concept just as much as he records an artist. In the vocabulary of film studies, the producer's purview is the mise-en-scène, in all of that term's mystery.

As a means of controlling the market for country music, four major record companies—Decca, RCA, Columbia, and Capitol—developed a studio system in Nashville analogous to Hollywood's. The catalyst that sped this integration of an industry was the Quonset Hut, an independent studio built in 1954–1955, and owned by Owen and Harold Bradley. The hits cut at this facility—especially those recorded by Owen Bradley (Decca), Chet Atkins (RCA), Don Law (Columbia), and Ken Nelson (Capitol)—were in a radio-friendly style that became known as the Nashville sound. It transformed the market for country from a strictly regional to a national audience. In fairly short order, RCA built its own "Studio B" in 1956. Columbia bought the Quonset Hut in 1962, and Owen Bradley converted a barn just outside of Nashville into another studio.

LEFTY FRIZZELL, *LOOK WHAT THOUGHTS WILL DO* (ORIGINAL RECORDINGS, 1950–1965; COMPILATION, 1997, COLUMBIA/LEGACY)

BOB IRWIN

A&R meetings are held at Sony Legacy, the same way they're held at Sundazed and every other record company on the planet. Ideas are put on the table, discussed, and fine-tuned. Everyone knew and was in agreement that there had to be a good Lefty Frizzell compilation out there. The only things available were packages done years and years ago with pretty lousy transfers.

Back in the '60s, when people started packaging country artists' past works—works taken from lacquer sources—the whole MO was to get rid of any semblance of noise. Therefore, they cut off the whole top-end and low-end of the performances. You were left with what the American public, to this day, thinks a 78-rpm recording sounds like: [cups hands] *like that*. Which is not what a 78-rpm record sounds like, if you have a good record. The same thing is true of transcription lacquers [discs for radio broadcast], but I'm getting ahead of the story.

I knew that I wanted to focus primarily on the early period. And once I started reviewing it, going over things, I really wanted to push for a double-disc set. That's not always, but very often, a tough sell to a record company that's marketing driven. But it was agreed that we should do a two-CD set and, eventually, at some point distill it down to a single CD set to sell at a lesser price.

My next step was to start putting together the A&R for the package, which has to be centered on the obvious songs, the hits. I've always been intrigued that certain greatest-hits albums live their own life. It's not only the *Buffalo Springfield Retrospective*. But that album to me and hundreds of other fans had a very deliberate sequence and deliberate feel of its own. It became an album unto itself, rather than just a collection of an artist's songs.

That's the way I've always tried to work when I'm doing a collection. After I have a centerpiece of the hits—the very obvious songs that have to be there—I try and disengage myself from popular opinion, from what other people expect you to put on there, and go with my heart. I go with songs that I think truly complement each other, and with what the artist might want people to hear. Indeed, if the artist is still with us, he's the first person you talk to. Which was impossible to do with Lefty.

That meant I needed probably two weeks of studio time where I did nothing but listen—listen in the truest sense—not by listening to the bogus, horrible-sounding records and discs that were out there, but by going back to original lacquers, playing through them to get overwhelmed with that feeling. There's not a better feeling in the world than sitting there with the transcription lacquer of a tune that someone's never heard before and getting a lump in your throat because it's so astounding. It's the best high in the world in my book.

Everything on that set was taken from the absolute original sources. Every single transcription lacquer was gone through by me. Every analog recording was gone through by me, up to that point—the early '60s—which was the set's predetermined stopping point. The earliest part of the disc, probably all of disc one, was very much discovery time. Nowadays, who cares if there's a little bit of noise on the top end? You want to hear the cymbals. You want to hear the low end. The sounds that they were able to capture to lacquer were astounding. The dynamic range is jaw-dropping.

What did you learn from the tapes?

For example, from October 19, 1951, the original logsheet: Lefty in the studio put down songs like "I Love You (Though I Know You're No Good)" "You're Here, So Everything's Alright"—one or two other songs. Next to each song in [producer] Don Law's handwriting is "NG" for "No Good."

You realize, that was a call. Don heard what was going on that day, and who knows, it could have been a million-and-one things. They were just plain old having a bad day. Lefty was having throat problems. Who knows? But Don brought Lefty back three months later, basically to recut all the songs. And those were the versions that were issued. That happens all the time.

MARTHA CARSON, "SATISFIED" (1951), *SINGS* (RCA/CAMDEN)

KEN NELSON

We used to record at the Tulane Hotel.* The thing about Nashville, you use mostly all the same musicians all the time, like Grady Martin and Harold Bradley and Pig [Robbins], the piano player. You had a group of musicians that you used on various sessions. I used Chet [Atkins] a lot when I first came to Nashville. He was playing guitar for me. In fact he did all the Martha Carson sessions. The artist usually knew who he wanted to use, and if he didn't, I would pick the musicians. It was just that easy, or that was just the way it was.†

HANK WILLIAMS, "I'LL NEVER GET OUT OF THIS WORLD ALIVE" (1952), *40 GREATEST HITS* (POLYGRAM)

CHET ATKINS

Hank had a lot of help out of Fred Rose. Fred was a great, great fixer. I had a long conversation with Gene Autry once. He used to write for Gene, you know, all those hits back in the '30s. Gene said, "You know, Fred's the greatest song fixer I've ever known. He's just wonderful at

---

* Recording sessions that took place in the Tulane Hotel were, more accurately, done at the Castle Studio located in the hotel. The studio opened in 1946. It was the first professional recording studio in Nashville.

† Nashville—as Music City, USA—is built on a foundation laid by Fred Rose, on songs published by Acuff-Rose, the company Roy Acuff and Rose formed in 1942. Most notably, it published the songs of Hank Williams, though Rose was, himself, one of America's great songwriters. His son, Wesley Rose, led Acuff-Rose Publishing after his father's death.

that." And he was. He wrote a lot of songs and gave them away. Half the time, he was upset at ASCAP [the American Society of Composers, Authors and Publishers], and he didn't want to put a song with them. He'd say, "Ah, you take it," and give it to the artist. He was a wonderful, wonderful guy.

BUDDY KILLEN

I worked with Hank. I did a lot of transcriptions with him and a lot of radio with him and some television and worked on the road with him. We recorded those transcriptions in WSM's studio. They shipped them out all over the country. We'd do mostly fifteen-minute programs. I don't remember if I cut a session with Hank. I was one of the busiest bass players in town. I recorded with everybody.

Let me go back. I came to Nashville as a musician on the Grand Ole Opry. Then, I wrote a few songs out of desperation. It gave me an opportunity. I was doing demos. Tree [Publishing] had just started, and they were paying me ten dollars a night to stand all night long and sing on demos of songs that announcers at WSM wrote. Of course, they gave the songs to Tree, but nothing was happening. The songs weren't getting cut, but by osmosis I started learning how to produce records.

I was a musician, and I was a songwriter. So I had sort of an innate understanding about music and songs. When Jack [Stapp, program director] called me down to WSM and asked me if I wanted to go to work for Tree [his company], I said, "I don't know anything about publishing."

"I don't either," he said. "We'll learn together."

That's how it got started. Because I knew that I had to get out there and get the job done, I didn't even have an office. I got Jack to get me a fifty-dollar tape recorder, and I went around. When I heard about a song or about a songwriter, I'd go see him and sign up a song with Tree. I found that I was capable of doing it all. It came together, just interlocked without any real effort on my part. I innately knew what I was supposed to do.

I made a lot of mistakes businesswise because I wasn't a businessman. They weren't devastating things, just little decision-making processes that you go through. But I had a feel for the song. I had a feel for the music. I had a feel for if someone was good or not. When you're a publisher or a producer, the most important thing you can have is an ear for the song. You must recognize a good song. I'm of the opinion that any producer who doesn't make it, normally, it's because he doesn't recognize a great song. It starts with that song, and you know what? It ends with it.

Cutting demos for Tree Publishing sounds like a
crash course in production.

You learn what you don't put on a record more than you learn what to put on it, because overproduction kills a record faster than underproduction. If you cover up the song, you've pretty well done some damage. You're going by your own gut feeling—that thing that hits your ear. You like it or you don't like it. All of us are playing twenty questions. No one's ever perfect in the assumption that they know what a hit record is. Sometimes, you'll think something is going to be a great smash, and it comes apart on you. But after having produced records for a while, you start getting a feel for where you're going.

When you go in to do a demo, you're trying to give the star the feeling that you think the song should have when he records it. Even without realizing what you were doing, you were producing a record that wasn't going to come out as a record but, instead, was going to come out cloned by somebody.

You've got to be careful about directing a demo toward one artist. Back in the early days of Tree, I tried to make the demo pretty generic, and yet present the song the best I could. If I did a demo directed toward Ernest Tubb, if he didn't cut that song, then who was going to cut it? To keep from taking it toward one guy, you'd just give the song what it needed, that special quality, that special feeling. I think finding the feeling that the song should have on the demo is more important than anything else. You can doctor it up. You can add horns, strings, fiddle, or banjo, but when you hear the demo, if the feel of the song doesn't grab you, then you've missed the most important part of it.

Hollywood may have employed a bunkhouse full of singing cowboys,
but until High Noon *(1952), film audiences heard country-and-western*
songs only when singers like Gene Autry and Roy Rogers were onscreen.
Dimitri Tiomkin's soundtrack to High Noon *altered that convention,*
announcing a new era in American cinema. It featured a Tiomkin-
composed popular song, "High Noon (Do Not Forsake Me)," sung by Tex
Ritter. It played as opening credits rolled. With that song Hollywood's
orientation toward "the popular" decisively shifted. The relationship

between song and score was reconceptualized, as was Hollywood's relationship to the recording industry. The notion that a soundtrack could be a collection of pre-existing (already recorded) pop tunes began with "High Noon."

TEX RITTER, "HIGH NOON (DO NOT FORSAKE ME)" (1952), *HIGH NOON* (BEAR FAMILY)

KEN NELSON

The first artist on Capitol Records was Tex Ritter [1942]. His first record was produced by Johnny Mercer, one of the founders of Capitol and a great songwriter.

I hadn't heard the soundtrack from the movie [*High Noon*], but I made the record. Lee [Gillette] heard it. He said, "Hey, you darn fool, you forgot the drums!"

I said, "What drums?" Lee was a drummer, and so we went in and overdubbed the drums on "High Noon." Overdubbing was pretty difficult at that time. I don't think there was tape, but I'm not positive. We did it from the acetate. It worked out. Of course, we had great engineers. We had John Palladino and Hugh Davies. Palladino was tops as far as an engineer—a mixer—was concerned.

I was there to get the best I could out of the artist. I believe that the emotion in a record is the important thing. It was my job to see that everything was under control and to listen to the sound. My main job was to listen for mistakes, listen for the balance. Microphone placement at that time was a lot different than it is today when everybody's got a microphone. We had microphones on the fiddle and on the steel [guitar] and on the piano, but the engineer would regulate it according to the sound. We didn't let anything overshadow anything else. We tried to blend them.

That's one of the problems with today's music. Musicians are listening to themselves and not to the artist. They're not listening as a group. I always said, "I want to hear every damn word." That was my philosophy. Today, they make musical tracks, and then the singer sings to it. And that's another thing that's wrong. There's no way that you can get the feel and the emotion. Then, of course, we didn't have charts most of the time. I'd write down where the fill-ins were to come in, like if the steel was to come in. Then I'd have this list of the fills, and I'd sit beside the engineer and tell him what was coming up.

I'd get with the art department. I had to approve pictures and liner notes. Sometimes I'd write them myself. Then I had to okay the record. I mean, after we recorded it, and it was put on a disc, I'd have to okay it—the sound and whether it was equalized correctly. That was all the job of the producer in the early days.

KITTY WELLS, "IT WASN'T GOD WHO MADE HONKY TONK ANGELS" (1952), *THE KITTY WELLS STORY* (MCA)

HAROLD BRADLEY

Paul Cohen came down here [to Nashville to supervise sessions for Decca Records] because it was cheaper to send down one man than it was to take Red Foley and his band—to pay for their transportation, their lodging, and their meals—to Cincinnati or to New York. It was cheaper for one man to come down. He'd stay for a month and record everybody in sight [notably, Kitty Wells, Webb Pierce, Ernest Tubb, and Red Foley]. It was kind of like what I call the shotgun approach. You're going to hit something, if you've got a wide enough shotgun. When he left Decca and started Todd Records, he didn't have the luxury of doing that. That's why he didn't have any real success at Todd. He could only do artists one at a time. Your odds weren't that good. Before, he recorded for a whole month. We [the session players] would be tied up for a whole month. We learned that Paul was really a good song man. He had no real musical talent, but he had a commercial ear for a song. If you sang a song to him and it struck his ear—he liked it—then, usually, he was right.

ELVIS PRESLEY, "THAT'S ALL RIGHT" (1954), *SUNRISE* (RCA)

ROLAND JANES

We generally worked on things until we got them pretty much right. That was one of the genius things about Sam Phillips. He was not afraid to take a song that wasn't perfect in some detail and release it, as long as it had a good, overall feel to it. For example, on Elvis Presley's record "That's All Right," in the middle he forgot the words. He goes into that "ah da-da de-de-de-de-de." That wasn't planned. That's just the way it was. But then, that particular take had the right feel, and Sam was not afraid to leave that in there like that. Most producers wouldn't have done that. They would've been scared to death. But Sam said, "No, that's the cut I want — the one with the right feel." That was what was most important to him. If the cut made you want to tap your foot or sing along, and the other cut — maybe it was a good cut — did not have that feel, then he would take the first one, even though it had one or two minor mistakes in it. I admired him for that.

THE LOUVIN BROTHERS, "WHEN I STOP DREAMING" (1955), *WHEN I STOP DREAMING: THE BEST OF THE LOUVIN BROTHERS* (ORIGINAL RECORDINGS, 1952–1962, CAPITOL; COMPILATION, 1995, RAZOR & TIE)

MARSHALL CRENSHAW

Some of those Louvin Brothers records are gorgeous in terms of sound, but some of the tracks that I didn't put on the compilation, like a few of the early gospel tracks, had this funny echo effect on certain chorus lines, used to create interest. There's one called "Pitfall" that's pretty gimmicky. And so, Capitol was a little bit into occasional gimmicky production effects. But not too much. I've said Ken Nelson was a purist type of producer, but he sometimes wasn't.

A couple of other tracks on the CD are from a Delmore Brothers tribute album that the Louvin's did. They're really simple recordings, but they're perfectly rendered and beautiful. Part of it has to do with the instruments. On those tunes, Ira Louvin is playing a Martin tenor guitar that belonged to one of the Delmore Brothers. It's a guitar with just the top four strings. Those Martin guitars from back then are delicate sounding. They have this nice top end.

KEN NELSON

Ira was more of a temperamental man, and Charlie was easygoing. Ira would get mad sometimes at Charlie—bawl him out once in a while—but never anything serious. Charlie, I guess, was just used to it. They were very easy to record. Whatever I said went. I was grateful for that.

Wesley Rose came to me and asked me to sign them. They were with Acuff-Rose [Publishing].

I said, "Great, I'll take them." Of course, I wouldn't have taken them if I didn't think they had some talent, but they were a fine team. Ira was a heck of a good writer.

Also, Wesley asked me to sign Roy Acuff. I did. But at that time, Capitol wasn't too hot on country stuff. It was called "hillbilly." I couldn't get any publicity from the sales or promotion department on Roy. He had a pure country sound. Anyway, I put out I don't know how many records but couldn't get off the ground. I made an album with him.

Finally, Wes came to me and said, "Ken, Roy just isn't happy. He isn't making it on Capitol. Would you release him?"

"Okay," I said. So I released him [from his contract]. And then, I had put this album out, and the darn album started to sell like crazy. One day, I was in with the promotion department. They asked me, "Why the heck did you let Roy Acuff go?"

I said, "Because you idiots wouldn't do a damn thing about him." I think the album is still selling.

FERLIN HUSKY, "GONE" (1956), VINTAGE COLLECTIONS (CAPITOL)

KEN NELSON

I went into the studio with Ferlin Husky, and I think I was about the first one to add a female voice to the Jordanaires [backing vocals]. We recorded "Gone." It was a smash hit, and as a result of that record, all the record companies—I just got a letter from Millie [Kirkham] the other day, who sang on the record. She said that since "Gone," which was, of course, many years ago, she'd worked her butt off. Everybody wanted her on their records.

MERLE TRAVIS, THE MERLE TRAVIS GUITAR (1956, CAPITOL)

THOM BRESH (guitarist/producer/Travis's son)

He was a real interesting character to produce. I've thought many times, what would it be like if he were here today with this kind of technology? It would be incredible what you could do. Today, you could take something like a Roland VS880 hard-disk recorder and a couple of mikes and go anywhere, just sit there at his house. Let him be real comfortable, get his ice-tea and his cornbread, and sit there and play. Say, "If you make a mistake, just play that part again, and we'll put it together."

Travis loved to edit, even clear back in the '50s when he was doing albums. There was a song he did on the famous, what they call "Yellow Album" for Capitol, which is *Travis Guitar*. He plays "Bugle Call Rag." In the middle of it, he's got this lick—really a hot lick.

People have tried to play it, but Travis says, "No, I did that with a capo on the second fret with an open position. We just cut [edited] that in. It was a technique so people would try to figure out how to do it." He said he played like hell and then, when it got to that place, he stopped [the tape]. He put a capo on the second fret and did this one little fill thing [and stopped the tape again]. And then, it went right back into the other tuning without the capo.

Everybody says, "How do you get that sound?" He just loved things like that. He had a couple of big Berlant-Concertones [tape recorders] that Capitol put Ampex heads on for him. He had those at the house where he would sit and record—woodshed some things out. He liked to overdub at the house. I don't know if any of those recordings got out. I heard a couple of things, but it's hard to tell whether they were them or not. He was always doing something with different tunings, or he'd do a lick and cut it in. He liked to cut things in. He said, "If people are going along playing [with the record], they'll say, 'How'd he do that?'"

He and Les Paul were both working with what he liked to call that Mickey Mouse guitar, where they'd slow the tape to half-speed [thus doubling playback speed]. Back then, Les was even doing it with [acetate] cutters, but Travis was messing with it at the same time. Of course, Les had it refined to a "T." Travis just knew he liked that, where you slow the recording down to half-speed and do these licks around it. He was an innovator as much as he could be for the time. It shows with the solid-body Bigsby [guitar] and different things that he did in his life.

Years ago, he was looking for a tape. He was having some drinks with Judy Garland one night. They both got rocking pretty good, and they cut at his home studio, I think he said, eight or nine songs. We hunted all over the place looking for that. He wanted me to hear it. One night, he was looking through all of these boxes of tapes, but they were all out of order. He said, "I just wanted you to hear this one thing Judy and I did. It was so good. We just had a ball that night." That would be something to find. It was done during both of their heydays. I don't think he was more than forty years old at the time.

ELVIS PRESLEY, "BLUE MOON" (1956, RCA), *SUNRISE* AND *ELVIS PRESLEY* (1956, RCA)

ROLAND JANES

Here's one of the mistakes that people make. They think the magic was in the room [at Sun Records]. Let me tell you something. Although it was a well-designed room, the magic was in the people at that particular time in history. Now, the room was suited for recording. It was a rented building, but Sam designed the ceiling and everything. It worked out well, although you were limited as to the number of instruments you could record. But we didn't record with the lot of instruments. The magic was generally in the combinations of people, and that included the engineer, the musicians, and what have you.

One of the secrets of good sound over there [at Sun] was Sam had the ability to add a little bit of slapback echo on whatever he wanted—usually on the vocal. Also you got a little bleed, even in the vocal, from the different instruments. You got that little touch of slapback echo that added a little body to what you were doing. It was part of the magic of the overall situation.

Sam had a way of recording. He had three tape recorders in the room. He had two Ampex recorders. He used one of them to record on, and he used the other one in case he wanted to run a copy of the tape. Now the third machine was a wall-mounted Ampex. He would record the desired signal onto machine number one. Machine number two just sat there unless you wanted to run a copy later. Machine number three, which was the mounted machine, he could take whatever signal he wanted from whichever instrument or vocal, and he sent that to the third machine, and it recorded along with the desired signal that went to the first machine. Then, at the same time that would be playing back through the console. So you had your desired signal. Then you had a slapback signal that came out of the third machine. You got that by delay. He recorded the third machine at the slow speed so you could get a wider delay in between the notes or what have you. That's how he created and got the slapback effect.

The way most people got it, they recorded on your one machine and ran it back through the board and then back to the same machine. When you did that, everything that went onto the machine had slapback on it. Sam, using the other machine in his method, he could have slapback on one thing and not on the rest of the band. Or whatever combination he wanted. That's the reason he had the good slapback, and he could have a good clean slapback. Everything wasn't slapping back all over the place.

We hung around the studio. Someone would say, "What are you doing tomorrow? You want to come in and record with Jerry Lee?" Everything was really laid back—not really laid out and planned out like the sessions are nowadays. It wasn't always the same musicians on sessions. It was a matter of whoever was available. If someone was out of town, we didn't let that stop us. We'd take somebody else and go ahead and do the session.

They were great musicians. Carl Perkins, I thought, was a fine musician. Of course there was Scotty [Moore]. Scotty had his own sound. We each had our distinct sound. But in the final analysis you can almost always tell it was a Sun Record sound, even though played by different people in a different manner. In a different style even. It still had the Sun signature to it.

The slapback might've had something to do with it, but everything didn't have slapback on it. Maybe the engineers had a lot to do with it. Engineers have a hell of a lot more to do with a good record than people realize—usually more so even than the producers. A lot of the records I've worked on over the years, the producer is out in the lobby on the telephone through about 90 percent of the session. So, basically, if you get good communication between the musicians and the engineer, then you're going to get yourself a pretty good session. It may not be a hit every time, but it will be a pretty good session. If the engineer has worked both sides of the glass, and a lot of the musicians out in the studio have worked both sides of the glass, they can communicate almost without saying a word.

CHET ATKINS

Elvis was one of the most talented people I've ever met. Goddamn, he was always shaking something on his body. I loved him. His first session [produced by Steve Sholes], I told my wife, "You've got to come down and see this dude. You won't get a chance anymore. He'll be so hot." So she came down and watched a few minutes and went home. I never did ask her, "What did you think?" Of course, she loved him. A lot of people love Elvis now who didn't love him back in those days.

I talked to Scotty, once, his guitar player. We were talking. I said, "Why'd he shake his leg like that?" He said, "You know, he did that instead of patting his foot." Most musicians will pat their foot to keep time, but he'd shake his leg, and it'd make the girls squeal. And so he'd exaggerate it.

What is now known as the "Million Dollar Quartet" was a chance gathering (and a casual recording session) of Mt. Rushmore figures—Elvis Presley, Jerry Lee Lewis, Johnny Cash, and Carl Perkins—at Sun Studios.

**THE MILLION DOLLAR QUARTET,
*THE COMPLETE MILLION DOLLAR
QUARTET* (1956, RCA/SONY BMG)**

JACK CLEMENT
I was there and sitting in the control room. I remember remarking to somebody, "I'd be remiss if I didn't record this." I got up, put a tape on the machine, went out, and moved a mike or two around. I already had some mikes out in the room hooked up. So I just moved them around a little bit, to where somebody was standing or talking or whatever. And let it roll for about an hour and a half. I remember I changed tapes two or three times. I had it set on the [lower quality] slower speed—7½ speed instead of 15—but it sounded fine. Otherwise I'd have to be changing the tape every fifteen minutes, and it might be right in the middle of something. So it was running for like thirty minutes a roll. Back then we used those small reels. We never did fool with them big reels. It was all seven-inch reels. But we'd run at 15-ips [inches per second], so you can only get four or five takes on a tape. But it was easy to deal with—flip another one on there real quick.

BILLY LEE RILEY, "FLYIN' SAUCERS ROCK AND ROLL" AND "RED HOT" (1957), *ROCKIN' WITH RILEY* (SUN)

JACK CLEMENT

I sort of knew the kind of music I wanted to work with, and I did actually produce a master record [Billy Lee Riley's "Trouble Bound" b/w "Rock with Me Baby"] before I went to work at Sun. I did it at a radio station, WMPS. They had a little bitty studio. I went in there a couple of times and cut tracks with Billy Lee Riley. That's what got me my job at Sun.

I took them to Sam Phillips to have him master them. We were going to press them up. He said that was the first time anybody'd brought him any rock 'n' roll that he liked. So I took him a finished record. I had produced it. It was all mixed. All he did was transfer it to a disc, press it, and put it out. I guess you could say that I was a producer when I went to work there. I mean, I hadn't done a lot of it, but I had done that.

ROLAND JANES

When I first met him, Jack was a singer-songwriter. When he got the job at Sun Records, Jack was hired, not actually to produce, but to audition potential material of artists that came in the door. In order to do that he had to turn on the tape machine: listen to them through the studio's microphones and the speakers. In the process he'd offer, maybe, a few suggestions, but he took what the artist brought through the door with him. Most of your really good producers, or a lot of them, started off as musicians and/or engineers. They slowly evolved into being full-time producers.

I grew up in the state of Arkansas and, later, in St. Louis, Missouri. Musicians over there were picking cotton or doing whatever they could to make a living. If they had a little bit of talent, they'd get together and form little bands and play at little gatherings and make a little money on the side.

All musicians are amateurs until they get paid the first time, and then they become professionals. A lot of the musicians you might classify as amateurs really weren't. They were good musicians; they were just playing in different styles and in their own way. In order to make a living, the musicians in this part of the country had to be open to all kinds of music. Everybody wanted to make a record, to make a dollar. A lot of them weren't schooled musicians, but they were good musicians. Some of your greatest musicians in the world came out of the hills of Tennessee or out of Kentucky and Virginia. Most of them never had a lesson in their lives.

In a small band—for example, in a four-piece band—if any particular instrument drops out, it leaves a big hole. Consequently, most of the musicians that come out of this part of the country, everybody played all the time. So at the session you never lost that bottom, that fullness of the sound. If you start getting bigger and more instruments, you can have a little more cohesive arrangement, but sometimes you lose the fullness of it. Different instruments are playing only in certain spots. Carl Perkins, if he quit playing that Carl Perkins rhythm, the whole damn thing fell apart. Or anybody else in the band.

Billy Riley's first record was a thing called "Trouble Bound," which he wrote—both sides. The second record, we looked around and found a song, "Flyin' Saucers Rock and Roll." We took it into the studio. The band worked up the arrangement. We cut it—of course, with maybe a suggestion from whoever was engineering at the time, whether it was Sam or Jack Clement; usually it was Sam. The band came in and worked up the song in the studio with everybody pitching in ideas. So it was a band-produced thing.

On that record, Jerry Lee was just getting started. I don't think his first record had come out yet, which our band played on too. He sat in with us on that session, played piano for two sides. We used to cut singles—go for two sides—before anyone got into the album thing. Jerry Lee had moved to Memphis, and we'd cut a session on him. It was waiting to be released, I think, or maybe it'd just been released. Anyway, he was still hanging around town, preparing to go out on the road. He played a couple of gigs with us, and he sat in on some sessions: one with Hayden Thompson, and he sat in on a Carl Perkins session where the Million-Dollar Quartet thing was recorded. He didn't do a lot of sessions because he got hot pretty quick and went out on the road.

"Red Hot," which was our third record, Sam had recorded it previously on the guy who wrote the song, Billy Emerson. His version was quite a bit different from ours. Sam gave us the suggestion that we might do that. Of course we took it. We worked up our own style of arrangement and, again, recorded it with a suggestion or two here and there from the powers that be. Basically, all of those things were worked up in the studio.

Did you have particular opinions about the way you wanted your guitar to sound?

Yeah, I wanted it to sound like a hit. No, I guess I did, but I didn't have any particular settings or anything. We'd adjust our amplifier to get the sound that we wanted. Sometimes, the engineer might suggest that we take off a little bass or add a little bass, or increase the volume or decrease the volume.

We might take one or two cuts [takes]; we might take half a dozen cuts. Everything was done mono at the time. There wasn't any punching in or anything like that.* If you notice the records back in those days, the solos were not all that long. Later, when you got into heavy metal and hard rock, you started having these fifteen-minute solos which said nothing. If we had anything to say, we had to say it in one short turn-around and get it done. They weren't anything elaborate, but they were effective and, evidently, people still like them.

ROY ORBISON, *THE SUN YEARS* (1956–1958, SUN)

JACK CLEMENT
Roy was the first one that Sam turned over to me—after "Ooby Dooby." Me and Roy got to be big buddies. I got separated from my wife one time. I had this little house. He lived there with me for a while. I really liked him and wanted to help him cut a hit record, but the stuff he was wanting to do was just a little bit more demanding than we had the musicians and singers for at that time. And studio. He needed vocal groups,

---

* During a performance, an engineer could push, hold, and release a button that would substitute what was being performed in the studio for what was previously recorded onto the master tape. This technique was called "punching in."

and he needed strings. He was thinking all that big orchestral stuff. I would've loved it, but we didn't have the players, the singers, and the studios to do it. So we limited him.

I did tell him one time that I didn't think he'd ever make it as a ballad singer. He never let me forget that either. Of course, I was delighted when he did. He was a beautiful guy, a lot of fun, but a hard-luck character. If there was an accident or something could go wrong, it went wrong for old Roy.

During the time I was around him, he wasn't having too much bad luck, but people would shit on him. One time he came in there [to Sun], before he moved to Memphis. He had this band, and we cut for a few hours in the morning. Then we went to lunch, and we were supposed to be back in an hour. An hour passes, and we ain't heard from the band. Where'd they go? Two hours passes, a little more. And then, we decided. That band, they'd done left old Roy sitting there. Being mean. Didn't tell him nothing; just left, went back to Texas.

DON GIBSON, "I CAN'T STOP LOVING YOU" AND "OH, LONESOME ME" (1957), *A LEGEND IN MY TIME* (BEAR FAMILY)

CHET ATKINS

We did them both—"I Can't Stop Loving You" and "Oh, Lonesome Me"—on the same day [December 3, 1957]. I knew or I thought "Oh, Lonesome Me" would be a hit.

Don was signed up for his writing with Wesley Rose [Acuff-Rose Publishing], and Wesley was one of those guys, "Keep it country. Keep it country"—and all that bullshit. So we did keep it country. We made a session—and nothing.

"Wesley," I said, "Don should express my ideas now. Let me record him, and we'll see what happens." First record was "Oh, Lonesome Me" and "I Can't Stop Loving You" on the other side. Boy, I've got a tape. A friend of mine made me a tape of all those Victor cuts to listen to in the car. Don was so damn good. God, what a guitar player! His hero was Django Reinhardt. He tried to play like that, and he could do it. Goddamn, he had a hell of a beat. He inspired the musicians to play on the beat with a lot of rhythm. God love him. He was on the first hit I ever made, "Oh, Lonesome Me."

I thought Don was the greatest thing ever, and I knew that other people would love his work. He wrote some beautiful ballads, too. If he had died like Hank Williams, he would be as famous as Hank is — or more. But he lived. He's still alive out here. He gets all kinds of royalties, I guess. He lives in one of the richest areas of town. He's got the prettiest wife in town, I guess. He's been married to her about twenty to thirty years, but he's married a bunch of times. When he was on drugs, he did some pretty wild things. But no more.

**JERRY LEE LEWIS,
"WHOLE LOTTA SHAKIN' GOIN' ON"
(1957), *18 ORIGINAL SUN GREATEST
HITS* (RHINO)**

JACK CLEMENT

Sam Phillips was in Nashville at the [Disc Jockey] Convention. It was in November. I remember it was on a Thursday, because . . . I remember Jerry Lee had come in on Monday, the second time [he'd came to Sun]. He'd been there before [Lewis's first visit to Sun], and I'd made a little tape with him. Played it for Sam. Sam liked it and everything. I was right on the verge of calling Jerry. I had his phone number right on the tape [written on the back of a tape box].

Before I got around to it, a few days later, he came back with his bass player — his cousin, J. W. Brown, who later became his father-in-law. So anyway, they came in, and I said, "I've been meaning to call you."

When he first came there, I'd told him that country music wasn't happening. That's what he was doing the first time. He was singing me George Jones songs and stuff. I asked him if he knew any rock 'n' roll.

"No, not really, but I can learn some."

I said, "You need to go work up some rock 'n' roll, 'cause country just ain't happening right now." I read where he said that I told him, "Rock 'n' roll is dead," but that's total bullshit. Why would I say something like that?

The fact is the people in Nashville were really worried. There was a pall over the Grand Ole Opry and all that stuff. Anyway, he came back [on Monday], and he'd written a song called "End of the Road."

I said, "Okay, that's rockin' enough." And he had a version of "You're the Only Star in My Blue Heaven" where he changed it from a waltz to "You're the only bomp, bomp, bomp." And I loved that. So I told him, "Come back Thursday. I'll have a couple of guys in there, and we'll cut some tapes." So that's what happened.

Sam was on his way to Nashville or was already over here. We went into the studio, and the heat went out that day. I had this little electric heater back in the control room. It kept tripping the circuit breaker on everything, and the board would go out. It was kind of chilly in there. But we cut that first record, which turned out to be "Crazy Arms."

I think we started with "You're the Only Star in My Blue Heaven." I just loved that one. It was really good. And then we did "End of the Road" and maybe something else. And then, toward the end of the thing, I asked, "Do you know 'Crazy Arms'?"

He said, "I know a little of it."

"Let's cut it," I said. So we did. He sort of made up some of the words, but at that time "Crazy Arms" had been a hit for six months or more. It had been a big hit with the Andrews Sisters—pop. Well, Ray Price to start with, and then a big pop hit with the Andrews Sisters. Everybody knew the song, but we put it out anyway. And it still sold 150,000 or something. It was a good first record. And it only had two instruments on it: piano and drums [played by J. M. Van Eaton].

The bass player was in the bathroom at the time. He comes in at the end [on guitar]. Old Billy Lee Riley had been playing bass. He [the bass player] was in the bathroom, and he thought we were just screwing around. He opened the door, walked out there, and the song was about to end. He [picked up Roland Janes's guitar and] put that little bad chord on the end of it. It's still there. But there wasn't any guitar on the song. It was nothing but piano and drums. But it has a sound to it.

I had put thumbtacks on the piano hammers. Well, that wasn't new. It was a spinet piano, and I got to miking it down underneath, rather than on top. So you didn't really hear that ping very much, but it gave it a sound. That was the sound we used on "Whole Lotta Shakin' Goin' On" and "Great Balls of Fire."

At RCA [in Nashville] they had an old upright piano with thumbtacks on it just for that purpose. A lot of studios might have one around. I had to put them in and, sometimes, take them out. They don't help the hammers. I didn't invent that process. What I did was mike it differently. It made it sound almost like a grand piano. On "Whole Lotta Shakin' Goin' On," you can't hear the ping. You get a definite ping with those thumbtacks, but it didn't record that way. So it was a neat sound.

The first time I played that record for him—Sam came in the studio on the following Monday—whenever he came in, I said, "I've got something I want to play you." We went back into the control room, and I put on "Crazy Arms." Before it ever got to the singing, Sam reaches over, stops the machine and says, "Now I can sell that!" And then he started it playing again. Of course, when he got to the voice, he loved it.

We made a lacquer, an acetate disc, right there in the control room, and Sam took it down to Dewey Phillips that night. In the meantime, we sent the tape off to Chicago to have it mastered. We had records by Thursday. But on Monday, Dewey put that thing on [WHBQ], and the phone lines lit up. It was kind of instant. We had records in some of the stores probably by [the next] Monday evening.

Now you think that wasn't fun? Cut a record . . . Conceivably, we could have put it out the next day or, maybe, even that night if we'd been in that big a hurry. Just press up a few singles.

The thing about Jerry Lee, if you see him on a show or see him in the studio, it's the same. He's the greatest I ever met for being able to go in the studio and give you the whole performance. Give him an audience of one, and he'll give you the whole show. Totally uninhibited.

I had a lot of fun with him back then. We used to hang out a lot together. In fact me and him and Roy Orbison all went and bought motorcycles the same day. And I used to throw these parties at my apartment, and Jerry Lee would come over. We'd get naked and dive off into the swimming pool.

ROLAND JANES

On the first session with Jerry Lee, we recorded probably fifteen or twenty songs. I don't know how many. It was basically supposed to be a demo session. We were searching for something to record. Out of that session, I think every song we recorded that night has been released in some form or another. His first hit came out of that: a song called "Crazy Arms." We came along with a totally different-sounding version.

THE EVERLY BROTHERS, "BYE BYE LOVE" (1957), *CADENCE CLASSICS: THEIR 20 GREATEST HITS* (RHINO)

CHET ATKINS

They're country boys. But Don [Everly] and I, we used to listen to "Bo Diddley," the song. We'd get together and practice that lick. Bo Diddley tuned the guitar in an open key. We'd play that, and Don would say, "You know, if I ever make records, we'll use that."

And so it happened. I saw him. They [Don and Phil] hung out down in the Alley back of the [Grand Ole] Opry. The Opry wouldn't have them on. They hung out back there. He told me one night, "Hey, we got a deal." We're going to record for — I guess it was — Archie [Bleyer] at that time. They'd recorded previously for Columbia.

By golly, that first session I played with him. We had a bunch of good players. He started that Bo Diddley lick, and I joined him and the whole rhythm section. And it was wonderful. God, I knew it was a historic thing.

Archie Bleyer was the greatest producer I ever knew. He recorded the Everly Brothers. I contributed, too. They always give me credit because they got mad at Archie, but he was wonderful. He'd take his demos home to New York. He'd married one of the Chordettes. She had a daughter about fourteen or sixteen or something. She had sock hops, they called them — get together and play records. He'd only let them play tunes that he had produced. He told me this. They'd get in a room and play the songs. They'd play certain ones of the Everly Brothers, and he was in the other room listening. They'd play the ones they liked over and over. I think that's how he had so much success picking hits.

JOHNNY CASH, "HOME OF THE BLUES" (1957), *SUN RECORDINGS: GREATEST HITS* (TIME/LIFE)

JACK CLEMENT

Johnny Cash was Sam's fair-haired boy. He loved Johnny Cash, talked about him all the time: what a great gentleman he was, all the appeal he had, and how easy he was to work with. He'd go out on the road and write some songs, work 'em up with his boys, come in, and be ready to go. Sam talked about the authority in Johnny Cash's voice. It really surprised me when they split.

It was a year or so after I went to work there that he finally let me record Johnny Cash. I know the record that I first cut. It was called "Home of the Blues." I don't remember exactly why Sam let me do that. After that, I did quite a bit. But I worked with Cash before I ever got into actually producing him. I was around there all the time when he was cutting, as sort of Sam's assistant. I was in the control room and all that stuff. Later, I played guitar on "Ballad of a Teenage Queen" and "Guess Things Happen That Way" [both of which Clement wrote].

Of course, Sam did "Hey Porter," "Cry, Cry, Cry," all that early, classic stuff. When I first heard Johnny Cash, I didn't like it very much. I thought it was kind of crude. He had a radio show, and it didn't sound all that great. I really got hooked on him when he came out with "I Walk the Line." That's when I really understood Johnny Cash.

BILL MONROE, "SCOTLAND" (1958), *ANTHOLOGY* (MCA NASHVILLE)

HAROLD BRADLEY

I'd never produced anything. We hadn't been long at the Quonset Hut over on Music Row. My brother was in New York for a company meeting with Decca. Like on a Thursday, he called and said, "Count Basie's Band is going to play Birdland tomorrow night, and I'm supposed to be doing Bill Monroe. How about you producing it?"

I said, "God, what do I do?"

"You just run the stopwatch, and Mort, the engineer, will do the sound."

I said, "Well, okay." So we did that in the Quonset Hut. Actually, getting back to figuring out what I was supposed to be doing, I did do something. The song was "Scotland." The way it was laid out musically wasn't a good form, and I asked Bill to change the routine. As I recall, it had three or four themes. He took my advice, and it was somewhat of a hit. I don't think my name would ever appear on the credits anywhere. My brother, naturally, would not have turned it in saying, "Produced by Harold Bradley." He had to say that he produced it, but that was fine with me. I got paid to produce it.

Later on, the same thing happened again. I don't know whether it was another year or two years later, but it was, again, Count Basie's Band at Birdland. This time we were at Bradley's Barn, and the engineer and I are recording Bill Monroe. We'd already done two tunes. We were sitting there, and the engineer said, "You know something? We don't have a bass fiddle."

I said, "You're kidding?" I hadn't noticed. I looked out into the studio, and we did not have a bass.

"What are we going to do?" the engineer asked me.

I said, "We're going to keep recording. If you'd wanted a bass, you'd have hired a bass."

You know what he [Monroe] said after we did "Scotland," every time I'd see him after that? You know he had that high voice? He'd say, "You and I know how to make a record. Don't we, boy?" I think that's what he called me.

"Yes, sir."

BUDDY HOLLY, "RAVE ON" AND "THAT'S MY DESIRE" (1958), *THE BEST OF BUDDY HOLLY: THE MILLENNIUM COLLECTION* (MCA)

BOB THIELE

I received a copy of "That'll Be the Day"—I don't remember whether it was a tape or an acetate—from a friend of mine, who was a music publisher. He said, "What do you think?"

I genuinely flipped. "This is a great record!"

When I went to the brass at Decca—which owned Coral—I said, "Look, you can't put this on Coral." The label had Lawrence Welk and the McGuire Sisters—people like that. That's when I got the idea to remind them that they owned the trade name Brunswick.

So "That'll Be the Day" came out on Brunswick. I don't think Buddy's name was on it; it was just the Crickets. And it took off like gangbusters! Of course, Norman Petty [Holly's primary producer] knew what he was doing. He made most of the records by Buddy and the Crickets.

Buddy was one of these soft-spoken guys—a real gentleman. I would hear from him from time to time. He was always calling to thank me for getting his records out, helping to build his career. One day, he called from Clovis. They were going to be there for maybe a week, making some records. He said, "I've got to do something for you. If you write a song, I want to record it." So two people that I wrote some songs with, we wrote a thing called "Mailman, Bring Me No More Blues," which he recorded. It's a trite song. There's nothing to it.

Then he said, "I would love for you to produce a couple of records for me." I don't think this made Norman too happy, but when Buddy was in New York, and Norman Petty was still in Clovis, we went in and did two sides: "Rave On" and the old Frankie Lane song "That's My Desire." We recorded at a little studio on Eighth Avenue here in New York [Bell Sound Studios].

We worked on "That's My Desire," but he'd been playing "Rave On." The guys were familiar with it. It was just a matter of getting the right interpretation, the right sound, and the right balance. We decided on the level of reverb we wanted and stuck to it.

DEL WOOD, *RAGS TO RICHES* (1959, RCA)

CHET ATKINS

The treble side is the important side on most tunes. So you use two mikes: one on the treble side of the piano, and a mid-range–type mike on the bass. Then you balance those. It's an easy endeavor to do that. I recorded Del Wood. She had a left hand—she played ²⁄₄. So I'd put a mike on the bass part of her left hand, but I hardly ever turned it on, 'cause she wouldn't hit the notes right. I always said her left hand was made for boxing. It sounded like she had on boxing gloves. It had a lot of treble and not much bass. So that's the way you do people that you have to balance. But anybody can do that.

GEORGE JONES, "WHITE LIGHTNING" (1959), *THE DEFINITIVE COLLECTION 1955–1962* (MERCURY)

DON PIERCE

There was a fellow named Jack Starnes from Beaumont, Texas, that managed Lefty Frizzell. He'd sold Lefty's contract, but he wanted to stay in the business so he started signing artists in the east Texas area. He acquired George Jones for the Starday label that was formed by me and Pappy Daily and Jack Starnes in Houston. Hence, the name Starday: Star for Starnes and Day for Daily. They made me president of the company because I'd had a lot of experience out with 4 Star Records in L.A.

Pappy did nearly all of the production work for Starday, and he got associated with Bill Quinn down in Houston. Bill had a little studio down there [Gold Star]; he used broken eggshells on its walls to get the sound he wanted. But when I moved to Nashville, I produced "White Lightning" by George Jones, "Treasure of Love," and a few others because he recorded in Nashville and I was there.

George had been on the road. He came back into Nashville. He said, "Don, I've got some tunes, and I've got some time. I want to record."

"Fine." I got the reservation for the studio over at Owen Bradley's, the Bradley Barn. It was an old residence that had been changed into a recording studio. George largely indicated which musicians he wanted to have. We got them for the session. Buddy Killen—who later built Tree Publishing and sold it to Sony for $40 million—was playing bass on the session. Of course, he knew George was a tremendous talent. Buddy had quite a lot to say about how things were going at the session. On the particular case of "White Lightning," you'll notice that the intro to the record is Buddy Killen playing bass. We took about ten or eleven takes.

We knew that we had a good cut in that third one where George had a slur and sang, "Sssa-lug." George didn't want to use it, but we were never able to get what we wanted in subsequent tries. By the time it got to about the eleventh try, Buddy Killen said, "My thumb won't take it anymore." It was about wore out. We went back and took the one with the slight imperfection in George's delivery. That probably helped the record.

I've been told that Buddy Killen said he produced "White Lightning." Is it possible to reconcile his claim with Don Pierce's story? Probably not, but it's my best guess that each man thought he was producing the session: Pierce as the superintending executive on the date and Killen as the musician leading the band.

JIM REEVES, "HE'LL HAVE TO GO" (1959), *THE ESSENTIAL JIM REEVES* (RCA)

CHET ATKINS

Jim and I, we'd get together and talk about the songs and what we'd do, maybe say, "Do you want to use Floyd Cramer on piano, or some other person?" We'd discuss things like that. But mostly, he trusted me to get the other people. We tried to get three or four songs in three hours.

There's always something memorable in a song that you can use for an introduction and an instrumental. That's all easy for me because I was an instrumentalist. I didn't pay any attention to the words of country songs for years. Then I found out the words are the most important ingredient of a record. People listen to the words. But the great combination is a great melody and great words. With the marriage of the two you get a tremendous hit.

I didn't imitate anybody. I never liked big bands and all that mess, and thank goodness. I thought I was just square, that I shouldn't even be producing. But come to find out, what I liked the public liked. I got so I recorded what I liked and, fortunately, a lot of times the public liked it too—which was small group. I always liked Benny Goodman and His Sextet and [Artie Shaw's] the Gramercy Five. That's the kind of music I liked. Thank goodness, I got to do something about it by making records the way I thought they should be made.

BUCK OWENS, "EXCUSE ME (I THINK I'VE GOT A HEARTACHE)" (1960), *THE VERY BEST OF BUCK OWENS, VOL. 1* (RHINO)

KEN NELSON

Buck was playing guitar with one of my artists, Tommy Collins, in Bakersfield. Buck kept bugging me. He wanted to sing. And I was, "Yeah, yeah"—like "Okay, get away from me, boy. You bother me."

One day, I told him to go into the studio. "Let's hear what you've got." He did about sixteen bars, and I said, "Okay, that's enough."

He came in the booth, and I guess he figured that I'd turned him down. But I heard the talent right away, and so I signed him [in 1957].

BOB IRWIN

It was one of those things where every single planet that could be aligned was aligned. I couldn't imagine a more studio-friendly artist than Buck showing up, and the chemistry with Ken Nelson was magic. That's rare. Buck will be the first one to say, "No one can touch those Ken Nelson productions."

It's amazing to see that chemistry live on. When you put on one of Buck's master tapes, from a studio perspective, from a technical perspective, they were so well recorded, it's scary. When I got the first batch of session tapes from Buck [for reissue], I put them on, and it was just jaw-dropping. They sounded so good. The bass was so well recorded. The drums were so well recorded. Don Rich's Telecaster was the clearest Telecaster to cut through on a record at that time and, as far as I'm concerned, defined that sound as much as [Johnny Cash's guitarist] Luther Perkins let the world know that the Telecaster was a country guitar.

JOHN PALLADINO

In time [1949] we moved out of Radio Recorders and went to Melrose Avenue, the first studio that Capitol really owned. That was the old radio station KHJ. Very fortunately, those facilities happened to fit right in with a lot of the things we were doing. They had what they called a "small studio" [Studio C]. In it things were miked on a rather close scale. We had twelve-position boards [mixing consoles] with rotary pots. Which was fine; they did a good job. The big issues at the time involved the use of echo-chambers. We developed really good echo-chambers there. So we had a small studio, a good echo-chamber, good equipment, and people who were interested in developing that equipment.

BRENDA LEE, "I'M SORRY" (1960),
THE DEFINITIVE COLLECTION
(MCA NASHVILLE)

HAROLD BRADLEY

She was around twelve, something like that [when Decca gave her a recording contract in 1956]. Owen did tell her to try to save some of the [vocal] tricks till the end of the song. Otherwise, if you do a trick up front, it's like telling the punch line at the beginning of a joke. He told her, "Save some for the end." But she did tricks. I listen to some of that stuff now, and I don't know what she was listening to or where all that was coming from. There were pickups and all kinds of stuff. It was unbelievable. And then, she turned out to be such a great ballad singer. "I'm Sorry," that and some of the others—just wonderful songs.

My brother made up that arrangement. I once heard a phone interview. They were interviewing Brenda, and they got Owen on the line. He gave her credit for all of that—the recitation and all that—when, actually, it was his idea. The Ink Spots, years ago they did those recitations. If you notice, on "I'm Sorry" it's like three verses. There's no bridge. So what he did was very clever. She sings the first verse, and then he modulates. He has a couple of modulations; then she has the recitation. I thought it created a great mood. It was all him. I can't say that. The arrangement to me was all him. But Brenda sang the heck out of it. My brother would never take credit for any of that stuff.

FLOYD CRAMER, "LAST DATE" (1960), *THE ESSENTIAL FLOYD CRAMER* (RCA)

CHET ATKINS

With Floyd Cramer, we developed that style. I knew it would take over the world. Nobody had played piano like that, except the guy that started it. That was Don Robertson, the writer. He would send me demo tapes, playing the piano like that, bending two notes at a time. We put it on a record with Hank Locklin, "Please Help Me, I'm Falling." Joni Mitchell or somebody stole that title. Don Robertson wrote that [song] and played piano like Floyd on it, pre-Floyd. It was a big hit.

I told Floyd one day, "Write yourself an instrumental like that, and we'll have a big hit." He came in the next morning, played "Last Date." I set up a session. We had an arranger, Cliff Parman, that I've heard the mafia chased out of Chicago because he did something they didn't like. So Floyd wrote the instrumental, and I talked him into putting it with Acuff-Rose Publishing because they had a promotion staff. I knew that would help a lot. He didn't want to do it, but I got him to put it with them. And we had a big hit, and he had a great career with other songs that he wrote and other standards that he played on albums.

HANK THOMPSON,
HANK THOMPSON AT THE GOLDEN NUGGET (1961, CAPITOL NASHVILLE)

KEN NELSON

We recorded the first live album; it was in 1961. It was Hank Thompson's *Live at the Golden Nugget*. I can't remember whether he suggested it or I suggested it. But I did an awful lot of live albums. I recorded Buck Owens in London, in Japan, at the London Palladium. I did him at Carnegie Hall. I did Merle Haggard at Independence Hall in Philadelphia. I did Tommy Sands at the Sands in Las Vegas.

I had a lot of artists here on the West Coast. I'd book dates with the artists that I was going to record in Nashville, and then go there and spend maybe two or three months at a time. Then I'd come home and record here, then go back to Nashville. I recorded—I'm told—about two hundred different artists during my career. For instance, in Nashville I had Sonny James, Jean Shepard, Roy Acuff, the Louvin Brothers, and many others. In Hollywood, I had Buck Owens, Tommy Collins, Merle Haggard, Tex Williams, all kinds of artists. I recorded Gene Vincent and Wanda Jackson, who was originally a country artist, but she went into rock 'n' roll.

With many people, I recorded just one, maybe two records. The reason for that was the sales department and the promotion department. They'd come to me every six months. They'd bring me the royalty statements of various artists. If there was no spark or if an artist was in the hole—the artist paid for his sessions; his session costs were taken out of money earned in royalties—so if an artist was in the hole too much, I'd have to drop him. Maybe I wouldn't want to. But the pressure sometimes was pretty tough with the finance department. You kind of had to go along with them. So that's why some artists, like Bobby Bare, I dropped him, and Jerry Reed, I dropped him. Golly, I can't remember how many. Some later on went to other labels and did terrific.

JIM REEVES, "THE BLIZZARD" (1961), *THE ESSENTIAL JIM REEVES* (RCA)

CHET ATKINS

I made it my business to get acquainted with all the good writers. I remember I wrote Harlan Howard a letter when he was in California and told him he should come here. He was one of my favorite writers. Could he send me some songs? He was working at a newspaper-printing place or something. And he kept that letter till his house burnt down. Then he wanted me to write him another one! I never did. But he moved here right after that. I saw him yesterday having a drink in a restaurant here. He's amazing. He's been real sickly, but hell, that booze helps him, I guess, get through the day.

HAROLD BRADLEY

Chet was extremely talented. He was a guitar player; he had a great ear. But he would sit in the control room, sometimes practicing classical guitar while we were playing. You'd think he wasn't listening. All of a sudden, he'd hit the talk-back [button] and say, "Somebody played a wrong chord there. Let's straighten that out." He was kind of like Owen [Bradley]. He wouldn't get involved unless the session needed direction. Then, he'd come out, pick up the guitar, and come up with some ideas. Of course, he had great ideas. He played on those Don Gibson records, "Oh, Lonesome Me" and other records that had a lot of guitar work on them, along with Hank Garland.

My brother used the same musicians until they died or retired. With Chet it didn't matter. He hired whoever was available. It could be a different set of musicians anytime. I walked in on a Jim Reeves session one time. We stood around listening to the song [the demo]. While we were getting ready to cut it, Chet turned to me, "Harold, we don't need another guitar on this. Go play vibes." The first thing you learned as a studio musician is you never say no. I didn't know how to play vibes, but I have a very fundamental idea of the keyboard. We were doing only three-chord songs. So I faked through some of those Jim Reeves records. I don't even know which ones I played the vibes on or which ones I played the guitar on.

ELVIS PRESLEY, "LITTLE SISTER" (1961), *FROM NASHVILLE TO MEMPHIS: THE ESSENTIAL 60'S MASTERS* (RCA)

HAROLD BRADLEY

On a session one day, Hank Garland said, "I'm working with Elvis next week. Can I borrow your Fender guitar, your Stratocaster? It twangs more than my Gibson."

"Sure." So my Stratocaster made it to an Elvis session before I did. That would have been 1961. That's my guitar on "Little Sister."

After Hank was injured [in an automobile accident], Felton Jarvis had me work with Elvis from 1962 to 1967, and in 1970, I overdubbed "Snowbird." By then, Elvis had gone to using his road band—James Burton. He'd fill in with a couple of guys. I'm not sure who all was at the session, but they didn't have an electric guitar-sitar. They hired me to come in and do an overdub. Elvis wasn't there. It was really a neat instrument. Reggie Young played one quite well in Memphis with B. J. Thomas and "Hooked on a Feeling."

PATSY CLINE, "I FALL TO PIECES" AND "CRAZY" (1961), *SWEET DREAMS: THE COMPLETE DECCA STUDIO MASTERS 1960–1963* (MCA NASHVILLE)

HAROLD BRADLEY

He [Owen Bradley] tried everything on Patsy, from backgrounds on "Young Love," where they just had Martin guitar fills, to Hank Garland, "Can't Rock 'n' Roll on Country Records." Finally, we found her sound. It did require some preproduction. Before that, we just walked in the studio and learned the song. Somebody played it on guitar or they had an acetate, a demo record. They played it, and we learned it, learned it by rote—no music and no number system [for indicating song structure]. We were still making up a lot of that [the head arrangements]. But when we started using the violins and voices a little more, there definitely was more preproduction and planning: going back to a particular song, sitting down with an arranger, and then coming into the studio and telling us what to do.

On a ninety-minute television show, the host baited Owen three times, wanting him to say that Patsy Cline was very temperamental and hard to work with. Actually, they did have their arguments. Everybody knows that. Really, it was frustration over those bad songs. Finally, the third time the host asked him, my brother said, "Patsy was no more temperamental than all the other artists I've recorded." Owen had a real problem with people saying, "Patsy said this to me and Patsy said that to me." He said, "How do we know what she said, you know?"

JAMES AUSTIN

Each producer had a different sensibility and was working with a different company. They had different musical tastes. One might like a lot of strings and a lot of production. Listen to what happened with Patsy Cline's material. You can hear what Patsy Cline sounded like on 4 Star [Records] versus what her stuff for Decca sounded like. [Decca's Owen] Bradley was someone who had a vision of what Patsy Cline could be.

HAROLD BRADLEY

The deal was Patsy had buyer's remorse. She'd hear a song and love it. Then, she'd record it and hate it—unless it was a hit. She wasn't thrilled about doing . . . Well, let's go back.

"Walkin' After Midnight" was the only hit she'd had on 4 Star because Bill McCall, who owned the label, let her do songs only that he published [the "bad songs" referred to above]. When my brother became the vice president of Decca in 1958, and Patsy's contract was up with 4 Star, he didn't know whether she'd sign with him or not.

But she called one day. His assistant came in and said, "Patsy Cline's on the phone. If we'll give her a thousand dollars, she'll sign with us." Owen didn't have carte blanche to do that. So he had to call New York and say he'd really liked to have this girl. They said, "Great," because they'd been following her career. Paul Cohen knew about her.

Owen signed her. She wasn't real thrilled over "I Fall to Pieces." There was a song that Freddie Hart wrote. I can't remember the name of it. Jan Howard pitched it, on Freddie Hart's behalf, to Patsy. She liked it. That was the one Patsy liked. Anyway, we did "I Fall to Pieces."

Patsy had the automobile wreck and was in the hospital. It took several months, though, for that song to sell. After it was a hit and Patsy was well, she poked her head in my brother's office and said, "I never did like that little ol' song anyway." My brother was stunned. He thought she loved the song.

There are two things going on with "Crazy." First of all, we recorded it after Patsy had the automobile wreck. Many years later, I called my brother because somebody from a magazine wanted to know why she couldn't sing it on the session. A normal session is three-hours long. We spent four hours on it, and all he got was one track.

He said, "I'm tired of talking about it."

I said, "If you don't tell me, I can't tell them, and nobody will know what happened."

"She couldn't hold that one note. It would hurt her every time she hit that note." He finally said, "Look, why are you beating yourself up?" By then we had three-track. He had the middle track open for her voice. He recollected that she came back within a couple of weeks, and she sang it through one time. He said, "When she got through with it, neither one of us wanted to do it again." They really didn't have to do it again. She nailed it.

The other part of the story is I was on a panel with Charlie Dick, her widower. His story is that Willie Nelson's phrasing on the demo gave her problems. So you have two conflicting stories. I'll take my brother's. I don't think Charlie Dick was in the studio when we cut it. I don't remember him being there.

RAY STEVENS, "SANTA CLAUS IS WATCHING YOU" (1962), *THE BEST OF RAY STEVENS* (RHINO)

SHELBY SINGLETON

"Santa Claus Is Watching You" by Ray Stevens was originally about three-and-a-half-minutes long. Because radio wanted records as close to two minutes as possible, we edited that up and got it down to two minutes and two seconds, or somewhere in that range. During those days, the artist didn't really have any say so as to what you did. I remember Ray got mad at me. I spliced the record up, reduced the size, and sent it to the plant to be pressed. Then I went on vacation in Acapulco. Ray called me up and told me I'd ruined his record.

BOBBY BARE, *THE ESSENTIAL BOBBY BARE* (1962) (RCA)

BOB FERGUSON

One of the techniques that I learned from Chet, he used it with Bobby Bare. Chet had a tune that he'd picked up. He had a drawer on the right bottom of his desk. He pulled out one the lacquers [a demo]. "Here's one, Bobby, that I think you might like."

He played it, and Bobby said, "I don't care much for that, Chet."

"Oh is that right?"

"Yeah, I can't get . . ."

Chet said, "Well, that's okay. I'll just put it back, 'cause that's a hit for somebody." Now listen, that'll get your attention.

"Maybe I better listen to that one again," he said.

Because this is what you ought to look for mutually. You don't want to force something on an artist. If they don't get it, they won't do it well, but if you believe in it strongly, then that can rub off, if you transmit that to them. They said that Bobby asked, "Why does Chet like this?"

I've always heard that Patsy didn't like "I Fall to Pieces," but Owen believed in it. Then, she was good for singing it. They did a good job, and it was a hit record. That illustrates the relationship with artists. If you do have a real hit, you need to give it that extra try like Chet did with Bare to transmit to them, "You may be missing something." You get a good relationship with your artist that way.

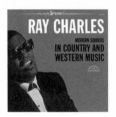

RAY CHARLES, *MODERN SOUNDS IN COUNTRY AND WESTERN MUSIC* (1962, RHINO)

SID FELLER

I lived in New York at the time. Ray was in California. He called me and said that he was thinking of making a country album. I wasn't prepared for it, but after I thought about it, I realized, "He knows what the hell he's doing." No title was mentioned at that time, but he asked me to gather together the best country-western hits of the last ten or fifteen years. This happened in 1961, a few months before the sessions.

I made calls to all the big country publishers, mostly in Nashville, but some of them were in New York. They sent me about two hundred or more of their best material on tape as well as sheet music with lyrics. I weeded through and found forty of them that seemed great for Ray Charles. I edited all those little tapes they sent me and put it all on one reel. I sent it and copies of the [sheet] music to him. From that forty, he picked twelve and that became *Modern Sounds in Country and Western Music*. But he picked them himself.

Then he asked Marty Paich to make the arrangements out there. So Ray picked the tunes out of the ones that I found for him, he picked the arranger, and he laid out all the routines. On that particular session I had no involvement until a few weeks or a month later I came to California and supervised the recording in the studio. Then I brought the tapes back to New York.

There was no editing. When we said, "That's it," that was the end of it. I brought home a master tape. At that time we didn't have mixing. The balances were made right in the studio at the time we made the recording, and that was my job to do. Ray was in the studio singing and playing the piano. He called the shots in there, and I called the shots in the booth. The engineer [Bill Putman] came with the studio [United Recording Studios]. We had recorded with him before. They had some great engineers.

After that, everybody in the country was making country-and-western music. Ray started that trend for pop people to make country songs. A lot of the people said, "Thank you for making us all rich men." A lot of publishers called me, "Thanks for giving Ray my song."

But the fact remains, Ray set his own agenda. No matter what the powers at ABC had in mind, it didn't influence him hardly any, as far as what he was going to record. Everything he did was his own idea. Theoretically, he didn't like interference and being told what he should record. He knew what he could record, and he knew what he did best. It was pretty difficult for anyone to tell him. I knew this from the front, before we even signed him. Our relationship became very solid because we thought alike.

Bob Thiele made the one album with him, a jazz album with Quincy Jones and some others [*Genius + Soul = Jazz*, 1961]. That was a pretty successful album as well. But that was the only other album [at ABC] that anybody else produced except me, until I left the company in '65, and went to California. Then, I worked with him as an arranger-conductor after that.

We'd sit in his office—both of us sitting on a big bench by his piano. I'd have a tape recorder going, and he'd start singing and playing the tune. We'd get it on tape. He didn't even know the words at the time. We'd stop the tape. He'd give me licks. I had paper. I'd write down exactly the figures and notes that he wanted. He'd say, "I want the first trumpet to play this, the second trumpet to play that. Here's where the strings come in." He'd dictate a whole line for one particular chord. He gave me the notes. That was from his old training, when he dictated arrangements to Hank Crawford. Hank used to write everything down, note for note, the way Ray told him.

I had many tapes of those routines. When one was finished, I had the routine all on tape. Later, I'd score it, and we'd record it just as he'd laid it out. I brought him the arrangement the way he wanted it to be, without having to correct it on the recording date. That's one of the reasons we got along so well. If there were any changes I wanted, I'd discuss them with him. I'd ask, "Could we do it this way?" He'd think about it a little bit, and if it was better than the original, he'd say, "Yeah, that'll work fine." Otherwise, he'd say, "No, I like it the way I had it."

He knew what he wanted, and ninety-nine percent of the time, it was the only answer. Once in a while, I'd come up with a suggestion. But I never did it over the PA system. Nobody else ever knew what we were discussing. I did general things over the PA—call the take numbers or tell the band, "I need a little more brass or I don't hear enough third or second [trumpet]." That direction would go to the instrument. If there was poor playing, nobody had to tell Ray. He knew immediately that something was wrong. He stopped it. He didn't wait for me to tell them that it was bad. I made directions for things that were miniscule, but if they weren't playing right, he knew it right before I did.

DICKEY LEE, "PATCHES" (1962), *GOLDEN HITS COLLECTION* (ROCK 'N' ROLL)

JACK CLEMENT

You remember that record "Patches" by Dickey Lee? I cut that in my studio in Beaumont, and I recall that it had about nine splices in it, from three different takes. I had a vocal group that had never sang on a record. They messed up a lot. Then somebody else would mess up—but mostly the vocal group. I worked around that with the scissors.

I did quite a bit of splicing, one track, one tape to another. All that was mono. We didn't even have a two-track, but you could still do it up to a half-inch. They quit doing it pretty much after it got more than four-tracks or half-inch tape, because it sometimes put a blip on the tape where the splicing tape goes across the tape head. We did it all the time back then, and everybody else did. A lot of times, you'd get right up to . . . and blow an ending, and then you'd go back. "Okay, let's just redo the ending." They had that down pretty pat.

Sam [Phillips] did it one day, and I said, "That's great. How'd you do that?"

"It's easy."

He didn't even bother to mark the tape with a red pencil, take it out, and then cut it. He would very delicately take little needle-nosed scissors and slip them in there—not touch the head—and snip the tape right where it touched the head. That's the way I learned to do it. I did it that way for a long time. Now, you can magnetize the heads that way, but we had somebody come along and demagnetize them fairly regularly. We did have a maintenance person who worked for Sam's radio station. He routinely came by and made sure that the heads weren't magnetized, but Sam never touched the heads. At Sun I was the engineer too. When Sam showed me how to splice tape, I played with it. I got real good at that. I could snip right in the middle of a word, a syllable.

HANK SNOW, "I'VE BEEN EVERYWHERE" (1962), *COUNTRY LEGENDS* (RCA)

CHET ATKINS

I was the champion splicer. I've always messed around with tape and discs and everything. All you've got to do is count time to learn to splice. A lot of the engineers couldn't, so I'd help them.

One of the great splicing adventures in my career was this song called "I've Been Everywhere" [1962]. It's an Australian song [rewritten by its author, Geoff Mack, for a North American audience and sung] by Hank Snow. In its verses it [the original version] names, I guess, every town in Australia.

"Hank," I said, "sing it until you tire out or till you miss it, and go on a little farther. We'll splice it. Then, we'll start again where you stopped."

In the meantime, Hank could practice the verses that he wanted to sing, the towns and everything. We'd start again, start with new cities— because it's a long song—and splice. That was a great endeavor on my part. It was easy for a musician, but I don't think Hank would have ever done that without me or some musician who could count time.

JOHNNY CASH, "RING OF FIRE" (1963), *RING OF FIRE: THE LEGEND OF JOHNNY CASH* (UNIVERSAL)

HAROLD BRADLEY

Supposedly, Johnny Cash heard that in a dream. When they did the song at our studio [the Quonset Hut], the studio was so small they put the two trumpet players upstairs in the office. Some guys say that on the record one of the trumpet players says, "Can you hear?" I've never heard that on the record. I don't guess my ears aren't that good. That was supposed to be Johnny Cash's deal. He had Bill McElhiney write the arrangement.

Don Law was a very laid-back producer, basically let Grady Martin, a great guitar player and a leader on his sessions, run the sessions. Unless there was something he heard that he didn't like—we worked it out in the studio with Grady, the music and everything—Don would approve it. He wasn't a musician. He didn't come into the studio. He wasn't hands-on, but he allowed it to happen. He captured it. Don was a wonderful guy to work for, because he let musicians create. It was just a different way of producing.

DON LAW JR.

I sat in on a number of sessions over the years. I used to go to Nashville, and at home we heard my father's recordings. He would bring them back.

He collected a lot of talented people around him. There were lots and lots of session guys who came in and participated. It was a very fluid, very relaxed creative process. There was a lot of sharing. He'd work with the Jordanaires, who were backup singers. Willie Nelson did session work—Carl Perkins, and Floyd Cramer. Grady Martin was quite astounding. My father said he could play anything with strings on it. He was self-taught and really brilliant.

They'd start with a song, they'd sit around, and Grady would pick it up. They'd start working on arrangements. I think in some cases they had charts, but most of the time they didn't. I was always amazed by the creativity of everybody: how they could take something that wasn't really very much and turn it into something that was really quite fun, quite good. And then, when they found that they could repeat it over and over again, they worked until they found the right pieces. They could create something from nothing.

Often, they got it [a usable take] within a fairly short period of time. Sometimes it took many takes, but a lot of times it was done fairly quickly. In comparison to modern production, where there's a lot of splicing, overdubbing, and so forth, it was a lot more spontaneous. There was a lot more interplay, as I see it. It was maybe less technical in some ways. They had a fair amount of fun; they worked long hours.

And there were some characters. Marty Robbins, who did those gun-fighter ballads, he was a real character. One day we were watching him sing. I think we were in the Quonset Hut—Owen Bradley's old place—that my father got Columbia to buy. Robbins finished his first verse. They started playing the bridge. To burn off energy, he ran full speed around the studio and picked up the ballad at the bridge. I also remember Johnny Cash being very hyper and very tensely wound, but obviously really talented. My father really enjoyed working with him. The artists, they were all pretty close-knit and knew each other. His artists really loved working with him. The creative environment really worked well.

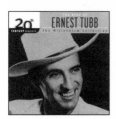

ERNEST TUBB, "THANKS A LOT" (1963),
THE BEST OF ERNEST TUBB:
THE MILLENNIUM COLLECTION (MCA)

HAROLD BRADLEY

When we started at the Quonset Hut [the Bradley's recording studio] on Music Row, we did not have the A-Team [of session players]. I'm talking about the musicians—the hot musicians. Some of us were starting to work together. Bob Moore and I were working together on basslines. Buddy Harman replaced Ferris Coursey on the drums. Grady came along. It was Grady Martin, Hank Garland, and myself on guitars. We were basically it; we were doing it. That evolved into being the A-Team musicians.

For about thirty years the A-Team took care of the town from Bill Monroe to Henry Mancini. My brother didn't care who came in. I was the guy who could read a little bit. He had the string-bender in Grady. And he had the great technician in Hank Garland. It really didn't matter as far as my brother was concerned. He thought we could handle anything that came along.

In many ways, my brother was a hands-on producer, and he was a terrific musician: arranger and piano player—accompanist. He tried not to do a lot of producing unless the session bogged down. It's like Conway Twitty said, "Any time Owen Bradley sat down at the piano, something was going to happen." On the other hand, you have people like Scotty Turner, a producer here [in Nashville]. When he first came to town, he asked my brother if he could go to a session with him. Owen said, "Sure." They went to RCA Studio B. They were doing Ernest Tubb. Owen and Scotty were talking in the control room, talking and talking.

Finally, Ernest said, "Owen, I think we're ready."

Owen turned to Scotty, "You see what I do?" All he did was capture what Ernest was going to give him, and then tweak it.

ELVIS PRESLEY, "IT HURTS ME" (1963), *FROM NASHVILLE TO MEMPHIS: THE ESSENTIAL 60'S MASTERS* (RCA)

BOB JOHNSTON

I found out who were the best musicians in Nashville. They were the ones who played for Chet and Owen and all those people. I didn't know that they pretty well did their own thing. So I hired them.

When I got in [the studio], I went around to Grady Martin, guitar player. "Can you play something, Grady, like an offbeat thing?"

He said, "Oh no, that wouldn't work. I'll take care of it."

I went around and asked the pianist. He said, "That won't do. I'll put something in there. We'll figure it out."

Every one of them said the same thing. So I paid them all double. Told them to rehearse the song. I'd be back later. I left—went to dinner and never came back. I never saw them again, except they did get paid double.

Prissy Reed—[guitarist] Jerry Reed's wife—had just moved in by us in Nashville. She told my wife, Joy [Byers], about Ray Stevens, Jerry Kennedy, Charlie McCoy, Pig Robbins, Kenny Buttrey, and all of those guys that'd came up from Louisiana, Missouri, Arkansas, and Arizona.

I said, "Well, let me try them." Joy was writing songs for Elvis Presley [e.g., "It Hurts Me," published by Hill and Range]. She had twenty-two in those movies they did with him. After getting that band, I went to see if I could get them to do the demos on those songs. I didn't want forty thousand people in there recording stuff. So I went out and asked the Jordanaires if they would do the backgrounds for me on demos.

They said, "Sure."

Then I asked the band if they'd play. And they said, "Sure." You hear the Jordanaires with the band, and I'm going, "Hey hey hey, baby" [singing Presley's part].

Elvis would listen to five or ten songs. He'd say, "That's one I want." It was my voice in there. He figured he could sing better than me any month! So that's what we did, and I learned how those people played. When I had the chance with Bob Dylan, I used them.

HAROLD BRADLEY

I played only one session for him [Bob Johnston]. When he got the job at Columbia, he said he wasn't going to use any of those old flip-flop musicians. And he didn't, which was okay because I was working somewhere else. What he did was good for Nashville. I give him credit. He had Dylan coming down. He had Simon and Garfunkel. I got an album the other day from the guy doing a biography of Peter Asher. We actually did an album with Peter and Gordon. We also did Buddy Holly, 1956. We've been rocking and rolling for a long time. I've worked with thirty people in the Rock and Roll Hall of Fame and eighty-three in the Country Music Hall of Fame.

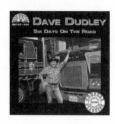

DAVE DUDLEY, "SIX DAYS ON THE ROAD" (1963), *SIX DAYS ON THE ROAD* **(SUN)**

SHELBY SINGLETON

Dave became popular in Germany. There was a group there called Truck Stop that had a truck-driving record. It was something about "I wish I could sing a truck-driving song exactly like Dave Dudley." Everybody thought Dave Dudley was just a fictitious character until he went over to Germany and did a television show. Then, all of a sudden, he became popular in Germany. Most of those records we cut basically for the German market; he played mostly German clubs and German venues.

Did you record "Six Days on the Road"?

No. That song was on Golden Wing, Dave Dudley's own record label. I called him up, and I told him that, because Mercury had [a subsidiary label called] Wing Records, that I was going to sue him if he didn't sell me the master. So he sold me the master, and we signed him as a recording artist.

PATSY CLINE, "FADED LOVE" (1963), *SWEET DREAMS: THE COMPLETE DECCA STUDIO MASTERS 1960-1963* **(MCA NASHVILLE)**

HAROLD BRADLEY

My brother [Owen Bradley] was a genius at putting singers in the right key. If I took a new girl singer and went up to his studio, he'd say to her, "Sing a song." He'd change keys several times and find the key that was best for her. He listened to the low notes, and he listened to the high notes, and he put it in the right key.

They might not think so. Dottie Dillard, our girl singer, when she came over from Springfield, Missouri, Owen asked her, "What key do you like?" She told him. He played, and she sang. He said, "Nope," and put her in another key.

I never tried to put anybody in a higher key. I tried to find the key where they were comfortable. I understand the psychology of having a high note and having people strain, but I thought it was more up to the singer. If he wanted to be where he could express himself with a high note, then he's going to tell me whether he can hit it or not. We're not going to spend all night trying to do some kind of ego trip.

Many times in the studio when we were learning, before the number system [for denoting song structures], we'd work on a song for forty-five minutes. We'd start cutting it, going for a take, when all of a sudden the artist would say, "Let's take it up a half step." You can use a capo; put it up a half step. But if you're doing the number system, it doesn't matter.

The funny thing is, when people's voices warm-up, they sing a little bit higher, but then you'll probably never hear the song again in that key. They go out on the road, and the song is, probably, back down at the key you started in. I think the artist should, to a point, choose the key, but I understand *American Idol*. When people get that high note and hold it for a long time, it thrills people to death. Patsy Cline used that [device]. That was one of the problems my brother had with her. She wanted to end every song up real high, but that didn't fit those ballads they were doing. For her, when she did "Bill Bailey" or "Lovesick Blues" and ended up with a high note, those were crowd pleasers. They were her *American Idol* moments. When she did them, people freaked out. That was what she was trying to re-create in the studio, and it wasn't working for my brother. Finally, she understood that. She started ending songs down low with a lot of feeling, like on "Faded Love."

BROOK BENTON, *ON THE COUNTRYSIDE* (1964, MERCURY)

SHELBY SINGLETON

I did an album with Brook Benton called *On the Country Side*. I recorded Brook, Clyde McPhatter, Dinah Washington, and Sil Austin, an instrumentalist [saxophone], and Richard Hayman, who played the harmonica—all different kinds of acts because I'm not a musician. I don't know anything about music. I looked at it from the standpoint of what would the people like and what would radio play, rather than looking at whether it was musically correct or not. I think that's how I got by with doing a lot of odd things that nobody else would've probably even tried.

I think when I cut "Forever" with Pete Drake on a talking steel guitar, everybody thought I was crazy. When I cut "Ahab the Arab" with Ray Stevens, they said, "That's weird. It's not anything we think would be a big seller or anything." Whenever I bought the master for Mercury of "Sea of Love" by Phil Phillips, it was like everybody said, "That's a strange record. Ain't nobody going to play that." But if one radio station played it, well then all the rest of them had to, because that just forced it. It had something that the people wanted.

ROGER MILLER, *PLATINUM AND GOLD COLLECTION* (1960–1961, BMG)

BOB FERGUSON

We [at RCA] were not always successful with our artists, but we tried everything. I remember Roger Miller was a close friend of mine and Chet's. We had him signed to the label.

Chet said, "Bob, I haven't been able to get a hit with him. You want to try?"

"Yeah, okay." So we met and had a ten o'clock session.

We'd get right to recording, and Roger would say, "I don't want to do this dang song!"

"Are you sure?"

"Yes, I hate this thing."

This went on, and about eleven-thirty or quarter-to-twelve—the session ended at one—I dropped over at Chet's office a minute. I said, "Chet, we're not getting anything."

He said, "What's going on?"

"Every time we get everybody rehearsed and ready to record, Roger doesn't want to sing. I don't know what to do."

Chet said, "Just go ahead and stay with the session till it's over. We could drop him, and maybe that'll shock him enough he'll go somewhere and get a hit." That was our attitude. These guys were friends and artists, talents. We recognized, it wasn't their fault, but for whatever reason . . . Chet said, "Maybe if we take him in a club somewhere and let him sing."

"Nah, we've tried." So we dropped him, and it did shock him. Roger went over to Mercury. Well, the first place he came after he got his hits going was over to our place, talking with me and Chet.

ROGER MILLER, *GOLDEN HITS*
(1964–1969, SMASH)

SHELBY SINGLETON

I signed him [in 1963], but I never produced him. I gave him to Jerry Kennedy to produce. The first session that Jerry did, he sent me a copy of it. It was all straight country songs.

I told Jerry, "Nah, this is not what we want. Make him cut all those silly songs he's always singing to us."

Jerry said, "None of them songs are finished."

"Make him finish them," I said. That's when they went in and did "Dang Me" and "Chug-A-Lug," and all that other stuff, and later on, "King of the Road."

Jerry was like my assistant. I moved him to Nashville from Shreveport, Louisiana, where we're both from. In fact I moved all of his furniture on the same truck I moved him on.

JERRY KENNEDY

I moved up here from Shreveport in 1961, with Shelby Singleton. He'd moved here to Nashville. He was a promotion man, working out of Shreveport, which is where we're from. They promoted him to A&R director for the South here, in Nashville. He asked me to move up here with him, and play guitar on some sessions. He said, "Maybe something will open up later." We moved here March of '61. April 1 of '61, I went to work for Mercury. I was really like his assistant. I didn't actually produce anything by myself until later in that year. We worked together on several projects.

But in 1962, this whole town exploded. That's when Smash and Philips came into being because Mercury was bought by Philips of Europe. They wanted to do some expanding as far as getting records on the radio. This is what a lot of these companies have done. You fragment the thing a bit, and you've got a better shot at getting airplay if they're not all on one label. That's how Smash and Philips came into being.

Roger and Tom T. [Hall] would show up. That was a thing where they did all the wood shedding, and I didn't have to worry about it. We might tinker with something just a little bit, but boy, they came in ready. The musicians were way behind when those guys stepped in the studio.

Roger was the first writer-artist that I worked with. I've always been such a song fan that it was really easy for me to get into a writer-artist situation. I'd sit back and applaud, actually applaud, when they were coming up with stuff. If I was involved in hearing fragments of songs, it used to knock me out, just to be able to hear that stuff as it was being born.

Roger was . . . man, what a writer! Song titles, lines from songs, his name, whatever, are mentioned in this town every day.

MERLE HAGGARD AND THE STRANGERS, *STRANGERS* (1965, CAPITOL/EMI)

KEN NELSON

I went up to Bakersfield to do a live album with a top man there, Cousin Herb Henson, who had a country TV show, the first one up there. It was very popular. So I decided to do an album. I had Glen Campbell. I had Merle Travis. I had Jean Shepard, Buck [Owens], and I don't know how many people. I recorded the album live.

Merle [Haggard] was on the show, but I couldn't use him because he wasn't under contract to me. I was impressed immediately with his voice. I went to him. "Hey, would you care to sign with Capitol records?"

"No," he said.

I said, "Oh. Why not?"

"Well, Fuzzy and Lou [Lewis Talley] gave me my first break, and I'm going to stay with them." They had a record label called Talley Records.

"Well, okay," I said. I respected him for that.

But then, pretty soon I started to notice this Talley Records on the *Billboard* charts. I said, "This is ridiculous." I called Fuzzy. "Hey, get down here. You're blowing your stack. You don't have the distribution or the ability to promote these records. Get down here and let's talk."

He came down, and I talked him into—well, I don't know, I guess they wanted to be on Capitol anyway. They realized that it was a difficult situation that they couldn't handle. So I signed Merle [in 1965] and bought all of the masters that he had. That's how I got him.

Certain artists, when they walked in the studio with material, I knew it was good for them. I never had to worry about their songs. They knew what the hell they were doing. Like Merle, there was no reason for me to sit down and listen to what he was going to bring in.

Fuzzy was his manager. It was only fair that I put him as part producer. I didn't have to. I just wanted to. I did the sound. In fact, Merle's the only artist that I would let anybody fool with. But Merle and Fuzzy were so close. And Fuzzy would be in the studio. He'd work with Merle, helping him with phrases and stuff like that, which of course I didn't like. I would never do. I believe that you hire an artist for what he can do. There was never anything drastic that Fuzzy did, but I decided—oh, what the hell—put his name on the record as producer.

Other artists, I'd have to suggest songs. Many would bring me songs. I listened, and if I felt that it suited them and worked for them, then okay. I'd say yes or no, "I didn't like it" or "It's not for you"—whatever the case may have been.

Merle wrote most of his own songs. Buck wrote most of his, and they were great. There's no question about it. See, that's the difference between me and Owen Bradley. Owen was a true musician. And Chet's the same way. To me, they're the two greatest producers that were in the business. They had musicianship. I was a musician too, but I didn't have the know-how of constructing songs like they did. They were up and above. That's the way I feel about them.

GLEN CAMPBELL, SONG DEMOS (1965) AND "I KNEW JESUS (BEFORE HE WAS A STAR)" (1973), *THE ESSENTIAL GLEN CAMPBELL, VOL. 1* (LIBERTY)

JIMMY BOWEN

Cutting demos was almost like the way I wound up doing productions during the last half of my career. It was staying out of the way of the song and the writer. You have the writer either be there and/or put it down with just their instrument, the guitar or the piano.

With Glen, if he heard a song once, he could then walk in and do it. He had the most incredible ear of any musician I've ever known. Of course, I knew him so well. We'd get bass, drums, and keyboard, or Jimmy Seals and some of the guys would come by and do different things. Sometimes you'd make the demo aimed at an artist. You're going to get one of Snuff Garrett's artists: going after Johnny Burnette or whomever it is. So then you point it that way, but the bad thing is, if you miss, now you've got to start over.

Basically, you wanted to go in and put the song down the way the writer or writers, the way it came out of them. That got me really wanting to do that. There wasn't much production there other than the little bit of preproduction. Just go in there: "Bam-bam-bam." You're doing them. Then, I'd walk across and watch Spector work on something for eight hours.

He was the first one, as I recall, who made people aware of that particular part of the art form. Snuff Garrett made a lot of hit records, singles. He and Phil [Spector] were both working at the same time: totally different kinds of stuff. I learned a lot from Phil, sitting around and watching him. He was always very nice to me. One thing I got from Snuff Garrett was Ernie Freeman—the arranger, magnificent! He was a brilliant talent with ego control. You could sit with him and ask for whatever, and he'd come up with it. He hand-held Snuff and me both with those big orchestra things.

THE ESSENTIAL PORTER WAGONER AND DOLLY PARTON, THE ESSENTIAL DOLLY PARTON, AND THE ESSENTIAL CONNIE SMITH (1965; COMPILATIONS, 1996, 2005, AND 1996, RCA)

BOB FERGUSON

The arrangement was, "Would I produce Dolly?"

I said, "Why, yes."

As time went by, I guess you'd say Porter wanted a bigger piece of the pie; he wanted more credit or whatever it is. We all were functioning in our roles. He was possibly what you might call an arranger. He had his own band, and they'd practice on the road. We'd have [additional] key musicians at the studio. I guess he wanted more and more of it. At contract renewal or when they made a new one—I wasn't there—he got himself listed as producer. Since that time, he's even had my name taken off some things that I produced. I always thought it was pretty strange. But the music business is very strange. I did my job as I saw it for the company—for them and for Dolly.

Finally, one day she came to me—Dolly, alone to my office. "Bob," she said, "can we talk?"

I said, "Chet and I aren't sure whether this place is bugged or not. We'll go somewhere." We went out to my car, and she said, "I know you and Porter are from the same place in Missouri or nearly."

"Yeah, twenty miles away."

"And you guys have been friends a long time. But I'm getting ready leave him."

I said, "You're my artist just like he's another artist. Whatever is the best thing for you, that's what we're going to do." It seemed that she wasn't in the negotiations with RCA about her own stuff. It was as if Porter was handling everything.

In fact a parallel example was Connie Smith. Bill Anderson brought Connie over [to RCA]. We made a lot of good recordings together, but in the early part of her career, she'd come to me about management. I think she had somebody in Texas in mind, but Bill wanted to manage her. She shrunk down at that and wanted some help.

I called Bill, and I asked him, "You talking to Connie about managing?"

"Yeah." Straightforward.

"That kind of worries her," I said, "but I think if you wouldn't take on the management part of her life, you'd always remain the knight on the white charger that brought her out." And so Bill backed off of that management thing.

Well, Chet and Porter had been together a lot, and Chet talked to Porter once about the same thing—about Dolly—about how you don't work with someone by holding them down. You let them fly, and you boost them from behind. Now this is probably the essence of production—the way I learned it from Chet, and the way I felt about it while we worked together. You fill in whatever is needed to boost artists to reach their aspirations. That was the way we felt about it.

Well, Connie was an example of being freed. Porter, on the other hand, Chet talked to him: "She feels like you're holding her down."

Finally, this was what she was telling me in the car. "Bob, I'm going to leave Porter. I wanted you to know what I'm doing." This was some time before it became visible. "It'll take me awhile," she said, "because we've got that publishing company together. We're doing the road shows. It's going to take me awhile, but I've got all these things that I want to do. He won't let me pick a note, sing a note that he don't okay."

We had some episodes in the studio where Porter made the announcement to the effect that he was the world's greatest producer. "Don't pick a note that I don't tell you to." The way I got it, Grady Martin packed up his guitar. Porter says, "What are you doing?"

He said, "I'm going home, hoss. I'm afraid I'll hit a note that you don't approve." He left the studio.

Anyway, I said, "Dolly fly. Do what you're going to do. I'll be right there."

"Well Bob," she said, "I just wanted you to know so you wouldn't sit there worrying."

I said, "I sure appreciate it, Dolly. Because there's a lot of goings-on." As Chet's authority was diminished and others came in, things happened, terrible things.

CHET ATKINS

Porter's an ambitious guy. He met Dolly, and he had a TV show. I don't remember how it all happened. I turned him over to Bob Ferguson. He worked out with Bob, or he told Bob, "I'm going to take over producing my records." Porter got into some drugs at that time, little blue pills or whatever the hell they are. I've never seen them. But he got a lot of confidence out of those things. Like they will do.

BOB FERGUSON

Some sessions I remember real well, but there was a period of time there when I was doing three sessions a day. You come out, grab a snack, and go back. Previously, I'd set up all the material and things for everybody. I'd be coming out. Chet would have his clipboard going in, vice versa.

Chet never did say a lot for me to do, but I rode shotgun with him a bunch. Once he was recording somebody. I don't remember who it was, and I was sitting there in the shotgun position. He asked me, "Did you hear something wrong?"

"Yeah."

He pushed the [talk-back] button and said, "Let's start over again." He leaned over and whispered, "Sometimes you hear something. You can't put your finger on what was wrong, but something didn't sound right. You trust yourself and just push the button and start over." That was one of the simple things that he told me. But we were awful busy.

It was kind of a rule of that time that you don't touch the engineer's end of the board. But you could communicate with him. A lot of times he'd say, "Bob, do that to where you hear it. Here's the one." Then he'd point at the knob. So you could do that, but most of the time, you'd communicate. We had good engineers so they knew what you were talking about. If you'd say, "Right after so-and-so, bring up so-and-so," they might say, "Reach over here and do it." Mainly though, we were limited to a talk-back button and a clock.

HAROLD BRADLEY

That's why Chet quit. People he was signing became close friends. They brought their problems to him, and it was more than he could handle to be their producer, to be their friend, and to keep his guitar playing going. It got to be too much for him.

He was the go-between. He was friends with all of them, and he took it personally. Don Gibson had problems, and his and Chet's roots went all the way back to Knoxville where they worked together at the radio station there. He took everybody's problems personally, and it got to be a problem for him.

BOB FERGUSON

When Dolly left Porter, I did her next session. She called me over, "Bob, I want you to sing a part on this." Which I did. We've remained very good friends. There again, I was doing my role in conferring with her. It's so complex, your role as the producer. There've been all kinds. Some of them say, "Come in and record this." I've seen that. I've known record companies that if they didn't get the publishing, they wouldn't record it. But Dolly and I had a nice, free relationship—a good understanding all the way.

CHET ATKINS, "YAKETY AXE" (1965), *THE ESSENTIAL CHET ATKINS* (RCA)

BOB FERGUSON

I did a record once with Chet in Studio B called "Yakety Axe." Right in the middle, the guitar starts doing rooster yodeling or whatever. I told the engineer, "Push up the echo to right here." I showed him where.

"Bob, you know the Chief don't like a lot of echo," he said.

I said, "He'll like it on this one."

"Okay."

So Chet did it. We made it like you hear it today. Chet came into the control room. He was standing between the speakers, looking down and listening. When it went to that high echo—where I threw it in—his eyes opened, and he looked at me. It got to the end. He said, "That's a lot of echo, isn't it?"

"Don't touch it," I said. "Don't bother it. Don't anybody do anything to it." If I can convey this: That was my job.

"Fine. Okay," he said. "You feel that way?"

"Yes sir."

He said, "Uh-oh, somebody here has lit up over this thing." That's the way we did.

Somebody once asked me, "What was great about recording Chet Atkins?"

I said, "It was a series of good listening enterprises, exercises." Chet counted on me to say just exactly what I thought: "That's good," or "Chet, we probably ought to do that over again."

Or before I could say anything, he'd say, "Let's do another one." While he was picking, he'd be thinking of a different way he was going to do something.

JOE TEX, "HOLD WHAT YOU GOT" (1965), "I BELIEVE I'M GONNA MAKE IT": THE BEST OF JOE TEX (RHINO)

BUDDY KILLEN

Country, from the beginning there were accepted parameters. Don't venture beyond this if you want to call it country. When they started using vocal groups and strings and horns, then people started venturing out. The so-called Nashville sound began to happen, and we found that we could push the parameters a lot further than we thought we could. But we still had to take into consideration, first and foremost, that the lyric was really so important. You didn't want to cover it up with too much music. Yet you always looked for just a little bit of something that was a little different sounding.

I always felt that R&B gave much more freedom to a producer than country did, even though I produced an awful lot of number-one country hits. If you'll listen to my records, you'll find that I used a lot of my rhythm-and-blues experience in my records. Rhythm and blues back in the '60s and '70s was real funky. It had a raw quality to it. If you started getting too slick, it wouldn't sell. So we'd go in the studio, and we'd come up with these real great grooves. Joe was really good at that himself. Most of the time, he knew what kind of groove he wanted on a song. He'd have some of those licks in mind. When I first started producing him, you talk about a gutbucket kind of R&B singer!

He and I fought in the studio for the first four years till finally, one day, we decided. It's a long story, but he wanted out of his contract. I said, "Let me record you one time the way I want to, and if we don't make it, then I'll turn you loose."

"Okay," he said.

That's when I cut "Hold What You Got." I mixed country with that real raw thing that he did. All of a sudden, we came up with a sound.

I cut that record down at FAME Studios in 1960 or something like that. By that time Nashville had added multitrack, like two-track, three-track, and four-track. Rick [Hall, owner of FAME Studios in Muscle Shoals, Alabama] didn't happen to have any multitrack machines down there at the time. But they were cutting all those R&B hits, and I just felt like that was the place to go.

And so that record was done mono. The piano player overdubbed, and Joe did a vocal harmony at the same time. There was a guitar overdub. We just went from mono to mono with about four or five guys over-dubbing at the same time. Nowadays you don't do that! A guy goes in; he's got his own track. But we didn't have tracks. We put everything on it at the same time.

Under normal circumstances we wouldn't have overdubbed anything, but I had this thing. I had a feeling, and I said, "Let's try this." When we did, I knew I'd hit a magic button. It gave us the sound that I was looking for with him. I lucked up on it. We used it many times thereafter. We maintained that sound for a lot of years with Joe, and we sold an awful lot of records. He was the original rapper. Listen to that stuff. Nobody was doing that back in those days.

I saved so many records by having the ability to figure out where to go with it. On "Hold What You've Got," everybody thought it was a failure. We'd finished about four or five o'clock in the morning. We said goodbye. Joe said, "Buddy, sorry we didn't make it," and Rick Hall apologized. I'm all downcast. But on my way home back to Nashville, I think, "I don't give up that easily." I went straight to RCA studios. I ran copies of those tapes and started editing.

On a mono tape, if you don't get it, you pretty much just didn't get it. But you could certainly edit, which I did many times. I'd tell the engineer where I wanted him to cut. "Hold What You've Got"—if you could see the white tape on that where I intercut pieces! I started with two tapes. We'd recorded two performances of the song, though neither of them was good. They were full of mistakes. I ran copies of the tapes. I'd cut a piece out of one tape and put it in the other one, cut a piece here, a piece there, until I finally put that record together. I found one chorus that held together. It's the same chorus every time you hear it. When I finally got finished, the tape sounded pretty good, and I'd gotten most of the mistakes out of it. But it was really manufactured. I put the record together, sent it up to Jerry Wexler [at Atlantic Records in New York].

He called me back. "Buddy, this thing is a smash. I'm going to put it out today."

I said, "We don't even have a label."

"I don't care," he said. We'll put one together. I'm just going to put a little interim label out there." He did it, just a one-color label. It was so easy to bootleg that we were bootlegged all over the place.

Joe called me a few days later. "Look here man. You said you're going to let me out of my contract. How about turning me loose?"

I said, "Joe, we've got a hit record." They shipped it. It sold fifty thousand the first day.

"Man, you put that piece of"—you know what—"out?"

I said, "Yeah."

He hung up on me.

A week later, he calls me again. "Look here, man. You done said you were going to give me my contract back. I want my contract back!"

"Joe," I said, "we've sold a quarter of a million records."

He said, "Look here, man—WHAT!"

"We've sold a quarter of a million records."

He said, "No kidding? What did you do?"

"Just some little electronic tricks."

"Buddy Killen," he said, "you're a genius. I ain't going to never question you again."

"I'm not a genius," I said. But in this case, I had saved it. I saved what would have otherwise been the end of a wonderful association. But in the studio—I've done this many times—you sit there and say, "What's wrong with this thing? Why isn't it doing what I want it to do?" Then, all of a sudden, "I know!" You just know.

I did a country album with Joe, *Soul Country*, and it was one of our biggest sellers. I did "Green Green Grass of Home," things like that with him. Joe loved country music, and he'd listen to country radio. He knew a lot of the songs, knew about them. Of course, we went through the Tree Catalog, which was one of the greatest country catalogs you could find. "Heartbreak Hotel" was one of the things [we recorded]. It was a good album. People really liked it.

Joe wrote most everything that he did other than with that one album. We'd get ready for an album. He'd come in, have some songs. He'd bring in some of his players. Most of them were pretty bad. They were road musicians. They didn't have that fine tuning that you need in a studio, but I stopped fighting. I let him use them, and then, when they left town, I took my own musicians in and replaced the tracks. I did that a lot of times. Joe would call me and say, "Man, what'd you do? That sounds great!" I'd say, "Oh, little electronic tricks."

BOB DYLAN, *HIGHWAY 61 REVISITED* (1965, COLUMBIA)

BOB JOHNSTON

I always said, "Let's go down to Nashville," the first day I was ever with him. We walked into the studio; all those suits were there. I was talking to Dylan about Nashville. "It's a good thing." I pictured the studio down there. "You don't have to fuck with anything. Nobody will mess with you. The engineers, I've got that worked out where we don't even have to have them sons-of-bitches."

He said, "Mmm, mmm." He never would say "yeah" or "good idea." He'd say, "Mmm," like Jack Benny with this thumb on his lip. He walked out.

[Clive] Davis and [Albert] Grossman, the manager of Dylan, and [Walter] Yetnikoff came over. "If you ever mention Nashville to Dylan again, you're fired."

I asked them, "Why? Why would that be? I was planning on bringing a bunch of people down there."

They said, "They're stupid down there. We don't want you starting off with Dylan, stupid in Nashville. Just remember what we told you. If you go down there, you're fired."

I said, "Good enough, you're the boss."

I took Dylan down there about six months later and cut the best album in rock history. So I have really no use for those fucking people—none of them at all. They're all crooked.

I told my artists to keep away from Clive Davis. I wouldn't let him in the room. I'd shut the door, turn the light out, or we'd go to lunch—anything to keep him out of there [the studio]. I told Dylan, I told all the artists, "I don't want those motherfuckers in there. You get them in there; you don't need me in there. Davis and Yetnikoff, they can't sing, write, play, dance, or perform. They can do nothing but give you the wrong advice for your career and for your salvation, and steal all the money from you."

CHARLEY PRIDE, "THE SNAKES CRAWL AT NIGHT" (1965), *THE ESSENTIAL CHARLEY PRIDE* (RCA)

JACK CLEMENT

I paid for the first session myself, which I have done a lot. I went in and rented a studio, hired the band, and produced the record with Charley Pride. I'd told Chet Atkins that I was going to let him have first crack at it. We were buddies. I'd worked a lot with him. We were cutting at RCA in his building. Of course, that didn't matter, but I told him I'd let him hear it first.

Well, he heard it and thought it was great, but then they passed on it. I was right on the verge of pressing it up myself, and then I ran into Chet down by the coffee machine there in the building. I had an office up on the third floor. So I'd stroll down there and hang out in the studio or down by the coffee machine. One day I ran into Chet. He asked me, "What'd you ever do with that colored boy?"

"Nothing yet. I'm thinking about pressing that one myself."

"Well, I been thinking about that," he said. "We might be passing up another Elvis Presley. I'll tell you what. I'm going to a big A&R meeting out in California next week. If you'll get me another lacquer of that, I'll play it for them." So I did, and he did. They loved it.

He came back and said, "They want to sign him."

He presented Charley the way I always did. It was fun. Play the record and then show them a picture. They don't believe it, you know. I had the only Charley Pride record in town for a while, and I had a lot of fun with it. People would come in. I'd put that thing on. It sounded great. I had these huge speakers in my office anyway. Play it, and I'd show them his picture.

Chet told me when he did it, everybody said, "No, the guy we just heard?"

"That's him."

But you know, they thought it was great. After they thought about it for a while, they decided they wouldn't even mention the race thing. They'd just treat it with respect. "Here's a really fine new artist." And let 'er rip. I still marvel that they had that much wisdom at the time. There was never any real rumbling about the thing.

He opened up in Louisiana and Texas. He was a good looking guy, and he had a straight speaking voice. It wasn't like a Southern person. It was like a Western cowboy. It had this drawl. He'd lived in Montana for eight years. I guess that's the reason. Anyway, he walks out on stage there in Louisiana, his first appearance. A hush falls on the crowd. He walks out, looks at his arm, and says, "Yeah, I do have this sort of permanent suntan." From then on, he's got them. It was the same way the next night in Dallas or wherever he was in Texas, Beaumont.

CHET ATKINS

He [producer Jack Clement] brought a demo record and played it for me. It was "The Snakes Crawl at Night." He kept telling me, "You've got to hear this guy sing."

So I'd see him in the street or in the studio, and I said, "When are you going to bring that black guy to see me?"

"Don't you worry," he said. "You'll hear him. You'll get him." Bye and bye, he brought that record and left it with me.

I went to an RCA executive meeting in Monterey, California. We'd all get together and play our productions that we'd made. So I play a few and then I put that one on. Of course, Charley's a great country artist, 'cause he has such an edge to his voice. That's what it took back in those days. You needed a guy with a real edge to his voice so you could hear him on the jukebox.

So I played the demo. Everybody said, "He sounds great. He's got a good voice."

Then I pulled the line, "He's black."

We had one guy there—he's dead now—but his name was Ben Rosner. He was head of the production staff. He just couldn't get over it. He just jumped up and down. He thought Charley was wonderful, because he liked black musicians. So we signed him.

I remember we had a long discussion. "What about the people in Mississippi? Are they going to boycott our records after we pull this on them?" Of course, we released it, and I think we put "Country Charley Pride" on the record. He pulled that off so well. I don't know that any other black artist could have pulled that off, because that's what he liked. He didn't like anything else. I asked him once, "Charley, why do you sing country? How'd you get that influence?"

He said, "Well, my daddy would turn on the Grand Ole Opry every Saturday night. I loved to sing those songs."

BOB DYLAN, "SAD-EYED LADY OF THE LOWLANDS" (1966), *BLONDE ON BLONDE* (COLUMBIA)

BOB JOHNSTON

Dylan went in the studio. "I'm going to write a song," he said. He wrote a song for a day. The night came, and the next night came. About four o'clock in the morning, he came to me and said, "Anybody awake in there?"

"Yeah, they're all awake." I went in there, woke them up. I told them, "If you stop playing, get your suitcase and all your stuff and go on out the door. You can get me a replacement, and we'll wait for it. But otherwise, I can overdub you all, but I can't overdub Bob Dylan. So don't ever stop. Don't ever ask him to play what he's planning—to rehearse it. We're not going to do that. Watch his feet. When he starts patting that foot and playing guitar, you can follow him along. Your job is not to play something that somebody tells you to play. Nobody is going to tell you what to play. You play what you do. People are either going to say, 'That's not worth a shit,' or 'Listen to that goddamn band.' And that's what they said, 'Listen to the band.'"

We made the first one [track], and what they did, they were all playing. I said, "Don't ever quit." Nothing in Nashville was ever done except for three-minute records. You couldn't have past a three-minute record because radio wouldn't play it. Dylan played the verse and the chorus. Then he gave a big ending like that was it. Everybody quit playing, and then he hit the next chord for the second verse. They didn't know it, and they jumped in again. More than eleven-minutes later, we finished the song.

"Did you hear that?" Dylan said.

"That's what you've got to do," I said. "Hear it back." We went in and played it back.

"Jesus Christ," he said. And that was it.

I don't ever remember cutting a song twice. Al Kooper always wanted to. "Let me overdub here."

One day, Al started, "One, two, three."

"What are you doing?" I asked him.

"I'm counting off."

I said, "Nobody counts off for Dylan. You're wasting time."

Kooper always said to Dylan, "Let me produce you. I can produce better than Johnston." Dylan would be waving his hands behind Kooper's back. He didn't want that son-of-a-bitch producing him.

**JERRY LEE LEWIS,
"MEMPHIS BEAT" (1966), *KILLER:
THE MERCURY YEARS* (MERCURY)**

SHELBY SINGLETON

Normally I had somebody working with me who would rehearse the songs with the acts before we went in the studio. Jerry Lee Lewis was a unique act. He was one of these instantaneous learners of songs. Other acts would have to go over a song many times. He had the ability to listen to a song, and then play it on the piano and sing it with his own style.

JERRY KENNEDY

Shelby signed Jerry to Smash in 1963 or '4. Then Shelby left Mercury in about '66 or '7. So that's when I inherited Jerry. I was a fan. That was one of the real neat things, being able to work with the guy that I'd sort of cut my teeth on.

We started off—back when we were cutting rock—I'd go to Memphis; Jerry would be coming through here. We'd sit down and talk about things. When we got into the country part of it, Jerry would show up an hour or two ahead of the session. I'd have a bunch of songs, and he would learn them right there, and we'd go in and cut them.

All those big, successful country things came from very little planning. In some cases he would show up at a-quarter-till-the-session and hear a song. He trusted us enough to say, "Okay, you guys find the songs. I'll sing them." He was a quick study on learning them. No sheet music— Jerry didn't read music. We'd have a good demo or somebody with a guitar to sing the song to him. That's how it happened. And he never did it the same way twice. Artistic liberties were running amok when he was cutting. He never said "me" very much. It was "Jerry Lee," because it rhymed.

Before we would even set up sessions, we'd start looking for songs. The minute we finished one project we were open to calling people and saying, "It's time to start looking again." We always had a stockpile of what we considered good songs before we set up the session. "Walking the Floor over You" and "Another Place, Another Time"—those were back to back.

A guy named Bobby Denton, WIVK in Knoxville, had been bugging the heck out of me to cut Jerry country. "Stone country," he said. "I don't mean rockabilly. I mean country." I spent about a year listening to him running that through.

Finally, one day, there wasn't anything else to do. In fact, Jerry's contract was coming up, and I wasn't sure they were going to continue with him. We just couldn't get anything going as far as pop. Jerry Chesnut brought "Another Place, Another Time" around, and Eddie Kilroy, who was the promotion guy at Mercury, heard it. He brought the song in to me, and I said, "Shoot it to him." He shot it to Jerry, I think, on a Thursday. Jerry got it on Friday. He was here on Saturday, and we cut it. It was the first time we'd used steel and fiddle with him. That was the first stone-country date he did. For a B-side, we cut, real quick, "Walkin' the Floor."

He was on! Absolutely on. In fact I'm going to guess that probably, from that record on, until the time he got through at Mercury, he never did any more than four or five takes on a record.

If I knew that three songs were definite, then: "Okay, let me get a mental arrangement going here. Alright, we'd better get a vocal group here." Jerry loved to have everybody in the studio with him. On anybody else I was working with, we could build tracks. We'd hire the basics and overdub all that other stuff. But Jerry loved to have it all happening with him. If there were strings, they were always there. I know the engineers would've loved to have strangled me back when we were doing all those things. We were working in a nice-sized room, but not that big. And Jerry—by God, he played so loud—it was hard to isolate him.

Mort Thomason and Tom Sparkman were two of the engineers that I used with Jerry. They did as good a job of keeping Jerry out of the piano and the piano out of Jerry as anybody I ever worked with. There was always a problem with other folks. I attribute a lot of that success, as far as being able to keep it as clean as we did keep it, separate as we did keep it, to those two guys.

We'd get a good take. We'd very seldom splice anything. That was something I hated to do, because you never really captured the same feel especially with Jerry Lee on different takes. I talked to somebody about this the other day. A bunch of old guys were standing around down at a hockey game. We talked about how we sacrificed perfection for feel back in those times. The feel was way more important than having that perfect ending.

1. Chet Atkins and engineer Bill Porter in RCA Studio B, Nashville. *Courtesy of Merle Atkins Russell, the Chet Atkins Estate*

2. Ralph S. Peer. *Courtesy of Ralph Peer II*

3. Owen Bradley in his Quonset Hut Recording Studio, Nashville.
Courtesy of Harold Bradley

4. Harold Bradley. *Courtesy of Harold Bradley*

5. Jack Clement.

6. Ken Nelson
and Wanda Jackson.
*Courtesy of Wanda
Jackson and Wendell
Goodman*

7. Sid Feller and Ray Charles.

8. Connie Smith and Bob Ferguson, 1964.
Courtesy of Barry Mazor

9. Shelby Singleton.
Courtesy of John A. Singleton,
Sun Entertainment Corp.

10. Jerry Kennedy.
Courtesy of Jerry Kennedy

11. Bob Irwin. *Courtesy of Bob Irwin*

12. (*left*) Jimmy Bowen.
Photo by Beth Gwinn.
Courtesy of Jimmy Bowen

13. (*below*) Bob Dylan,
Johnny Cash, and Bob Johnston.
Photo by Al Clayton. Johnston
(Bob) Papers, di_01912, The Dolph
Briscoe Center for American
History, The University of Texas
at Austin

INTERLUDE
STUDIO MATTERS

JERRY KENNEDY

I'm going to guess that I was happier when we were cutting mono. When the red light came on, you started picking, and when the red light went off, that was the record. It had a feel. Everybody knew that their part couldn't be done again. Everybody was on top of their game. I'm talking pickers and singers too. They knew that was going to be it. There was something magic about everybody being there. Singer feeds off pickers; pickers feed off the singer. It was just a special thing. There were no earphones then either. Everybody was hearing the real thing that was going on.

It made for some tense sessions as a player. You knew, "I don't want to be the one to blow it here in the last eight bars, because we'll all, probably, have to do it again."

Now that kind of went away in '66, '67, somewhere around there. Before the multitrack thing, we'd run things down, and then when we got ready for the take, I'd go out and sit in a chair and do it then. That never seemed to be a problem. It's certainly not that I thought I was better than somebody else, but if I heard something, why would I beat a guy to death showing it to him, when I could just do it, either right then or after the session? That's how I ended up playing [guitar] on a bunch of those things.

JIMMY BOWEN

When I was in L.A, I was using the best musicians in L.A. They didn't know who the hell I was. I had to have people skills. The first time I used a big string section—twenty people just in the string section—I wanted to make a change. I walked over. Ernie Freeman was this great arranger that I worked with. I walked over, and I'm trying to deal with it. And I could hear the Dodger baseball game playing; one cello player had it in his earphone. Then, I heard something else over on the other side of the section.

I thought, "Oh boy, I've got to get these people's respect. I want them to be a part of this. I don't want them to be here in body, but not in mind and spirit." Everything had been going really good. Violin sections get tuned so good.

"Alright, let's take our break," I said. Everybody sat their instruments down very carefully. I went over to the second violin, not the first, and I detuned him just a little tiny bit, one string—I forget which one now— detuned him a little.

I got them back in. I stood right there where they were, in their section of the room. When they came back in, I was rather demanding. "Okay, quiet, quiet. Absolutely quiet, please." One guy started to check his tuning. "No no, absolutely quiet. I've got this thought. I've got to hear the letter B. Let's go to bar twenty-two. On the downbeat, 1–2–3 and . . ."

The strings went "reeeeooooowww."

I said "Whoa, whoa, whoa. Hold it! Jesus. Right over here. Checked the tuning, would you?"

Indignantly, he went "eeeeaaaah." He looked so embarrassed. And he brought that baby back up to play.

"Alright guys, let's try that again." They ran that one little section again. "Thank you very much." I turned around and went back into the booth.

I never had trouble with the string section the rest of my time in L.A. They assumed "if that son-of-a-bitch can hear that good, we'd better listen." Because I was a kid.

I'd watched Jimmy Webb take hours trying to get what he wanted out of the string section. They knew he was a brilliant-but-crazy artist guy trying to work with them. These were old guys who did movies and television, anything musical.

That worked. I don't know why I thought to do that, but it worked.

DAVE ALVIN

I get into big arguments with some of the acts over sonics. There's a tendency with more roots-oriented acts or retro acts to want to go into the studio and make records that sound exactly like a Bob Wills record, 1948. I don't like to do that because it can't be done. You can simulate it, but when it comes to the greats of yesterday, when they went into the recording studio, they were trying to use the best technology that was there. Bob Wills didn't go into a recording studio in 1950, saying, "Could you make my record sound like a Jimmie Rodgers record from 1929?" To me, authenticity is in the notes you're playing, in the way you're playing them, and in the heart that you bring to the music. When Ken Nelson was producing Buck Owens and Merle Haggard in the mid-'60s, that was state-of-the-art sound. That's one of the reasons why those records sound so great today.

I learned this the hard way with the Blasters. We'd go into a recording studio and be frightened to death of all the technology. We wanted our records to sound like Sun Records or Chess Records or Starday Records. We'd bring in tapes, and we'd be in some state-of-the-art, expensive studio in L.A., trying to make it sound like one room at Sun. The reason you can't replicate that sound is Sam Phillips or Pappy Daily or Leonard Chess knew their little rooms. They knew where the piano sounded best. They knew where the drums sounded best. They knew where to place that mike. That's where that sound came from — the knowledge of that room. It's hard to beat that into people's heads.

JACK CLEMENT

Now, it's too many machines. They use computers to tune up people's voices — change their phrasing. I still like a pretty simplistic way of recording. "What kind of mike do you use?" By the time you get it all mixed, a mike is a mike, pretty much. I have a few favorites, but mikes ain't that important. Somebody asked me how I miked the drums at Sun. If I was lucky, if I had a mike and an input — we had enough mikes, but we had only five inputs — so if I was lucky, I could have one for the front and one for the snare. A lot of times we used just one mike. You had to put it so you'd get some of each [part of the drum kit].

The room had a lot of leakage. When I was working there, I didn't know as much about acoustics as I learned later. I've built about eight studios since then, including one down the street here [in Nashville] which was one of the most successful studios that's ever been in town. It was the first sixteen-track — kind of revolutionary for the time.

By the time I went back [to Sun] with U2 in '87, I'd built all those studios [Clement co-produced several tracks on *Rattle and Hum*]. I knew about baffling and everything. Besides that, the first time I went over to Memphis with U2, they had only an Akai twelve-track machine there. Somebody had to transfer those tapes to twenty-four-track. So we talked them into letting us bring those tapes here and transferring them. While we had them here, we got to sit here and listen to that room over there track by track, where you can punch up a solo on the drums, or you can solo the voice. It was like being able to go back into the past with equipment from the future. It was like being able to plug a present-day studio into that room back then. The room sounded the same, and I understood it.

When I was working for Sam [Phillips], I kind of thought he was full of shit about that room sounding so good, having a distinct sound. But it does. When I went back there with U2, I realized that it does have a sound. And what it is, there's almost no separation in there. Everything is kind of equal. But by the same token, it's not big enough to have that out-of-phasing thing you get from the back ends of microphones and from leakage. But the leakage was the big part of it. That's what made it really, really good.

Nowadays they do everything they can to get rid of all the leakage—put the drums in a separate room, all that earphones and stuff. I hate earphones. I can use them for overdubbing, but if I'm producing something, there ain't no earphones. But that's getting harder and harder to do because there ain't many people around that remember how to do that.

JIM ROONEY

Jack [Clement] was my real master mentor. I met him in 1976. What I really got a feel for—there were many things—was songs: the quality of the songs that were being generated in Nashville. He had a wonderful publishing company, and I listened to a lot of songs. That helped me refine my standards about songwriting. Material is very important for an artist.

Jack told me that I needed to learn how to run the board [at Jack's Tracks]. I resisted. I said, "I'm not inclined that way—technically." He insisted that I do it. So I did. I asked the two engineers who were working with him at the time where the on/off switches were.

Jack gave me some very fundamental advice. At the time there were VU meters with needles. "Just keep the needles in the middle," he said. He was clear about not interfering with the signal from the microphone to the tape. When I was at Bearsville [Studios in New York], I watched people putting limiters, compressors, gates, and all kinds of equipment on the signal—both going in and coming out. I thought there was some mysterious process that I didn't understand. Jack disabused me of that notion. "Just get that signal on tape as clean as you can," he said. "Then you can deal with it later on if you want to."

That was a huge help to me psychologically. I'd thought there was stuff that was too mysterious for me ever to figure out. He said, "You've got good ears. You know what music should sound like. Just trust yourself." Then he threw me into the deep end of the pool. I started recording whoever came into his place. I did that for several years. That was my journeyman's experience.

Johnny Cash's daughter [Roseanne Cash] was coming over like once a week to demo songs. We'd cut eight songs in two- or three-hour sessions—and that was with overdubs. Then I mixed them the next day. I had to work fast. You get used to making all these little decisions very quickly, on-the-fly. You don't put it off until tomorrow. Up in Bearsville a lot of people were working with pretty substantial budgets, and there was a lot of deferring of decisions. That doesn't work for me. I like to have a bit of energy going in a recording session. I dislike the attitude, "We're going to fix this later"—that, somehow or another, all of this is going to get done at some other time. I want it to get done now, and I want everybody to be on their toes.

Jack was very much like that. When we rehearsed, he'd say, "Be here at ten o'clock in tune and ready to play." He didn't mean 10:01; he meant 10:00. At the stroke of ten, he'd walk through the door. We were expected to be there in our places, ready to go. One thing I really learned in Nashville was this work ethic. It wasn't like we were working under slave conditions; we were all enjoying ourselves. But we got there early. If we needed to put strings on our guitars, we got them on early. You could have your coffee, tell a few jokes, and get settled in, but by God, you'd better be ready to go at ten o'clock. We got a lot of work done. I liked that; it suits my temperament.

Learning how to run that board was invaluable experience for me. If there was down time in the studio—Jack was very, very generous—it was mine to use. That's something people pray for. As a result friends started asking me if I could help them record. I was doing things very cheaply and very efficiently. I could make a record that sounded really good for very little money.

JIMMY BOWEN

I'm not an engineer by any stretch. I always had to have an engineer with me to hook up all that shit. Every time we got a new piece of gear they had to tell me at least twenty times exactly how it worked. I had no retention for that kind of stuff. But I wanted to do the sound on the artists and the instruments myself. I studied the vocal—the sound of that singer. By doing the EQ [adjusting audio-signal frequencies], I knew what frequencies were their strong points, what frequencies were their weak points, and if the vocal needed any help: adding a bit more in the middle, in the top or the bottom, or in all of the different frequencies we had. Once I got that in my head, then when I was doing the drums— when I did the initial sound of the session of the drums and when we did the mixdown later—if there was anything in the drums that hurt any of the frequencies in the vocal, then I downplayed them in the drums. Therefore, I did not hurt the singer. You want the singer to be the focal point of it all. I loved to do it all myself. Every instrument was EQed to be complementary and not negative to the singer. I'm sure that's what most engineers do. We used to laugh; they had to do all the dirty work. I got to do the sound part and the final mixes, but I had four or five great engineers with me in Nashville the last four or five years.

When I got to Nashville [in 1977], the studios were antiquated. In pop music the studios stayed on top of the development of sound in every aspect: the microphones, the soundproofing in the studio, and the speaker systems that guided you. Nashville had been doing it the same way for years and years. They didn't have the money to stay with the times like L.A. and New York. It was a matter of coming to the modern world inside the studios. There was no one down there doing that. Basically no one could afford to do it.

From the day I got there, it was a slow battle of change, change, change. I got accused of owning studios because some of the people down there did. That was the most ridiculous thing in the world. First of all, why would you want to own the studio? There's no profit. You get that shit paid off, and it's out of date. So you go back in debt again. If you're in there and something blows up, who are you going to holler at? Yourself? I didn't want an artist mad at me because my goddamn equipment didn't work. That's minor, minor, minor money. There's not much profit in studios.

What I did, I went to the owner of Sound Stage [Ron Kerr], and I said, "If you'll spend money to modernize your studio, I'll guarantee you

X sessions for X period of time." I had no risk, and I came out the other end with a more modern studio. I did that with about four studios. I had to have it because I always had three or four albums going at one time. Actually, the most modern studio in Nashville during that period was Ronnie Milsap's. But it was just him. It was his studio. He wasn't booking it out. But I did quite a bit of stuff over there, using his studio. He'd built it in the modern era.

I got [engineer] Tom Headley to build the one studio at Sound Stage without a wall between me and the musicians. It took away the "them" and "us." It was just us. I had two big speakers on hydraulic lifts. So you had the same big speakers you'd have in any other studio. But I worked mostly in the earphones. That's where the music was happening. That's what I cared about, how it sounded in there. I got each instrument sounding right—you'd do that up on the bigger speakers—but I didn't need the big speakers. You walk into a session and big speakers are blaring. Guys are out there playing in their little bitty earphones. I always hated that. I wanted to get that wall out of the way. So when technology got to a point where I could, I said, "You build it; I'll use it. It's yours. But I want it this way." When I quit and I went to Maui, I was over there about two months and Ron Kerr called me. He asked me, "Are you sure you're not coming back?"

"I'm positive."

"I need to put a wall up," he said. "Nobody else wants to use that damn studio."

I said, "Well quick, put the wall up for God's sake."

JIM ED NORMAN

Country artists making records and constantly on the road set in motion an interesting kind of dynamic in the work process. You may have heard mention of "number charts." First off, you've got, in the song form [of country], a fairly simple harmonic, rhythmic, and melodic structure. What changes in the music, if you go back ten, fifteen years ago [to the late '80s, mid '90s], what changed was the lyrics. You had melodic differences, but harmonic changes, rhythmic changes remained somewhat the same. The melodies and lyrics were different.

What happened is a kind of system developed in Nashville. There was an efficiency in the number-chart thing. You had a performer who was able to devote only a limited amount of time in the studio to recording, and you had an economic necessity, in terms of the number of records and albums that were sold, to get four songs done in three hours. (By union rules you were allowed to do four songs in a three-hour session.) Everybody tried to max that out so, essentially, an album could be recorded in the time of about three sessions.

If the artist showed up, knew the material, was ready to perform, you'd walk into the studio, and the way you would then communicate with the [session] musicians—and it made it easy for them to communicate—was to write a number chart of the song. That enabled them quickly to change the key. If, all of a sudden, the singer decided the chosen key was too high, you could lower the key a half-step or a step. The number chart remains the same; your key relationship changes.

I grew up in Los Angeles, musically, where charts were written in historical, typical chord symbols. So if you were in the key of C, then C, F, and G were written on the chart, as opposed to I-IV-V [or, in Nashville, 1–4–5]. If you found yourself having to change the key, you actually had to sit down, and people, depending on their level of proficiency, sometimes would literally have to rewrite the entire chart in the new key, rather than just being able to automatically make those transpositions by looking at the chord symbols and then by making the subsequent transpositions necessary to be in the new key. The system is, once again, an indication of how much one was trying to accomplish in the amount of time that you had, as well as an indication of the simplicity versus the sophistication of the chord changes and symbols. In pop music you had different harmonic progressions, different approaches to what was going on musically. With country it was a little more straightforward.

The other thing I would point out is that you also began to see the development of a number chart written almost in song form. You began to get an almost visual image of what the song was in its relationship of verse to chorus to bridge—that kind of thing. So there's a kind of song consciousness that developed in Nashville years ago. The Nashville Songwriters Association, their motto is "It All Begins with a Song," and that is something that has perpetuated and insinuated itself into the entire process. Everyone knows it and accepts it and feels it—that it all begins with a song. The focus of what happens in Nashville, in terms of making music and putting things together, is song-driven. It's about the song and about how the artist participates with the song and brings it to life: renders the performance and sings and communicates with people about the song.

It's interesting how this emphasis carried over into production techniques with the number system. It's helped to perpetuate a feeling that goes on in the studio, about the song in its most simple way, even by differentiating between verse and chorus, such that when the chorus comes, it's visually apparent. You see where you're headed as you are playing along. I'm not suggesting that people who read music in a linear manner can't feel a chorus when it's coming, but it's not quite as evident visually as it is when charts are written out on a simple piece of paper.

I remember the first time I proposed the idea of a number chart in Los Angeles. Everybody thought I was crazy. I quickly had to move away from a number chart kind of consciousness because it was so foreign and difficult to people. They were really uncomfortable with it. Since a producer's responsibility is, I think, to create an environment where people can be comfortable and perform, I had to move away from the number chart concept. But I preserved a little bit of what I had begun to understand about song consciousness. I wrote out letter charts, but instead of writing them in a linear way on staff paper, I started writing them on plain pieces of paper. You now had these letter charts and a shorthand way to represent what was going on in every measure. If on occasion it was required that I actually write specific notes that people needed to play, I might have to resort to staff paper or, possibly, even sit in at times and quickly scribble a staff and notes on a page.

HAROLD BRADLEY

Neal Matthews of the Jordanaires, he'd have a yellow tablet. He wrote down the chords in the number system, but it was in Roman numerals. We'd walk by, look over there, and see he had his pad, but we didn't pay any attention to it. They were singers. They weren't musicians, so we didn't fool with them.

I was the leader on a session one day, and all of a sudden the session kind of stopped. I looked over, and Charlie McCoy was down on his knee. He and Wayne Moss were talking. Wayne was a new substitute guitar player, just working his way into the A-Team. I went over and asked, "Hey, what's going on?"

Charlie said, "We're writing the song down in numbers." So Charlie was the first person I know of who transferred the number system to the musicians, only he didn't write it in Roman numerals. The reason being, if somebody is playing you a demo and you're writing down the cords, it's pretty fast. You don't have time to write in Roman numerals. We just wrote it down in regular numbers.

Arrangements had been done at the sessions. I walked away when they said, "We're writing the song [its structure denoted in numbers]. I thought, "You sissies." We'd been memorizing them all those years. But when I became leader, I realized that it saves you fifteen minutes on the session. You'd do four songs—you'd play four demos—and everybody would write it down. They didn't always write down the same thing. So if I was the leader and I could talk to the A&R man or to the artist before we went in, and he could tell me what the songs were, then I could write just the cords down in numbers. When we walked in, I handed out the numbers. Then, that's like the framework of a house. Everybody takes it from there and fills in their parts.

MULTITRACKING
CONSTRUCTING THE PERFORMANCE,
1967-1991

Multitracking means that sound can be edited not just horizontally, with one piece of tape joined to another, but vertically, with the tracks stacked or layered. Notable record albums of the mid-'60s were effects of experiments in multitracking that used four-track tape recorders: *Sgt. Pepper's Lonely Hearts Club Band* (1967) is the definitive example. But it was with eight available tracks that multitracking became the rule, not the odd exception. Around 1967, recordings changed. From that point on, they were almost never actual records of single musical events. They became instead, almost always, composites of many musical events— "virtual" records. The performances heard on records were more constructed than caught. In this paradigm of production the producer as auteur could emerge, impressing his signature sound onto recordings.

But there's a catch, and it's something of a paradox. There aren't many auteurist producers. Multitracking may have revolutionized the way records were made—they weren't cut; they were built—but it rarely sounded that way, especially within the kingdom of country music. With maybe one or two exceptions (see the discussion of Billy Sherrill that follows), producers rarely foregrounded their labors or their sonic visions. Consider the comments in this chapter either as a guide to how producers dutifully stoked the star-making machine or as a series of rare glimpses at their typically invisible working methods.

• • •

On "Tramp," one of Otis Redding's Stax/Volt singles, Carla Thomas's job is to taunt the singer. "You know what, Otis?" she asks.

"What?" he snaps.

"You're country. You're straight from the Georgia woods."

To which, Redding replies, "That's good."

He wears "overalls and brogan shoes." Thomas makes fun of Redding's clothes, but she could have cut closer to the truth and told him that he had a gift for countrifying R&B.

OTIS REDDING, "(SITTIN' ON) THE DOCK OF THE BAY" (1967), *DOCK OF THE BAY: THE DEFINITIVE COLLECTION* (ATLANTIC UK)

STEVE CROPPER

At Monterey, I knew we'd found a new audience. That same crowd probably was the original crowd for the Grateful Dead and all that stuff. On that show was Electric Flag—Bloomfield and Buddy Miles and all that bunch. That's more of a hard-rock, blues-type stuff—very San Francisco influence. At that time those people hadn't heard "Dock of the Bay." They didn't know the connection would come later, not too far away, that Otis was going to write a song about San Francisco. Actually, he wrote about Sausalito, which I found out many years later.

I'd been telling the story that I knew based on what Otis told me about how the song originated. He and I, we never had a confrontation about anything, and this wasn't any kind of a heated confrontation. It was just my theory against his theory, and it was in the lyric "I watch the ships roll in; I watch them roll away again." I said, "Otis, if a ship rolls, it's going to sink. You can't roll it. You can float one, bob one, bounce one, but you can't roll it."

"It's gotta be roll, Cropper. It's gotta be roll."

He never explained to me what he was talking about because he had it wrong from the get-go. He was writing about a ferry, and he called it a ship because it was a big boat. "I watch the ships." If he'd written, "I watch the ferries come in," it probably wouldn't have been a hit. Thank God he didn't. But he was talking about a ferry.

It took years to figure that out. Neil Young backed it up. He came in the dressing room one night, and he said, "Man, I've been reading this book, and you were in there telling a story about how 'Dock of the Bay' was written. I just wanted to let you know I stayed in that boathouse the week after Otis did."

"Really?"

"Yeah," he said. "I played there after Otis. Bill Graham put me in his boathouse. I was there." Neil told me that in '92. So how many years was that from '68, the year I started telling stories? So there's a guy, the only living soul that can validate that Otis was in a boathouse in Sausalito and came up with the idea for "Dock of the Bay."

My contribution to the song was that I wrote the bridge. I came up with "I left my home in Georgia." I was always writing about Otis. He was writing about ships; I was writing about Otis. "And headed for the Frisco Bay" because he was going out there to play the Fillmore West. In those days Bill Graham—usually, when we played out there, we stayed in a hotel called the Jack Tar on Highway 100 [Van Ness Ave.]—he'd put most of the musicians up there. But the headliner, he'd let you stay there or you could stay on his boathouse in Sausalito. It's beautiful out there. I never got that chance. But a lot of the artists that worked the Fillmore got to stay in Bill Graham's boathouse.

Jerry Wexler argued with me on "Dock of the Bay." He wanted me to remix it. I couldn't do it. The thing was, when we mastered the stereo, it had a 3 dB [decibel] rise in the vocal anyway, which I already knew. If you listen to it on radio, Otis is in your face, but you do hear every lick in there.

We'd been searching for a long time for a song we thought would be a crossover for Otis. We hadn't reached it. We tried several times with cover songs, from "A Change Is Gonna Come" to "Cigarettes and Coffee" to this, that, and the other. I think we even did a Jackie Wilson ballad one time. Was it "A Woman, a Lover, a Friend"? Anyway, we were always trying things that we couldn't write. We were writing so much dance music, real-deep R&B dance music. We were having trouble writing something that could be crossed over.

I think Otis and I knew it. He knew he had a hit [with "Dock of the Bay"]. He called me straight from the airport and said he wanted to make sure I was in the studio because he was coming right down there to show me this song.

When we recorded it, I said, "This is it. This is the one that's going to do it for you, man. We've got it." It had been in the can for probably a couple of weeks. Everybody thinks it's the last song he recorded, but it was on the last recording session. It was one of the first songs on the last recording session. We were there working for a couple of weeks. We had never had Otis that long; he wasn't on tour.

The story I had was he'd just gotten over a throat operation. I think after Monterey he went in and had them work on polyps. He couldn't sing for a while; wasn't allowed to go on the road. He did a lot of writing, and I think the Fillmore was one of the first gigs that he did. And God was he in great shape, wow. Ronnie [Capone, recording engineer] and I noticed the difference in his voice right away. It was still Otis, but it was so clean.

At night, we started pulling out all the tracks that were sitting on the shelf and having him re-sing them. So we had about fifteen or sixteen sides in the can, sitting on the shelf, that hadn't been released with Otis's brand-new voice on them. That's the good thing. We had some stuff stockpiled.

But did we know or were we lucky? Was it a good guess, and it turned out that way? Or did we actually know what we were talking about? I tend to think we knew. I've heard it said by more than one person—I've seen it in writing—where they said, "It's sad we lost Otis Redding, but 'Dock of the Bay' would have never reached greatness had he not passed away." I don't believe that. That song was a hit song.

JOHN HARTFORD, "GENTLE ON MY MIND" (1967), *EARTHWORDS & MUSIC* (RCA)

TOMPALL GLASER

We had published "Gentle on My Mind," which became BMI's first big, million-performance song. I recorded John Hartford's original version, but Hartford wanted to put out the record himself. He had a deal with RCA, but they didn't promote it.

Glen Campbell's producer [Al DeLory] out in California heard it: different group of people, different line of thinking. They cut it immediately after they heard it, and put it out.

We could've beat everybody out with it. We'd published it, we had a studio, and we had a band. But the thinking here in Nashville was they didn't like the song. They weren't going to promote it. They didn't think it was country. Nashville gets so inbred. It gets to be a clique of people like is in there now.

THE BYRDS, *YOUNGER THAN YESTERDAY* (1967, COLUMBIA)

BOB IRWIN

Gary Usher is one of my favorite producers. We had a friendship before he passed away, as I'd begun working on some of his material [readying it for remastering and for reissue]. The first place I remember seeing his name and knowing that a producer very obviously contributed something to the sound of a record was the Byrds' *Younger Than Yesterday* album.

Speaking more specifically, I know for a fact that Gary didn't necessarily bring the Byrds around to country music. That was a natural progression brought to the Byrds through Chris Hillman and, of course, eventually Gram [Parsons] and other people. Roger [McGuinn] had folk roots, as did the other guys. But Chris Hillman had bluegrass roots, and country was very much a natural progression. *Younger Than Yesterday* was also the first time that Clarence White performed with the Byrds. And boy oh boy, once Clarence White walked into the studio, how could you help but not feel the influence of his playing? I think that's what set the light bulb off over, certainly, Chris Hillman's head, because Chris was writing songs like "Time Between."

Gary Usher helped them define and refine that. Along with being a wonderful producer, he was the best diplomat and arbitrator you've ever seen. When you go through the session tapes, a lot of them are not pretty. It's just trying to hold that damn boat together. But I think Gary was born to be the Byrds' producer, although I'm fond of other producers' work, especially Terry Melcher's. But that's another lifetime of the Byrds.

I don't know if they chose Gary Usher at the beginning, or if he was assigned to the band. But as soon as you put on *Younger Than Yesterday*—coming from *5D*, which was an album full of marvelous songs and wonderful ideas that suffered from the production end of things—it's as clean as country water. It's an absolutely flawless production in the sonic sense of the word. And that's the magic to me. Very often a producer can attain a clean, wonderful sound, and the recording puts you to sleep. It's sterile and not exciting. But having a well-recorded album that still pushes all of your hot buttons in terms of performance and the choice of songs and just the sonics of the album, that's where Usher's magic was. He didn't drain the band artistically. He pushed them artistically, kept them in top form and put out a sonically wonderfully record almost every time.

JACK RENO, "REPEAT AFTER ME" (1967), *MEET JACK RENO* (ATCO)

BUDDY KILLEN

My experience, which grew through the years, helped me recognize not only a star or a person capable of being a star but also the song that fit him, the song that would work for him. I argued many times with singers. I'd say, "I want you to do this song."

They'd say, "I don't like it. I'm not going to do it."

"Well, why don't you at least try it?"

Many times they'd argue, "Well, I'll sing it, but I'm not going to sing it good."

"Well, you can't sing good anyway!" I'd say, kidding with them. But I'd force them to do a song, and it turned out to be the biggest song of their career.

There was a guy named Jack Reno. I had a song called "Repeat after Me."

"I don't like it," he said. "I don't want to do it."

I said, "I want you to do it anyway." I finally got him to do it, and it was a top-five hit for him.

Normally, if a guy doesn't want to do a song, you'll say, "Okay, fine."

But if there's one of those that you just know "This is a hit," you've got to stay on him until you convince him. "Look. Cut it. If it doesn't come off, we won't put it out. Okay?"

Usually they'll go along with you, but they'll say, "That's not my style."

"What is your style?" I'll say. "You're not hitting. If you're not selling records what is your style? Maybe this will give you one." That has happened so many times through the years.

JEANNIE C. RILEY, "HARPER VALLEY P.T.A." (1968), *HARPER VALLEY P.T.A.* (SUN)

SHELBY SINGLETON

Tom T. Hall had written this song, and there was a demo of it by a girl. I believe her name was Alice Joy. I'd heard the song, and I liked the song. But I didn't have a girl singer that I thought it fit. I had it in a desk drawer for three or four months.

A disc-jockey friend of mine was managing a girl name Jeannie C. Riley. He brought me a demo of her singing. "Bring her by here," I said. "I've got a song that I think is a hit if she's got the image that I want to sing this song."

She came by. I talked to her. I thought that she'd fit the image. I said, "Okay, you learn this song, and then we'll go in the studio and record it."

We set up a recording date, and it was what we called a split session, two sides by her and two by somebody else. I was in business for myself, and I was trying to save money—get as much as you can out of what you spend.

The night that we cut that, right at the last moment, my wife at that time, she said—*Laugh-In* was very popular on TV—she said, "Why don't we change that last line to 'That's the night I socked it to the Harper Valley P.T.A.,' instead of 'I put down'?" I think that was what the original lyric was. So we changed it. That night we knew the record was a hit, but we didn't realize how big it really was. You know it's a hit when you're staying around after a session, playing back takes, and all the musicians stay too. None of them leave. They keep listening to it over and over.

CONWAY TWITTY, "NEXT IN LINE" (1968), *GOLD* (MCA NASHVILLE)

JIMMY BOWEN

When Owen was recording in his studio down there [the Bradley Barn], I went out a couple of times to where he did Conway and Loretta, duets and singles, Patsy Cline, and some of those marvelous records.* They didn't necessarily make marvelous albums—full albums—but they made some great records. The music business back then was a singles business. Nobody sold a lot of albums anywhere. Albums were still $1.98, maybe up to $2.98.

HAROLD BRADLEY

Country music had gone as far as it could. Elvis came along and knocked us [Nashville country] off the charts [in the mid-'50s]. Buck Owens came back with "Tiger by the Tail" [in 1964, the "Bakersfield sound"]. He had five or six musicians doing hard country. Owen and Chet thought they could do something to gussy-up country music [what became "Country-politan" or the "Nashville sound"]. Chet later said he was sorry he did it, and even later on said, "Nah, I shouldn't have felt guilty about that." Owen merely said, "Hey, we tried it the other way, and it didn't work. So we tried something different." He never was apologetic about what he did, because it took years to find what he did. We had a seminar at the Country Music Hall of Fame. I was on the panel. Some people wanted to know what Owen changed. He'd said, "I had the same musicians. I had the same studio, the same engineer; the only thing I changed was the songs."

JIMMY BOWEN

Owen had a group to work with all the time, as we all wind up doing. I'm sure he paid fifteen guys that did most of his stuff. When I was in Nashville, I had about twenty-five or thirty different people to do all our stuff,

---

* "Next in Line," produced by Owen Bradley, was Conway Twitty's first of forty number-one hits.

because I like rhythm sections that work good together. But then, you had to cast the right rhythm section for each individual artist.

When it came to Tony [Brown] and me, to our era, it was totally different. The productions became thirty-, thirty-five-, forty-minute projects. I always looked at an album as a concert, as a musical presentation. It needs to open, needs peaks and valleys, and needs to close. It's difficult to do that because it's in a short period of time. But I wanted to sell albums. And that's how you get a following so you sell X, whether you have a hit single or not. People are waiting for the next Hank Junior album, not just the single. It became quite different in that regard. When Owen was working, of course he didn't have big budgets. He worked faster; we worked slower.

PORTER WAGONER, "THE CARROLL COUNTY ACCIDENT" (1968), *THE ESSENTIAL PORTER WAGONER* (RCA)

BOB FERGUSON

I wrote "The Carroll County Accident" coming down to the Choctaw country. At the time, I was dating my wife-to-be. I was driving pretty fast as I came out of Nashville and into Carroll County, Tennessee. I thought, "If I don't slow down, I'm going to be the Carroll County accident," and then I thought, "Boy, that sounds like a song if I can figure it out."

I got the first two lines as I drove along: "Carroll County's pointed out as kind of square. The biggest thing that happens is the County Fair." I said, "Yeah, this here is some kind of a story." All I've got to do is figure out what it is.

First of all, when I write, and it's true today, I first get an idea of what I'd like to write. Like, I would like to write a story. That will dwell with me for a while, and then things just happen.

I've written most everything while I'm driving somewhere. I get a few miles out of town. My mind is free. So by the time I got down here to where I live, I felt like I had a song. I'd stop for a little bit and write down a few more verses. I had the beginning and the end figured out, and I had to go back and put in the middle part of the story. You can do that when you've got a good lead and you know kind of where you're going. I said, "When I can, I'll go back and put the middle into it." So I did. I wrote that song in that way.

When I later got back to Nashville, I told Porter [Wagoner] I had a song that might be good for him.

I was very slow to push any songs I'd written onto my artists. I just didn't believe in it, but by the same token, I thought if I had one that might work, I'd be remiss not to show it to him.

Porter said, "Just put it on my desk." He had an office upstairs in the building.

I called one of our engineers. He met me at the studio. I put it on tape—me and a guitar—and I left it on Porter's desk the next morning.

When he got in, he called and ran down. "How soon can we cut it?" he asked.

I said, "Anytime."

"How about Friday?"

"Fine, that's good."

So we went in. We cut it. The fiddle led off. I think it was Mack Magaha. Porter went on the road for the weekend. He came back Monday and asked, "What'd you think of that cut on 'The Carroll Country Accident'?" I hesitated a minute. "Me too," he said. "Let's do it again."

He said, "Buck [Trent] has figured up a lick on the bus." He was a banjo player, with a pedal banjo. Anyway, we went back and did it again. That time it really felt good, although the other one wasn't bad the first time through. But that's the way "Carroll County" came about.

I've done that with all of my songs. If the artist doesn't flip over it, forget it. If they do, then you go ahead. Everybody's thinking about what could be a hit. Finding a good song is the hardest thing in the world.

JOHNNY CASH, *JOHNNY CASH AT FOLSOM PRISON* (1968, COLUMBIA)

BOB JOHNSTON

Johnny Cash signed with Sun Records—Sam Phillips. He went in the first day and told Sam that he had a marvelous idea. He thought it would be his stairway to the stars.

Sam asked him, "What is it?"

"I want to go to a prison to record an album."

Sam said, "If you go to a prison to record an album, I'll either drop you or I'll make sure you don't record for anybody else for five years. It's a horrible idea, and it will ruin your career. Forget about it." So he forgot about it.

Five years later [in 1958], when he got off Sun, he went over, and he signed with Columbia.* "I've got a great idea," he said, and he told them.

They said, "That's a horrible idea. You can't do it. If you do, we will fire Johnston, if he does it. We will close the office down there, and we will get rid of you. You'll either not record for anybody or you'll have to wait five years to record."

Johnny came over. He told me he had a great idea. He said, "You probably won't like it either."

I said, "What the fuck is it?"

He told me. I picked up the phone and called Folsom and San Quentin. I got through to Folsom, got the warden, Duffy. I said, "Duffy, you don't know me. My name's Johnston. I'm from Texas. I'm with Johnny Cash here."

"Holy God!" he said.

I said, "Johnny Cash is going to come up and do a live record and a fucking concert for you! What do you think about that?"

"God Almighty, when?"

"Ask him," I said. I handed the phone to Johnny and said, "Johnny, talk to the warden at Folsom and set it up." So Johnny set it up, and I left. I went to Florida or something, and I got back.

* In 1967, Johnston replaced Don Law as head of Columbia's Nashville office.

Five or six days later, Johnny called me. He said, "I just called you to see if there was anything you could do. The CBS people came to me and said that they'd fire you and get rid of me, and I couldn't record anymore for five years. If I did that concert, it would ruin me." Just wondered if you had any idea . . . ain't nothing anybody can do with those power-structure people, but I wondered if you had any idea."

"Yeah, I've got a great idea."

"What is it?" he said.

I said, "If I was you, I'd quit messing around. I'd go out, and I would get me the biggest goddamn suitcase I could find, and I'd start packing the motherfucker." I hung up on him.

About a week later, he called me back and said, "When are we going?"

"In two weeks." I'd never said anything about it. We just got in a plane or bus and went up there and did the album.

DUSTY SPRINGFIELD, *DUSTY IN MEMPHIS* (1969, ATLANTIC)

REGGIE YOUNG (guitarist on the album)
Tom Dowd could pretty much create on the spot: "Okay, we'll have the marriage of the drums and the bass here." We'd get a little groove going: "Okay, Reggie, you find something to play in this section." We built it up, but Dowd was the creator of stuff. He'd give ideas, and we'd see what we could come up with. They [producers Dowd, Jerry Wexler, and Arif Mardin] had songs picked that we were going to do on Dusty.

TOM DOWD
We were in each other's face all the time [Dowd, Wexler, and Mardin]. We shared space, and there was never any ego or animosity. If Jerry was hell-bent on a song, and I didn't like the song, I'd figure, "Well, he knows something that I don't know, or he's sensitive to something I've got to learn more about." I'd back off and let him do his thing.

I had no problems with Dusty, though I, all of a sudden, recognized that she was an exquisite, pitch-sensitive musician. Like Mel Tormé or

Don Eliot. And she was a devil for "I can do it better" or "I am flat." You say, "That sounds great. Leave it alone." It was later revealed that Dusty thought I was an egomaniac, an overpowering human being, and I never had words with the woman. Years later, when I was doing Rod Stewart, Dusty came by a couple of sessions, and she and I are good friends. She has a reputation for being a wicked old witch, but not by me. I can't say anything bad about the woman.

REGGIE YOUNG

She sang in the studio with us. As a matter of fact, she was very uncomfortable. In England she'd always have a production; everything [instrumental tracks] would be cut. She had a singer who sang the songs [a "tracking vocal"]. She'd come in later and put her voice on. In Memphis, when she showed up, I remember asking her, in the middle of something, "What do you think about that, Dusty?" Just getting her input. Did she like it or not? She'd never had the opportunity, I don't think, to participate in producing her own record. It kind of scared her. Paranoid might be a good word for how she was in Memphis. There were so many people in the studio who had stepped in there, and here she comes. But as it turned out, that album still sounds great.

After the week we worked with her, we had a playback party of the stuff we'd cut. It was absolutely really good. And then, they took it to New York and redid her vocals and all of the strings. It made it better and better and better.

TOM DOWD

She was originally, the Springfields were originally country singers, and she had exquisite pitch. Oh God, she had exquisite pitch. And as she describes it, she was always accustomed to walking into pre-prepared arrangements. She'd say, "I like that. Make this softer on top—that part." And then she'd sing over the arrangement that had been prepared. We were throwing her into this impromptu, jazz-type environment. "Here are the chords, guys. Here's the way she's going to sing it. Va-boom-boomp. That's it. Next song." She'd look and say, "What do you mean? That's it?"

When we finished recording *Dusty in Memphis*, I struck for Miami [Criteria Recording Studios] on another project, and Arif and Jerry went back up to New York. Jerry wanted to add some strings and maybe double Dusty's voice in places. I had two or three cuts, and I said, "Jerry, the Memphis Horns are coming down to record." I don't know whether it was a Dr. John or a Wilson Pickett record. I said, "I've got an idea for Dusty." He said, "Okay, put them on." I remember sitting in an airplane with a cassette in my lap and a piece of manuscript in front of me, and I sketched out this part for "Son of a Preacher Man." When the horns showed up in Miami, I said, "This is what I want to do." I played them the cassette [of what had been recorded in the Memphis studio] once or twice. I said, "I want to voice it this way," and so forth. They listened to what I sang and to what I played them on the piano. We ran it once or twice. I made an adjustment.

They said, "Why don't you try this?"

"That's a great idea." Boom, boom, boom and it was done.

LORETTA LYNN, "COAL MINER'S DAUGHTER" (1969), *THE DEFINITIVE COLLECTION* (MCA NASHVILLE)

HAROLD BRADLEY

The ultimate in being a producer is the ability to take whatever people give you. Some producers are so schooled musically that they can't accept what people give them. They see no value if it's not exactly correct musically—either meter-wise, or a little out of tune, or not what they were expecting. For instance, people talked to my brother about Loretta. She sang, "I was borned a coal miner's daughter"—b-o-r-n-e-d. Somebody mentioned that to Owen. They asked, "Why don't you correct her English?" He said, "Because it sounds like Loretta to me." If you think about it, Ray Price sang, "There's a starm a-brewing somewhere"—"starm" instead of "storm." But that makes it unique; it makes it different.

Owen just tried to capture what she could give him. He didn't try to make Loretta into Patsy, because she wasn't Patsy. He never tried to make singers be other people. He signed them to be themselves. He wanted what they could do. I think that's really important as a producer. In the beginning we couldn't do any overdubs. But later on, I'd be ready to leave the studio, and I'd hear him say, "Loretta, you need to sing this sentence for me," or "this word." She'd do it, and it would sound fine. It might be a little flat or something, but it fit right in. It sounded right.

He wasn't there to make them into fantastic singers. They were good singers to begin with. In Loretta's case, she was already a woman when we started to record her. I think she already had three children. When we recorded her, I went into the control room. After the session, I told my brother, "I don't know what it is about that woman but what's in her heart comes out her mouth."

"I know," he said. "That's why I signed her. I thought she was sincere."

We were both right. Whatever is in her heart comes out her mouth, and she is sincere. That's what Owen caught. She truly believes what she is singing.

ROGER MILLER, "ME AND BOBBY MCGEE" (1969), *GOLDEN HITS* (SMASH)

JERRY KENNEDY

Kris [Kristofferson] was still writing "Me and Bobby McGee" when Roger cut it [in 1969]. We didn't have a second verse. Kris brought the second verse to the session: "From a coal mine in Kentucky"—all that part we didn't have. We knew there was going to be another verse, so we were rehearsing the thing. He came in. If it was a two o'clock session, he came in like at three o'clock with the second verse. Then we kept him there and had him sing on the fade.

I can't ever remember filling up but one tape with sixteen tracks. I loaded up "Me and Bobby McGhee." It was the first time I ever recorded on sixteen-track. But hey, I'm the guy who looked at a tape when I was in Berlin in 1963—it was eight-track—and I thought it was the biggest thing I'd ever seen in my life. I said, "If we can ever get that, that's all we'll ever need." And boy, that blew by us a long time ago.

ELVIS PRESLEY, *MEMPHIS 1969 ANTHOLOGY: SUSPICIOUS MINDS* (RCA)

REGGIE YOUNG (guitarist)

I remember [Chips] Moman making the statement one time. "I'm not a producer," he said. "I'm a waiter." In other words, we'd run the song down. He'd say, "Ha! That's what I'm looking for." He called himself a "waiter." But he knew what to wait for. He knew it when he heard it. He had that talent.

Mostly, to get his part right, Elvis wanted to sing it [a song] over and over again. He'd been cutting movie tracks—all that stuff. He hadn't had a hit record in eight years. He really wanted it to come off. It was the first time he'd been back in Memphis [to record] in a long time. We kind of sandwiched him in. We were cutting a lot of acts at the time.

Everybody was sent home. There wasn't anybody there but the band, Moman, Felton Jarvis, and the engineer from RCA. All the entourage that came with Elvis was asked to leave. It was just down to basics: let's cut some records. That's what we did. There wasn't any horsing around— party time or anything. I think we cut thirty-something sides. That was his comeback album. He always said that. It got him back out on the road. He tried to hire us, but nobody wanted to go out and be a road dog. I didn't want to do that. That's when he got the TCB band to go out.

On "Any Day Now" Elvis sings toward the top of his range. Would Moman suggest a key or did Elvis make all such choices?

I'm sure it would've been where it was comfortable for Elvis. I don't remember Moman pushing him. Of course, he might have. I just don't remember. On those "Elvis in Memphis" sessions, he really did try harder than what he'd been doing. He finally had some good songs, and he wanted to make the best of it.

A year earlier you'd already cut "Suspicious Minds" with Mark James, its writer. Did Elvis hear that record, use it as a demo, or did the band play things for him?

It's almost the same arrangement. We knew that song pretty well, but we never played anything for Elvis for him to choose. If they played anything, it might have been Mark James's record. We'd never say, "Listen to this." We never did any of that.

[Of Young's guitar part] Dan Penn said, "That's Spooner Oldham's lick." But it's not. If you dig into it, it's nothing like it. Spooner played a thing on the song "Sweet Inspiration." Penn would always say, "Man, that sounds like Spooner's playing." But it's not. They were totally different. I wasn't even thinking about "Sweet Inspiration" when we did "Suspicious Minds." Matter of fact, on Mark's record I started out playing that lick, and Moman had me not play it. I didn't come in until halfway through, and Bobby Emmons played the lick on the organ—that same fill thing. Then, I came in on the second half of it, but on Elvis's version I started off with it.

Who's the most underrated producer you worked with?

In Memphis, I'd have to say Chips Moman. I don't know if he brought any of that on himself by not conforming. Seems like everybody in Memphis was favoring Stax or Hi [Records], but we never got the publicity at American that we should've gotten. I think we cut more hits than the other two studios put together. We cut 122 top-forty pop and R&B records in a five-year period, but we kind of got swept under the carpet.

Moman got fed up with it and said, "Let's move to Atlanta." That was the worst mistake we ever made, but it was the best thing that ever happened to me. I quit in Atlanta, and I came to Nashville. I didn't really make any money until I moved to Nashville. We didn't have a time limit on sessions in Memphis. Everything was nonchalant: "We'll start at three o'clock." We might not start until ten o'clock.

But my idea of Nashville was what I saw on TV—Porter Wagoner or something, everybody sitting around on bales of hay, playing music. I thought, "That ain't for me." But I had a lot of friends here. The funny thing about it, when I moved here, I didn't change anything I did. The thing that changed was the singers. I still played the same guitar style— R&B stuff. I didn't have to play hayseed kind of stuff. I played the same style I always did, only it had a country singer on it. Some of the first stuff I did when I got here in 1972 was Dobie Gray [the guitar part on "Drift Away"]. Then, I did other people—George Strait and Merle Haggard—but I just kept playing the same thing I always did.

I remember the first day I worked here in Nashville. I showed up at the studio. A guy came over, an assistant, and said, "Mr. Young, where do you want your amplifier?" I said, "What?" At the end of three hours, you signed a card, and you got paid scale. It wound up being double scale. Everything was always very businesslike. One thing [Jimmy] Bowen told the people who worked for him, he always said, "Don't mess with the creative people." He was talking about the musicians. "Make sure they're happy. That's where we get our music." Even though it's head arrangements and stuff, keep them happy.

RAY PRICE, "FOR THE GOOD TIMES" (1970), *THE ESSENTIAL RAY PRICE* (SONY)

DON LAW JR.

My father was very close to Ray Price. They did Ray's biggest record, "For the Good Times," when my father was sixty-eight years old. It really remade Ray Price's career when nobody wanted him. I was thrilled that at that age he could take an artist that nobody wanted, who was frankly on the scrap heap, and turn his recording into that big a deal. Ray Price never forgot it. He was devoted to him.

But my father stayed close to a lot of artists: Carl Smith and Lefty Frizzell. I remember seeing Little Jimmy Dickens when I went down to the Hall of Fame. He got all teary talking about my father. Everybody liked him. He was a very affable person.

My father didn't view it as a business. He had to deal with New York. He had to deal with accounting and legal and the rest of it, but it was the music—the artists, their personalities, and making good records—that he really loved.

KENNY ROGERS, *KENNY ROGERS &*
THE FIRST EDITION GREATEST HITS
(1971, HIP-O)

JIMMY BOWEN

That was the only group I ever did for very long. It was great fun because I was doing all that big orchestra stuff with Sinatra and [Dean] Martin and Sammy Davis. It was really great fun to work with the kids, because that's what Kenny and the band were at the time. I didn't enjoy doing groups. I did the first session with them, and they almost had a fight over a harmony part, which is typical for groups.

"Kenny," I said, "I need to see you at ten o'clock at the house tomorrow morning."

He came over. "What did you want to see me about?"

I said, "From now on it's going to be Kenny Rogers and the First Edition. Otherwise, it doesn't make sense. You had the hit, 'Just Dropped In.' I don't want a group with four or five lead singers." Of course, he loved that.

He asked me, "You going to tell them?"

"No, you're going to tell them." He looked at me like, "What?"

I said, "The only way it's going to stay together is if you can pull it off. If I tell them, the group will last sixty days. If you go tell them, some will stay, some will leave, and you'll go forward. There's a good chance they'll all stay." And they did. He figured out a way to handle it with them.

Most of the sound things [e.g., on "Just Dropped In"], I credit to Eddie Brackett, who was the engineer I used in L.A. He was marvelous. I'd ask for something, and he'd come up with something. But so many things came out of the musicians.

If you can get a rhythm section, five or six guys, if you can get them hooked together and committed, to be a real unit for three or four days on a project, they'll come up with those great things for you. That's really what happens. Well, that's the way I like it to work. With Kenny and the First Edition, that was when I was starting to switch from the Bacharach approach of production, where you take total responsibility, into helping the artist and learning how to get the musicians into the project. Once you get them into it, they do wonderful stuff.

THE ALLMAN BROTHERS BAND, *THE ALLMAN BROTHERS BAND AT FILLMORE EAST* (1971, ATLANTIC)

TOM DOWD

The Allman Brothers were a very unusual combination of elements. They had the Southern tradition, they had a church empathy, and they swung. Think about it. You don't get country mixed in with jazz, mixed in with church that swings too often. But the Allmans were the essence of all of that. On the early Allman Brothers' albums, Dickie Betts plays Stéphane Grappelli–type solos on the guitar. He's playing violin-type solos.

Of all producers in popular music Dowd was the best suited to produce the Allman Brothers live. He understood the band musically, and it didn't hurt that, one year earlier, he had engineered Live Cream *and produced* Layla and Other Assorted Love Songs.

NITTY GRITTY DIRT BAND, *WILL THE CIRCLE BE UNBROKEN* (1972, CAPITOL/EMI)

WILLIAM MCEUEN

The roots of *Will the Circle Be Unbroken*, our record, can be traced to the Ash Grove in Hollywood. From about 1959 until he closed the club ten years later, Ed Pearl, the owner, brought the greatest American musicians. Suddenly, they were in this room in the middle of Hollywood: Bill Monroe, Earl Scruggs, Muddy Waters, Doc Watson, Sonny Terry and Brownie McGhee, Lightnin' Hopkins, Roscoe Holcomb, and Rev. Gary Davis. The list goes on and on. I was there half of the time. My brother and I were either playing on stage, sitting in the audience, or hanging out backstage.

I grew up listening to that music. It was something that I'd always loved. I'd followed those artists that we ended up recording with. They were a part of my life. In a way I kind of forced the project on the band so I could meet those people. I made the deals. I was the producer. I put the whole thing together. My brother, John McEuen, was in the band. He was the banjo player.

I had a lot of help and a great engineer, Dino Lappas, who was the chief engineer at Liberty Records. He ran the studio there on Third Street. He was a very big part of making that album. Dino had spent many years recording artists live in a folk, natural, documentary fashion. I brought him to Nashville because I wanted to know, when I walked in there, that I could get exactly what I had envisioned.

Nashville at that time didn't really appreciate acoustic music and didn't really care much for bluegrass at all. Chet Atkins had kind of laid down the law that there would be no steel guitars on RCA Victor records. All of a sudden, we had to listen to strings and arrangements. There was this push to make it more accessible — to take the country out of country is the way I viewed it.

Our goal was to extract the regional, mountain sound — what we thought of as ethnic music. We grew up in the hardcore folk era, coming out of Folkways Records, listening to field recordings. Moe [Moses] Asch was the owner of that label, but Samuel Charters was the man who went out, discovered the artists, and made the records. Sam Charters and guys like that — documentarians — were my inspiration for the *Circle* album. I had very specific notes about things I wanted on the album. These were the songs that meant a lot to me, and at least half of them were my selection. The other half were songs that the artists selected. There were certain fundamental things that had to be on there, or it didn't work for me.

Those artists — Maybelle Carter, Roy Acuff, Merle Travis, Doc Watson (well, Doc was younger then), and Earl Scruggs — they were not young. They were in the middle of their careers, and in fact, when you're in the middle of your career in the record business, you're at the end of your career.

I wanted to make sure that I got to meet them. My brother [John McEuen] and I were in love with their technique. Playing Carter Family music was our inspiration for years. Just to get started doing anything, you sit down and play "Wildwood Flower." There was a sense of "I can't believe these people are willing to talk with us, much less to record with us." John and I and Dino [Lappas, an engineer] walked into Nashville, and in two weeks we came out with that record on tape, cut live on two-track at 30 ips [inches per second], not multitrack, no overdubbing at all, and no electric instruments, period. Everybody live. That's why it's called *Will the Circle Be Unbroken*.

We went to a couple of different houses, but a lot of it occurred at Earl Scruggs's house on the lake out in Henderson. We rehearsed at Earl's house for maybe a week. People would come and go, and we'd run through two or three songs. Earl was very helpful in pulling the project together. He knew Vassar Clements, and he knew Maybelle [Carter]. We didn't know these people. We knew their music, but we didn't know them personally. John [McEuen] knew Doc Watson.

Roy Acuff wouldn't record with us until he'd heard. It came down from Acuff-Rose that . . . I had meetings with them, and I told them my goals. I said I wanted to record a lot of Acuff-Rose music, which got their attention. Wesley Rose said, "Well, you know Roy's not sure he wants to do this, but he's willing to come in and listen to the first week of recording. If he likes what he hears, he'll do it."

I played back the first week for him, and we were all in the control room, just like the pictures there on the record. We were all gathered there and played back a lot of songs, and Roy Acuff turned to me and asked, "So what do you call that music, son?"

"Country," I said.

He said, "Damn right, let's do it." His stuff was all done in like one day, maybe even half a day. He was obsessed with doing things the first time, just like he says on the record. "Let's get it the first time, and to hell with the rest of it." Those are the lessons that we learned. Unfortunately, everybody's forgotten those lessons, thanks to multitracks. That's the reality of the thing.

There's a picture—that I created actually—where I shot, through the control-room window, the Dirt Band in a circle with Doc, Earl, and a few people. I sepia-toned the photo. But in the lower half, I cut out, I removed the console that was there at Woodland Sound Studios, and I stripped in a photo of an old console with three big dials from 1926 or '27. (I got permission from Glenn Snoddy, owner of Woodland, to copy a picture hanging on his studio's wall.) I made it look like that was the board we had made the record on. It was very significant image in that three-record set, but nobody has ever commented on that alteration—not even the band. They don't get it, but that was my secret message:

what we're interested in here is the history of recording more than anything.

The artists were legends to us. It was analogous to walking into Hollywood and, in two weeks, coming out with a movie with ten of your favorite stars. When we came back with that tape and I did the editing at Third Street Studio in Hollywood, I was listening to this thing on the speakers, and I thought I'd had a dream. It just didn't seem real—that this thing could sound so damn good.

Nashville had nothing to do with that album, by the way. There was no effort at all to accommodate Nashville. It was financed by United Artists Records. It cost thirty thousand dollars. The money came out of Hollywood, because I had a deal at UA to do whatever I wanted. At that time I was doing the Dirt Band and Greg and Duane Allman and a few other people.

Except for the artists coming in and playing, the corporate side of Nashville didn't even know we were there. We were in and out of town before they even knew what happened. There was a big story in *The Tennessean* about the session, but it was over by then. We didn't have to relate to that system at all. We couldn't have done it if we had to. They wouldn't have let us, not with their money.

Today it's routine to do eclectic projects at a price, if you have the right names. Back then, I was working at a label, as an independent, producing records at UA, a label that had ELO and War and I think Don McLean might have been there; a lot of jazz, a lot of R&B, and a lot of jive pop—Hollywood music. They didn't know what this was. In fact when I played the album for fifteen people [record-company executives], they were looking at their watches most of the time: "When's this fucking thing going to be over?" Then it went out and sold 2 million records, and they said, "How did this happen?"

It was all because of FM radio. At that time FM was willing to try and do or be anything. It went crazy for that record. Stations would play the whole thing. College radio was new then. So all of that rebel, outlaw radio—that I think has been fairly well contained—was the reason the *Circle* album got to have an audience. It was an interesting era.

Let me tell you something. That record's been out thirty years [forty, now]. This is the first time anybody's ever called me about it. I've made multi-platinum records in comedy and music, and I've made movies. I've got a lot of product out there, but this is the first time anyone has ever asked me, "How did this happen?" They've talked to the band members. I think people have the feeling that the band made this record. They didn't make this record.

Al Green might not be some folks' idea of a country singer, but early on he made the odd foray into country territory: "I'm So Lonesome I Could Cry" (Hank Williams), "Funny How Time Slips Away" (Willie Nelson), and "For the Good Times" (Kris Kristofferson).

AL GREEN, "FOR THE GOOD TIMES" (1972), *I'M STILL IN LOVE WITH YOU* (HI/THE RIGHT STUFF)

WILLIE MITCHELL

When I got Al Green, I had worked out a basic sound, but I gave him another sound. Everybody was so hot then. Stevie Wonder was hot. Marvin Gaye was hot. Stax was there. But I was searching for another sound to get away from all that. So I said, "I'm going to give Al some jazz chords, and see how he works with this." We kept on messing with jazz chords and what have you—writing songs around them. He finally caught on to it.

At the time I got him, he was singing real hard. I said, "Al, you got to lighten up and be more pleasant." I gave him some Charlie Parker records. I gave him Jesse Belvin records and Sam Cooke. I told him, "You need to soften up. You're singing too hard. You've got to float. You can't sing hard like this." At the time, he was more interested in Sam and Dave, and Otis Redding. That's how the sound came up on Al Green. I tried to get a real top on the music that was pleasant, but a thunderous thing on the bottom. That was the formula I was trying to put together.

Al and I spent lots of time in the studio [Memphis's Royal Studios]. When I came off the road, I had my band. They were there all the time. Once we started working on something, we kept on pursuing it to see what would happen with the thing. Once we got it in another place, we put it down on tape. There was a whole lot of rehearsal on that stuff.

CHARLIE RICH, *IT AIN'T GONNA BE THAT WAY — THE COMPLETE SMASH SESSIONS* (1965-1966, ACE)

JERRY KENNEDY

Charlie was somebody who wanted to work a good while before he ever went to the studio. We spent a lot of time wood shedding, working out stuff. "What's going to go here?" He needed to know that because of what he would be playing. Jerry [Lee Lewis] was more spontaneous. You worked around his freedom. Charlie was more structured, I think, than Jerry was.

Of course, Charlie played piano and had, maybe, a guitar, drums, and bass with him. We brought in everything else later, the vocal group, and strings later on. That's the way Billy did it too, Billy Sherrill [Rich's subsequent producer at Epic Records].

We wondered why we weren't more successful with Charlie than we were. We had the one hit, "Mohair Sam." But to me, that was probably not really Charlie. "Nice and Easy" [a Kennedy-produced single] was a strange song to throw out for all the pickers that day. They were, maybe, not the right group to have in the studio, but we fumbled through it. But that was Charlie. If he did a set in a club in Memphis, you were hearing 90 percent jazz.

Pig Robbins played piano on "Behind Closed Doors" and "The Most Beautiful Girl" [Rich's breakout sessions at Epic Records]. All that intro thing was Pig. A lot of people don't know that. I played [guitar] on most of that stuff over there, too. I was working sessions for Billy. We're good friends. That was the one account that I kept with Mercury's knowledge. It wasn't a problem with them.

That's Jerry Kennedy's guitar on Tammy Wynette's recording of "Stand by Your Man," a song Wynette co-wrote with Billy Sherrill, her producer.

CHARLIE RICH, "BEHIND CLOSED DOORS" (1973), *FEEL LIKE GOING HOME: THE ESSENTIAL CHARLIE RICH BEHIND CLOSED DOORS* (COLUMBIA/LEGACY).

LAWRENCE COHN

I used to be one of the heads of Epic Records. Because of the way we were set up corporately, [Billy] Sherrill, who was in charge of the Nashville operation, reported to me. I was his boss. Billy changed the face of country music. What can I say? Good, bad, or indifferent, he had a vision. He heard things a certain way in his head. He's a great producer. He's a great musician. He's a great songwriter. And he doesn't need me to trumpet his skills.

In the Charlie Rich case, Billy had no constraints. He could do what he wanted. Before Charlie hit with "Behind Closed Doors" [1973], Billy and I were discussing the fact that we both thought that Charlie was absolutely a superstar. We just couldn't get a big thing going with him. It was bothering both of us.

Billy called me one day. He said, "Look, I don't know what else to do. He's essentially a blues artist and a jazz artist. That's always the way he's perceived himself. Why don't you try to produce something on him, and let's see what happens."

"Let me think about it," I said. I thought about it and called Billy. "Look, I'm going to call B. B. King and see if we can do an album with him and Charlie. That would seem to be a nice marriage between the two of them."

Then, in two weeks' time, I think it was, he hit with "Behind Closed Doors." That was the end of my concept. Hitting successfully with that song, there was a real duality. It was a double-edged sword. Charlie finally got recognition. He finally was making a lot of money. But I think it really eroded his soul. He was not for Las Vegas. He was for clubs where he could play blues piano. This is what the guy really did. All of a sudden, he's with those shitheads in Las Vegas. It's like performing puppets, so to speak. That may have contributed to his demise. But that's just my opinion.

REGGIE YOUNG (guitarist)

Sherrill had a studio band, if you want to put it that way. Pig [Hargus Robbins], the piano player, he had a style of playing. They had a way of playing—a bass guitar and a bass—they locked in and played. There was a formula they played. The left hand of the piano played the same thing the bass and the bass guitar did. It's that Nashville sound. Steel-guitar players were usually Pete Drake, and he'd use two or three other guys. I got to play on a lot of that stuff. Sherrill would have about three guitars—a couple of acoustics, electric lead. He was a song guy. He really picked good material. The dynamics of how you'd get from a verse to a chorus, the verse could be really low key and then, when you hit the chorus, it would be wide open. There were dynamics throughout most of the stuff that Sherrill cut. That was the way he signed his signature on anything he produced.

JIMMY BOWEN

Billy Sherrill was like the country Phil Spector. God forbid he ever heard me say that. But when you listened to a Billy Sherrill record, there was just a ton of Billy Sherrill. He probably wrote the song. He wrote great songs. He did the music with the musicians. The person learned it, came in, and sang on the track that was being played. That was a different era.

B. J. THOMAS, "HOOKED ON A FEELING" (1973), *THE SCEPTER HITS AND MORE 1964–1973* (ACE)

REGGIE YOUNG

I just showed up and went to work. I play guitar, and I played guitar. That's what I do. Nobody gave me any direction. In Memphis [at American Sound Studio] that was an in-house thing I did with [Chips] Moman for five years. We were all like a group production company. Nobody sat down and said do this or do that.

But you played an electric guitar-sitar. How was the decision made to use it?

I probably just picked it up, was noodling around: "Ah, this'll make a great intro." I remember that song was kind of chopped up. Moman took the ending and put it in the middle as a solo. But the intro was just off the top of my head. Somewhere in the middle you can hear where the tape was cut, and another part of the solo was added. He probably took it from the ending.

A lot of that stuff, we didn't sit down, do it, and five minutes later we had a record. Some of those things took three or four days—sometimes all week. They were all head arrangements. Most of it was spontaneous. Nothing was written out for us to play. We just played off each other, trial and error, and then we'd try stuff. It's not like we'd play that whole time. We'd cut it and listen to it, come back in the next day, and if we didn't like it, cut it again—four or five, six times.

Especially in Memphis, when we'd do things over and over, it was usually the singer who wanted to change something, maybe even re-write something. We'd cut it again. As long as it was getting better each time, we did it, fine. When you started going downhill, it was over with. We'd take the best take and, then, finish it out, go from there.

Nashville was a little more organized. We had three hours to do a session. I know in the case of—I worked with Jimmy Bowen—sometimes we listened to a demo, sometimes we'd just listen to the song and write our number charts. Sometimes it would be a person's second take, while we were running it down. The talk-back would come on and say, "I don't think you can get it any better than that." That's what we'd take.

We had a basic rhythm section that we cut. A lot of times I over-dubbed solos after we did the basic track. It might be on another session. Many times we went in and cut the song, first or second take, and we were through the first hour. You still had two hours to go. We'd go sit in the lounge and wait for session number two to show up. The players were such high-quality and they were so fine-tuned, including myself, because we played all the time. It's hard to come in off the street and get in that rhythm section. You'd better be on your toes because everybody was so homed in on what they were doing. So we'd cut the basic rhythm track, and then sweeten it and overdub stuff on it.

DON WILLIAMS, *THE DEFINITIVE COLLECTION* (1973, MCA NASHVILLE)

ALLEN REYNOLDS

If something is really good, no matter what genre it is, it tends to travel better than you would anticipate and into places you wouldn't anticipate. So before Don Williams, there was Jim Reeves. He was huge—absolutely huge—in South Africa. There may be something in that culture that makes them like that resonant baritone. Because then along comes Don Williams, and it's the same kind of thing. But there's also a certain melodic appeal to a great many of the songs that Don Williams did that might have its similarities to Jim Reeves—a certain, without trying to get too analytical, a certain mellowness or something. Or it could be many other things. But it has played well in South Africa.

I got back together with Don in 1990 or '91, and we did another album. During that time a group from Zimbabwe, called the Bunda Boys, came through here and came to the studio and wanted to cut a record with Don Williams, who was their hero. It was a happy, wonderful day of working with these guys. We cut a couple of things. They just loved the guy, loved his music. We cut "You're My Best Friend" and a couple of Don Williams things with those guys playing. It was a nice reminder how you shouldn't construct barriers in your mind because music travels on its own, with its own logic.

Years ago, when *Don Williams, Vol. 1* was complete, and we were distributing it here in Nashville, I was with the label owner, Jack Clement, in New York. We were talking to a guy from Polydor. He had just come from being the head of Polydor in Britain to be the head of Polydor in the U.S. I was talking to him about the Don Williams album and about putting it out in England. He said, "They don't like country music over there."

I said, "Well, Faron Young just had a number-one record with 'Four in the Morning.' I'd call that pretty country."

"Well," he said, "there's always the odd exception."

Within six months the music subpublisher of some of those songs kept nagging the radio stations over there, and Don Williams broke wide open with "I Recall a Gypsy Woman" from the very album I was talking about. He was like Elvis over there. It was huge.

I felt like the Brits would love him. I don't know why, but I was right. And they continue to. He goes over there today and plays concerts and draws big, respectful, happy audiences. If the music's good, people are going to like it even if they don't normally listen to that kind of music. I've had the experience, all my life, of people hearing something I've worked on and going, "Is that country? I like that."

As if, "Wow, I really like that, but is that country?"

"Yeah, that's country."

So I've always had faith that if you make it really good, the best of its genre or up there in the spirit of the best, then you don't know what's going to happen. Anything can happen. I've got so much faith in the audience out there and so little faith in the marketing men that stand between me and that audience.

TOMPALL GLASER, *THE GREAT TOMPALL AND HIS OUTLAW BAND* (1976, MGM)

TOMPALL GLASER

My adult, tax-paying life has been spent in Nashville. I worked with Marty Robbins for quite a bit. He produced the first records that I did with my brothers. He sold the contract to Decca. We'd been on *Arthur Godfrey's Talent Scouts*. So we came into Nashville after winning that talent contest. It was a big deal in those days on CBS [television]. You stay on CBS for a week. We got to come into Nashville little stars already. Right away we went on the Grand Ole Opry. It kind of spoiled me. I thought I was better than I was, I think.

When did you build your studio, Hillbilly Central?

I never called it that. Hazel [Smith] called it that in her [gossip] column. I didn't start producing until I produced myself on MGM in '67, '68. We built a little four-track studio and then built it up to eight tracks. We started doing some stuff in there. In 1969 I built the new place—Glaser Sound Studios—started building it [at 916 19th Avenue South, Nashville]. In the middle '70s we did all of our records up there. Hazel said once, "You could expect Elvis to walk in any day." There was a lot of traffic. A lot of different people from different parts of the country came in there and hung out.

WAYLON JENNINGS, *LONESOME, ON'RY AND MEAN* (1973, BMG HERITAGE/RCA)

CHET ATKINS

Waylon was on drugs, I guess, when he came here, but I was really impressed with him. I thought, "Boy, I've found me a star." The way I found him was Bobby Bare and Skeeter Davis and a lot of people kept saying, "You've got to sign this guy in Phoenix. He's great." So I called him on the phone, and I asked him, "Would you like to record for RCA Victor? This is Chet."

He said, "Oh yeah, I'd love to." He was on Herb Alpert's label. I don't know what he worked out with Herb. I've never asked him.

So he came to Nashville [in 1965] to record. [Ronny Light and Jennings produced *Lonesome, On'ry and Mean*.] And he was so good—and handsome. But by and by, he got on drugs really bad, and he hated me. They'll do that you know. Don Gibson did too. They'd get on drugs, and they hated me. But when they'd get off them, they loved me.

One day a few years ago, I was in the vicinity of Ray Stevens's office, and Waylon came by in a convertible something. He yelled at me, "Hey Chet, I'm off drugs!" And he was. He hasn't been on them since. I was so happy for him. A lot of those guys quit cold turkey, you know. Roger Miller did too.

WAYLON JENNINGS, *HONKY TONK HEROES* (1973, BUDDHA)

TOMPALL GLASER

I used to like to play pinball; at the time they were gambling devices. Waylon liked the freedom, and he knew I had the freedom. He wanted to get in on it. So I taught him how to play pinball. He didn't even have a bank account at that time, didn't know how to start one up. Amazing! That's in his book.

That Outlaw movement: my idea was to find somebody like Waylon who needed to get in there and do his own thing, and then throw up a guard around him. Like a movie producer would do: keep the record company away from him and give him all the studio time he needed. Hide the clock. Get him in there with the band. That's how he got his hits.

Waylon was a guy who was starved to do what he wanted to do, but he never got to do it. The most important thing I did was to keep him in my studio and keep the record label away. They didn't know, most of the time, when he was cutting. My job was to keep the influences away so he could try to discover his own music. He did come up with that "boom boom," that eat-shit bass.

That's what the Outlaw movement was all about. Things had gotten so bogged down that a lot of good music was just sitting out there waiting to be heard, and nobody could hear it. That's when a producer has the most fun. That's when he can help some of that stuff emerge.

We never really got credit for it either. They hated us, especially me. I really fought it hard. I got so sick of it that I probably said too much. Me and old cocaine talked too much. I naturally talk a lot. Get me some speed help, and I really go at it. But I'll tell you the truth. We were pretty strung out. We didn't do as much editing as we should have. There was a couple or three years in the middle '70s that I kind of veered to the left. The ideas came easy that way. Waylon could work pretty good on them [pills and cocaine] on the first couple of days, but on third days nobody can do anything. I couldn't work on them. I had to quit early in the game, by about '77. Waylon went up and on into the middle '80s.

There weren't as many country radio stations back then, but there got to be a lot more of them after the Outlaw movement. For years, as soon as something really started selling, record labels wouldn't call it country anymore. They'd turn it over to their pop divisions to sell: for example, Jim Reeves, Marty Robbins, and Bobby Helms. I worked with Bobby about six months before he died, and he still couldn't figure out why they never thought he was country. They sent him out on pop tours all the time.

The Outlaw thing changed all that. They sold the first platinum country album [*Wanted! The Outlaws* (1976)]. It went over 4 million before it was all said and done. They sold it through the country channels. That was the biggest market that it made. It let country music grow up. It brought new fans, a new generation.

JIMMY BOWEN

Tompall was the only one . . . He had a studio; he had this great knowledge of the history of country music—musically and politically. When I went down there [1977], I lived at his place for a year. I'd record some country instrument, banjo and one or two fiddles, and Tompall would come upstairs. He'd be in the back listening. I'd finish, and he'd say, "Let's go downstairs and have a drink." Then he'd say, "Let me play you how that ought to sound." And he would! He'd play me some famous old country guy who I didn't know anything about. I didn't know the history of country music. I was coming in on the middle of it, I guess, from what it was to what it is now. He and I, we had such a great time together. He enjoyed teaching me, and I enjoyed learning it. Plus, he laid out the town for me—the politics.

He knows how important he was, how I felt about him. But he wasn't just important to me. He was important to what I was able to do down there, and to what happened to country music. He believed it could be big. He was the original. He was a true outlaw. Waylon [Jennings] fell into it and developed into it, and so did Willie. But Tompall just was. Everywhere in his life, I'll bet he was an outlaw.

Why do you think cocaine was such a lure to musicians in Nashville, and marijuana much less so?

I wondered about that immediately. Their first thing was booze, as it was in California and New York. Then the pills came into play. Pop acts go out and do a tour. Country musicians were on the road all the time. They've got five hundred miles to make, leaving at one in the morning for the next gig. So they had the pills: the L.A. turnaround pill. They used to joke about it. You could drive to L.A. and back on this one little pill. That's speed. All you've got to do with a guy who does pills is give him some cocaine, and you get the same effect, although of the two, the pills are better for you. But booze was the base. You add cocaine to it, and it made sense. It didn't make sense to smoke a joint and lay back. You certainly couldn't do that and try to get down the road.

[Johnny] Paycheck called me one time. He'd been up six days. "Bowen," he said, "I want to come over there with you."

I said, "Johnny, I'd love to have you. Have your lawyer call me. I'll see if we can work it out."

His New York lawyer called me. "Hell, Bowen, he owes five more albums to Columbia."

I said, "Why don't you call and explain that to your client, please."

Paycheck called me back in a little while. "Bowen," he said, "that's bullshit. I can deliver all of those albums by Christmas." There's your cocaine working.

WILLIE NELSON, *PHASES AND STAGES* (1974, RHINO ATLANTIC)

CHET ATKINS

I recorded Willie; he sang better then than he ever has. But we couldn't get him off the ground. I guess, RCA, they had all these promotion men, but back in those days you promoted people that you thought would sell. They didn't have a lot of confidence in Willie because he sang so far behind the beat and everything. But I tell people Willie didn't start selling till he got ugly: beard and hair. Everybody tried to record Willie and couldn't bring it off, because the public wasn't ready for him yet.

BOB FERGUSON

Chet had been recording Waylon a long time. They just couldn't get a big hit. The company was pressuring him: "You better drop this guy."

Chet said, "No, I know he can hit. We'll try him another year."

Same way with Willie Nelson. I don't think from reading Willie's autobiography that he realized this, but I remember our meetings at RCA: "What are we going to do? I've tried this. I've tried that." We hired another producer—Felton Jarvis—and put him over there with him. Felton tried to get some hits with Willie. Felton was producing Elvis. So he tried.

But all of us had the same kind of experience. We'd look and see if the chemistry was there. We'd pass an artist around. "You want to try him? You got any ideas for him?" This was our cry. Later, Willie wrote out against RCA in his book, but actually he had been the subject of many a discussion: "What are we going to do? How can we get this guy going? He's a good writer and everything. Good singer." Finally, he made it on his own down in Texas, which was probably where he was supposed to be. But he came back with us in another way when they started doing the Outlaw-type material.

JERRY WEXLER

They're doing a documentary on me, and they just interviewed Willie last week.* I just got the tape. The interviewer asked him your very question, "How did Jerry Wexler relate to you in the studio?" I wish I could give you Willie's answers because they'd be better than mine. He says, "Jerry Wexler listens to my songs and then devises the best way to frame them in the studio. And also, after the song is done, to do the best with it with the mixing and the equalization, the engineering and so on."

Do you know John Morthland's book, *The Best of Country Music?* I want to read you something. Here's a quote: "Though *Shotgun Willie* was supposed to be the album that freed Willie Nelson from the Nashville assembly line, it turned out to be a slap-dash affair. But on *Phases and Stages*, the 1974 follow-up, Willie turned the trick." That's why I'd like to get away from *Shotgun Willie*, which was just a smorgasbord. Then he goes on to say [of *Phases and Stages*], "Nearly everything about the album represents a departure. It was recorded at Muscle Shoals, Ala-

---

*Wexler signed Nelson to Atlantic Records in 1972; in 1974, the company shut down its country music division.

bama, using primarily the same session musicians who cut much of the great soul music of the late '60s and early '70s. It was produced by Jerry Wexler, who made his name working with R&B and soul artists from the '50s and '60s. The album is also rife with contradictions. It's got more jazz inflections than anything Nelson had done, yet it's still true to his country roots. Finally, this is a concept album whether you're listening to the words or not."

On a tape Willie recalled how we first met at Harlan Howard's house. There was a party every Christmas. All of the pickers got together, and they played their current material. I was there, my first meeting with Willie. He played *Phases and Stages*, the whole thing. I was very impressed with that, though I didn't need to be. All I knew was that Willie Nelson was unsigned, which was an unimaginable opportunity. He played *Phases and Stages* on his guitar, and that led to the signing.

One cut on Phases and Stages *features strings. How did they come into the recording process?*

I imagine that came up retrospectively, after we looked at what we had. We decided the ballad needed the strings. And Morthland said very nice things about those strings. In so many words, to paraphrase, it wasn't the usual Nashville glop.

In that album I hear possibilities that Booker T. Jones revisited and developed when he produced Willie Nelson's Stardust *[1978].*

You want to know how that happened? This is amazing. Willie, at that time, had an apartment or a condo in L.A., and Booker T. had an apartment there too. They met at the pool; they started to talk. One thing led to another. I felt that fate screwed me out of the opportunity to do that album. To me that's an album I should have done. Don't get that wrong. I love Booker T., and I'm very happy for him. He probably made a million dollars from it. This is just a little rueful side remark on my part. It's an obiter dictum. Can you see how I feel I could have done a job with that particular album, given my knowledge of standard songs, my interest in the great tradition of American pop song?

Your work with Doug Sahm and Willie Nelson should've been regarded as the birth of the Outlaw movement.

Ray Wylie Hubbard and "Up against the Wall, Redneck Mother"*—all of that, to me, was one of the most hilarious, self-conscious put-ons in the history of music: people deluding themselves. 'Cause Willie had one earring and a pigtail down to his ass, this made him an untouchable? Great! Wonderful! So they don't like you, Willie, in Nashville? I love you. Come with me.

I'll give you one quick one about Ray Wylie Hubbard. At that time, my apartment was a penthouse in the Essex House on Central Park West. It was very elegantly furnished. So Ray Wylie Hubbard's manager at that time was this football player—he was like a second-string player with the Cowboys. He was associated with Warner's. Anyhow, he brought Ray to my apartment, and we're sitting in my living room talking, and suddenly Ray says, "Man, you got a Mason jar?" Here he is with his chaw spitting into the Mason jar. So I signed him up, and I sent him to Muscle Shoals, but not for me to produce. I forget who was going to handle him. He arrived in Muscle Shoals like on a Thursday, and on a Friday he was out of there, and that was the end of him. I thought there was something there.

DOLLY PARTON, "JOLENE" (1974), *JOLENE* (RCA)

BOB FERGUSON

Each artist has a different set of capabilities, and I always presumed my job was to help the artist bring out who she wanted to be and to fill in any of the gaps. Some artists didn't need much help in choosing their material. Dolly was like that. Of course, Porter brought her to RCA, and I was producing Porter so I became her producer and their producer. Porter himself would be well prepared for a session when he came. He and the band, when we did use his road band . . . There's another thing. Some of the artists didn't have a road band, and a producer helped fill

---

*Jerry Jeff Walker recorded Ray Wylie Hubbard's Outlaw anthem in 1973. It amounted to a shot across the bow of Nashville hegemony.

in and hire the musicians, which helped formulate the persona that the artist was going to present.

But they would go out on the bus — Porter and Dolly, for example — and they would've rehearsed a lot and discussed a lot of things as they traveled during those road dates. So my job with them was to find out what they needed. It wasn't like it was with some of the artists. Dolly wrote songs, and she wrote good songs. It was just a matter of listening to how she did it and approving the takes and encouraging her and being something of a confidant to her. Porter had a strong personality, and Dolly would sometimes mention things to me, privately, that she had aspirations to do. My role was to urge her to continue her writing and to do those things.

You know those tape machines with voice-activated, automatic recording controls? I had an idea once of trying to produce a record where the voice would come out when the artist was singing, when they were loud and up close to the mike, and it would knock down the sound of the music. As soon as the artist quit singing, that automatic volume would raise the music's level back up and grab the instruments.

I talked to our engineers at RCA, who were the best, and explained this idea. I got a call one day from Al Pachucki: "Hey, what are you doing? Come down to the studio."

I went down, and he said, "I think I've figured out how we can do what you've been talking about." It was a production technique whereby we got the same effect on the voice — in this case Dolly's voice — as on the lead instruments. But the rhythm, we wanted to keep that steady. We didn't want the piano, bass, and drums going up and down. So they weren't fed through this system. It gave us some very effective sounds.

"Jolene" [1974] is probably the best example of that technique. Al and I got in the studio alone, when Dolly and Porter were on the road one time. We remixed the tape that way. It was a knockout. I was delighted with it, and I think the public was too. The meter doesn't move 10 dBs [decibels] all the way through the song. When she's singing, that automatically pushes down the lead instruments, and when she quits, it pops them right back up so they're right in there with her but out of the way. It's a tricky technique. You can't use it on everything. If you tried to do that when you had a string section, it sounded terrible. But it sounded good on "Jolene," and I believe we used it on "The Mule Skinner Blues." It's compression, that sort of thing.

In that case as a producer, I didn't have to worry about the songs, the material, the instrumentation that was brought in, and so on. I had to worry about how we were going to mix the recording to make it something special.

GEORGE JONES AND TAMMY WYNETTE, "(WE'RE NOT) THE JET SET" (1974), *16 BIGGEST HITS* (EPIC/LEGACY)

BOBBY BRADDOCK

The demo on "(We're Not) The Jet Set" goes back to a time when I had sort of gone on strike against my publisher. He got it in his head that there should be somebody on staff with the writers when they did demo sessions. I refused to do that. I said, "Screw it. I'll do my demos with just a piano." They sounded pretty crappy at first, but they got better and better. I started adding musicians. I got a Moog synthesizer, added a bass; the engineer was a drummer. Then I had a good string of success. By the time I had a full group of musicians, I was getting what I wanted to do anyway. I had to take a long time and go through the back door. At that time, then, the demo on "(We're Not) The Jet Set" was not very sophisticated. I don't think it was all that good; it was me on electric piano and not much more.

"He Stopped Loving Her Today" was not a good demo either. The original was not even the final song. Billy Sherrill, I have to credit him with that. He took liberties as a producer. If he didn't like a line, he would change it without even asking the writer. In most cases that would be a terrible thing to do. In Billy's case, with "(We're Not) The Jet Set," there's a line he threw in. I had nothing to do with it. It's at the end of the song; it goes, "The Jones and Wynette set / Ain't the flamin' suzette set." That was Billy Sherrill. He added that. There is another case, in "Golden Ring," that he changed a line. I hated it—still do. But in most cases when he changed a line in a song it was for the better. He was an anomaly though.

EAGLES, *THEIR GREATEST HITS 1971-1975* (ASYLUM/ELEKTRA)

JIM ED NORMAN

There was never any real purposeful effort on the part of Nashville to start trying to copy Southern California. All of the changes that have come to Nashville are the sum product of the experiences of all the people who are here working today and what they feel is important to bring to the music. The purveyors of the artform are the ones who get to set the strategies or get to set the tone for what the artform is going to be, rather than some outside judging body that says, "This really isn't this, and this isn't that, and this is this, and this is that."

The goal here is really that the artists themselves, as they come together, propose through their actions and their work and their art what the sound is going to be. It's always a sum of their experiences and ideas being worked out. In the studio you have an idea and say, "Hey, I heard something on a record the other day that reminded me of something we did fifteen years ago. I can still remember the motivation for that part and where it came from." You begin to see relationships between particular sounds where, after a while, they can invade a genre. You can then build some connections about where these things came from and how they turned into what we have today. I think those forces, however, are at work in every genre and happening all the time. It's not something that's exclusive to Nashville.

Prior to getting into arranging [for the Eagles], I was in a group called Shiloh. This group consisted of Don Henley, and along with Don [were] Richard and Michael Bowden, and Al Perkins. Richard went on to play with Ronstadt, Fogelberg, and then to form a comedy duo called Pinkard and Bowden down here in Nashville. His cousin, Michael, became Emmylou Harris's bass player for years in the Hot Band. He then went on to play with Patty Loveless and now is an executive here in Nashville. Al Perkins is still playing steel and dobro.

We [Shiloh] made an album for Amos Records, Jimmy Bowen's label. Our producer was Kenny Rogers. He and I found ourselves in the studio with roles reversed, almost twenty years to the day [recording *Some-*

thing Inside So Strong]. It was really something to have that kind of experience, to be working together in partnership again, with different responsibilities this time.

THE EARL SCRUGGS REVUE, *ANNIVERSARY SPECIAL* (1975, COLUMBIA)

BOB JOHNSTON

I always demanded that people be open-minded, willing to work with each other. With Earl Scruggs, I had Billy Joel, Alvin Lee, Albert Lee, Duck Dunn, Roger McGuinn, Cissy Houston, Joan Baez. I had about thirty people down there—all of them in a room.

I said, "Were going to do this song now."

Leonard [Cohen] would go, "Let me sing on this one."

Billy Joel would say, "I'll play piano."

I got together a bunch of them, and we'd do the song. Somebody came over to the studio, went back, and said that there was a bunch of major artists who didn't know what to do, wandering around in the studio.

They came over there to take care of it, and I locked all the doors. They couldn't get in their own goddamn studio till I got through recording, which was two days later. It was a wonderful album—Earl Scruggs's twenty-fifth *Anniversary Special* album.

TOM T. HALL, "I LIKE BEER" (1975), *THE DEFINITIVE COLLECTION* (MERCURY NASHVILLE)

JERRY KENNEDY

He was the first disciplined writer that I ever ran into. He'd wake up at five o'clock, five-thirty every morning, go down to his barn and write.

After he had six, seven, eight things, he'd call me. "Can I come in?" That was always a big thrill when Tom would call.

I'd say, "Alright, man. I'll clear the calendar. I'm ready to hear some new stuff."

He'd come in and paint seven or eight beautiful pictures: just knock me out every time. He never failed to surprise me. He told me once that he never left a song unfinished. He would go ahead and finish it and get it out of his system even if he knew it was bad after four lines. He's a special guy.

He had a lot of fans back in the early '70s, rock groups. The people at Mercury said they'd come by offices in Chicago or in New York or wherever to pick up his latest stuff, to get it as quick as they could.

If Owen Bradley called me for a session, I knew what he would tolerate and wouldn't. What he wanted. Basically, if you heard the song, you knew how he wanted us to act. I think that probably the engineers that I worked with were familiar with the records. And this came after a few years of doing things. But they kind of knew what you wanted, and they would set up. The engineers would take a great interest: "Hey man, who are the players?" They wanted to know who was on drums, who was going to be playing and everything. That had a lot to do with it, too, as to how they would set things up.

THE STATLER BROTHERS, "FLOWERS ON THE WALL" (1975), *THE DEFINITIVE COLLECTION* (MERCURY NASHVILLE)

The Statlers cut "Flowers on the Wall" first for Columbia, and then later for Mercury with you as producer. Did you make money when Tarantino used the track in Pulp Fiction?

JERRY KENNEDY

As it turns out, that was the Mercury cut used in *Pulp Fiction*. The royalties of anything I recorded while I was there, I'll get forever. Some of those deals end when it's over. But no, the contracts I had are forever. That's nice. That's mailbox money, we call it now. On occasion, these box sets they put together, that just adds to it too. That was one of the real nice things about the time that I spent at that label. There were some really great people in Chicago and New York that we were working with. You won't hear very many folks in Nashville make a statement like that.

GEORGE JONES AND TAMMY WYNETTE, "GOLDEN RING" (1976), *GOLDEN RING* (RAZOR & TIE)

BOBBY BRADDOCK

I was on a TV show with Marijohn Wilkin and Danny Dill. They wrote "Long Black Veil." We were on the show together, and we were talking about "Golden Ring." I said, "My publisher was talking about suing on Conway Twitty's 'I'd Love to Lay You Down.' It's so much like 'Golden Ring.'" And then I said to Marijohn and Danny, "I told my publisher, 'Don't do that. Marijohn Wilkin and Danny Dill will turn around and sue us.'"

Marijohn said, "We came close; we came close to doing that."

But I think if you go back far enough you'll find some old gospel song that sounds like that. I wanted to write a song for George and Tammy that sounded like—there was an old gospel group called the Chuck Wagon Gang. It was old-timey Baptist, or maybe even Pentecostal-type singing, just them and a guitar. I wanted to write a song for George and Tammy like that.

I got with Rafe Van Hoy. I had started the song, but I was stuck on it. I called Curly Putman to see if he wanted to come in. He didn't want to leave his farm. Rafe walked in the door, and his mother worked at a jewelry store. I said, "Why don't you write this with me?"

I don't think Rafe wrote a lot on it, but he made up for it by . . . I was going out of town the next day. I knew George and Tammy were recording soon, and I wanted to get the song demoed. Rafe is a great singer and guitar player. I asked him, "Why don't you go in there and sing a bunch of parts on it? Do it kind of like the Chuck Wagon Gang—hillbilly gospel."

My God, the little demo he did on that is wonderful. My publisher produced Bill Anderson. He tried to find Bill Anderson—couldn't find him. So he went ahead and followed my instincts and pitched it to Billy Sherrill for George and Tammy.

They recorded it a few days after it was written, and a very few weeks after that—maybe three or four weeks—it was playing on the radio. Billy cut it in that spirit, but he did his own little things on it. He had the Gatlin Brothers doing the answer harmony. A wonderful, wonderful record: it had a great guitar intro. He did the first verse without bass, then the bass came in afterwards. He changed a line in it, which I didn't like. Aside from that . . .

JENNIFER WARNES, "RIGHT TIME OF THE NIGHT" (1976), *BEST OF JENNIFER WARNES* (ARISTA)

JIM ED NORMAN

I've always told young, aspiring producers, "Spend the vast majority of your time looking for material, the least amount of your time in the studio actually making the record. Making a record is not that hard. You don't have to be a genius to make a record. You're competent already. You're smart. You know what you're doing in the studio. The thing that will distinguish your work is going to be the kind of material that you bring to the artist."

As a producer, you find that the material that gets done in the studio is always a co-op between you and the artist. There've been very few times in my career as a producer that I tried to make an artist record a song when they didn't want to. Typically, when an artist is dead set against something, they're not inclined to render the kind of performance that it would take to make the song communicate and connect with people.

Jennifer Warnes didn't want to do "Right Time of the Night." I tried to intellectually express why I thought that song could work for her, why it had potential, how it could be done. "I would do my best to make sure that she got what she wanted," et cetera, et cetera. It took several dinners and meals to finally get her to kind of relax and say, "Okay, okay."

There's always a co-op between the producer and the artist when choosing material. Occasionally, you end up trying to press a little harder for a song if the artist is on the cusp, and you feel strongly about it, but you can only go so far. More typically, the artist can feel strongly about a song and feel that they really can render a performance. They want to do a song, while you as producer may feel less excited about its potential. You, then, assume your managerial, organizational responsibility and make sure that the artist gets what they're trying to get.

**JERRY LEE LEWIS,
"MIDDLE AGED CRAZY" (1977),
*THE JERRY LEE LEWIS ANTHOLOGY:
ALL KILLER NO FILLER* (RHINO)**

JERRY KENNEDY

A couple or three times Jerry Lee relinquished the piano to Pig [Robbins]. He's one guy those guys didn't mind saying, "Hey, take it." But like "Middle Aged Crazy"? That was a tough one for Jerry to get into for some reason, and I always had Pig there on like a B-3 [Hammond organ]. He'd do little pads underneath stuff that was going on. So it was easy to say, "Hey, why don't we move Pig over there [to piano] and let you concentrate on the singing?" That's the way that would happen. That worked fine with Jerry as long as I threw in "so you can concentrate on singing." Nothing about "This is a tough one for you to cut, man" or "This one's going to give you a problem."

CRYSTAL GAYLE, "DON'T IT MAKE MY BROWN EYES BLUE" (1977), *WE MUST BELIEVE IN MAGIC* (CAPITOL NASHVILLE)

ALLEN REYNOLDS

Crystal was Loretta's youngest sister, but there's probably fourteen years' difference in their age, and Loretta grew up in Butcher Holler. Crystal was born there and then moved to Wabash, Indiana. Her heroes included Loretta Lynn, for sure, and a lot of real sure-nuff country influences, but it also included Leslie Gore, Brenda Lee, and Joni Mitchell. As you get to know somebody, you acknowledge these influences. It helps you find the right kind of material.

Everybody was there, and they weren't too isolated. I like a little ambience. I had two keyboard players, bass, drums, acoustic guitar, and I don't think I had anything else. I'd have to double check. It was like a five-piece rhythm group, which is basically how I like to work—five or six pieces, on down to as few as one.

That vocal on "Don't It Make My Brown Eyes Blue" happened the first time we rolled tape. We had run it through maybe two or three times, and the first time we ran tape, we got that record. The only thing I did was add strings later. The only other thing I did was give Crystal time enough to come back and try to re-sing it and see if she could improve it, 'cause she thought she could. Ultimately, we left it alone. Those are the moments that you pray for.

Once you've got that moment, you've got to work at messing it up. If you're going to mess it up, you've got to really try. From then on, you can add something and take it off. Add something, and if it works, you keep it. In other words, you can putz around with it, but getting that moment of inspiration is the thing. Once you've got that, you've got a record. You can do many things to it to enhance it and then flesh it out. But you can never put that spark in there if it isn't there to start with. And if it is there, you can hardly mess it up. Least that's what I think.

Again, to look at "Don't It Make My Brown Eyes Blue," that identity lick on the acoustic keyboard? That was the gift of Pig Robbins, Hargus Robbins. When he threw that in early on, it was like everything gelled.

All of a sudden it just began to fall into place—everything. The drummer was doing this wonderful, real simple work with the brushes. The other keyboard player, Charles Cochran, who later wrote the strings, was playing the Wurlitzer. And if you listen to the record, the Wurlitzer is really playing the horn parts. But I couldn't have planned that lick or conjured it up. That took Pig. When that happened it was like magic. It was like sparks. Everything happened fast after that. That often is the way it is if you're working with good material to start with.

There's no measuring the contributions of Pig and many like him. I can't tell you how continually impressed I am. My engineer and I, after the sessions, we're working on things, maybe it's mixing, and we're shaking our heads in disbelief and in happiness at the work that these guys have come in and just tossed off.

ANNE MURRAY, "YOU NEEDED ME" (1978), *THE BEST . . . SO FAR* (CAPITOL)

JIM ED NORMAN

Fate brought Anne Murray and me together. It was a wonderful opportunity and a wonderful relationship. I was in the early stages of my production career. I had worked with Jennifer [Warnes] and Jackie De-Shannon.

"Right Time of the Night" was at this point out and on the air. At the same time, I was at Wembley Stadium conducting the orchestra for the Eagles. I'd written string arrangements for their songs. Backstage, I met Anne Murray's manager. He asked, "What are you doing?"

"I'm conducting the orchestra here, but I really want to be a record producer."

He asked me, "Have you done anything?"

"I've done only one record so far that you might be aware of—'Right Time of the Night.'" As fate would have it, it was playing in England at the time. The manager was Canadian, over there on some separate business. Back in Los Angeles three weeks or a month later, I got a call saying that Anne wanted to have a meeting. It turned out that she was a fan of "Right Time of the Night." Her manager told her that he had met me and that I was interested in producing.

We had a meeting. She had done records with Brian [Ahern], but in between Brian and me, she'd made about three albums. She had worked with Tom Catalano, a producer in Los Angeles who had done Helen Reddy. He had tried to make more pop-oriented records with Anne. In my meeting with her I suggested that—if she were prepared to go back into that mass-appeal, country-based thing—I felt like I could do a good job for her. If she still wanted to work within a pop arena, then I didn't think I would be the right person for her.

A couple of weeks later, her manager got back in touch. Anne wants to work with you on this next record. Let's work out the particulars." That album was the last album of her deal at Capitol.

Because of Anne's Canadian roots and the level of success she'd had, the deal that had been put together allowed her to choose the single, which was at that time unusual. It was a contractual provision, rather than a "we'll work this out together" thing. The record company, as always, trying to come up with something that was spirited and going to work in the marketplace, wanted an obvious, up-tempo, positive love song. Anne, the manager, and I reconnoitered and decided that for the next single we were going to insist on the song that was by the record company's notion a dirge. It was a song called "You Needed Me."

We were fortunate. While it was a long time coming, that record finally crawled up the charts. A female program director in Georgia (I think it was) started playing it on a pop station. It ended up going on to be not only a successful country record but a number-one pop record. Working with Anne at that point in her career, working together the way we did, going through that experience, really helped form a great working relationship between the two of us. We ended up doing ten albums together. Anne's voice is one of the best voices in the industry.

The first five or six albums we did were all done in Canada in Toronto. As I began to do more work in Nashville, I might've proposed the idea that we do some recording here, but I don't think we departed from our typical process, which was to cut a basic track live and then do Anne's vocal. I'd be left to organize all of the various and sundry overdub and layering kinds of things.

"Comping" is short for "composite." To comp a vocal is to cobble together the best bits of a number of vocal tracks to create one ideal recorded performance. This method of production is now standard practice for recording all popular music, having been automated by digital-editing technology.

MEL TILLIS, *I BELIEVE IN YOU* (1978, MCA)

JIMMY BOWEN

By the time I came into his life, he'd been making records for a long time and writing songs. What I felt he needed was a different rhythm section, with a new energy and a new excitement, working with him and vice versa. That was one of the things I needed to do. Mel hardly did anything unless he wrote it and/or his writers wrote it, because Mel was into publishing. When he first got to Nashville, that's what he learned. There's nothing wrong with it if you have good writers, and he had some pretty damn good writers. But I needed to get him a new rhythm section and a total new sound.

His music had been the same for ages, and I was changing instruments that I sweetened with. He'd never had any string sections. I put a flute on one ballad he did. I put on saxophones. Instead of one or two fiddles I had a whole section on a couple of things — different stuff.

Somewhere in the third year Mel asked me to come by the studio. He was taking his band in and recording some stuff for — I forget now what it was — a TV show or something. I got down there, and it was a decent-sized studio, but it was crammed full. I looked around. "Damn Tillis, how many buses you got on the road?" I think he had three. Every time I put something new on one of his records, all those strings, he added some strings, or a flute player. He didn't know you could get a keyboard player to simulate all of that.

"Bowen," he said, "by the way, don't put any new fucking things on my records. You're breaking me!" Because every time I added anybody, he hired somebody else for the road! Oh God, he was the funniest man that I worked with in Nashville.

We never actually had any way to change the tuning. Except with EQ sometimes, you could have your vocal come in on your board on two different tracks. For example, at one word where someone was really flat, you could take some frequencies and kind of exaggerate them [manipulating the pitch]. Then you threw in that one note, that one word or piece of word [on the corrected track], using what we called fine faders. For example, take the word "forgot." Well, "for" was great, but "got" was out of tune. So you corrected that second syllable the best you could [using EQ], and then with the faders, when the singer sang "forgot," you made a very fast switch. You threw in your corrected "got" and, of course, went back to the original track from then on. Then you could mess with the echo. But it was a real hard thing to do. You could never do it satisfactorily.

The artist was, of course, live. That was usually where the majority of the master tape came from. I'd give the band a break, and have him sing it two more times. Sometimes with Conway [Twitty] and a few other people, he'd say, "Let me have one more." So I had three or four vocals to work with. If there was leakage on the live track, you wouldn't allow leakage on the overdubs. Then I'd make a "best of" those three or four vocals. And again, you go back to that live one where that music is happening, but whatever is wrong, you fix that using one of the other two or three takes, with faders or switches. Nowadays, they just tell a computer, and it does it; they tell it once, and it does it forever. It used to take us hours to do those fixes. But I wanted to max out every piece of the record, and that was the way you did the vocal.

Mel Tillis was the first one I did it with down there. He came to one of the sessions where I was comping his vocal. "That's a . . . what's tha . . . how did you do that?" he wanted to know. But every time I took a vocal cut and did the combine, as soon as I finished, Mel had it. No matter which take I chose for the final vocal—it was always the best dub—the next time you saw him that's exactly the way he did it. Sometimes on stage with a live vocal, Mel played with the melody in different places, but not where I'd comped. I went to see him live, and he did it exactly like the comp. It was a win-win for everybody to take the time and spend the money.

MERLE HAGGARD, *BACK TO THE BARROOMS* (1980, MCA)

JIMMY BOWEN

I really liked Merle. He so distrusted anybody in Nashville, but I wasn't from Nashville. Maybe that helped. I caught him right on that cusp, like when I had Dean [Martin] and Frank [Sinatra]. The age was right. He'd already done to death what he'd done. You don't need big, but you need slight changes. With Haggard, he's just documenting his life. One of my favorite albums is *Back to the Barrooms* with "I Think I'll Just Stay Here and Drink." That project was great fun. I had such great musicians to work with down there.

What I did, I went out and got one of the live albums of Haggard's. I had the band there a couple of hours before Merle. We just sat and listened to him and the Strangers. I told them, "This week, you're going to be the Strangers, but you guys aren't the Strangers. You're not that old." Reggie Young could play country guitar like he knew everyone that ever lived. He knew how to play like them. We finished that album. Merle brought the band in, and old Roy Nichols, his guitar player, sitting on the couch, listening to the playback, he turned to one of the other guys and said, "Damn, I don't remember us doing that." He thought it was him! That's how good Reggie was. That's the way that whole album was done.

GEORGE JONES, "HE STOPPED LOVING HER TODAY" (1980), *THE ESSENTIAL GEORGE JONES* (SONY)

BOBBY BRADDOCK

Originally, when we [Braddock and Curly Putman] wrote it, we didn't have the recitation in there. We had the verse, and then the chorus came, another verse, and then chorus. Billy [Sherrill] wanted the chorus to wait, which sort of breaks a cardinal rule in songwriting. If you go pitch somebody a song, and it takes a long time to get to the meat of the song, sometimes they'll turn the player off and won't listen any further. But he wanted the chorus to come later; that was his idea.

Then we had a recitation verse that we wrote. Billy holds to this day . . . he believes they started recording that song a year and a half before it got finished. It took George that long. I keep journals, and that is absolutely wrong. I've tried to tell Billy that, and he will not listen to it. He's got it in his mind, and he believes it.

We wrote the recitation verse two or three days before they recorded in 1980. I remember Curly Putman and I going back and forth in the snow to Billy's office, taking him the different recitation versus. It took four or five until we got one that he really liked. So why would he, a year and a half before, say, "Let's add an extra verse here, just in case Bobby Braddock and Curly Putman happen to write a recitation a year and a half from now, which I have not yet asked them to do"? There's no way.

But the production . . . I think "He Stopped Loving Her Today" was a good song. I don't think it was the best country song ever written. But maybe it was the best country *record* ever made. I think Billy's production and George's singing elevated it. Billy had a reputation back then, with the critics, for what they felt were schlocky arrangements. They thought they were too embellished, there was too much instrumentation, and they were too slick. In truth, looking back on it, he's now thought of as the producer of some of the greatest traditional country music of our time. It's just traditional country music that was a little more sophisticated, a little more polished.

I tell people the best part of that record is the string section. They have this room full of cellos and violas and violins doing this ascending-movement thing. It sounds like the guy's soul is going up to heaven. That was Bill McElhiney's string arrangement. Billy [Sherrill] told me the recording sounded kind of flat; it just laid there. He thought, "This needs strings." Bill came up with the string arrangement. That's the best part of the record. The second best part is Millie Kirkham doing the "Angel of Death" vocal. And George performed perfectly. He's a great singer. He doesn't always nail a song, though. He nailed it that day.

Were you invited to that or to other sessions?

Billy Sherrill did not issue invitations to his sessions. He ruled his sessions with an iron fist. The only Billy Sherrill sessions I went to were when he asked me to come in there for a reason. One time, Kent LaVoie—who was known as Lobo back in the '70s—he and I wrote a song called "Our Boy George." It was about George Jones. Billy wanted George to record it, which made no sense to me. Since they didn't put it out, I guess it eventually didn't make sense to them. Billy wanted me to come in and sing it in George's key to George so he could learn it. And George was there while I sang it.

Another time he did a thing on Tammy Wynette, a song of mine: "They Call It Making Love." He called me up. He said, "I don't know why, but Tammy wants you to come in and sing this part you did on your demo. Come on in and do it." So I did.

Then, Deborah Allen and I wrote a duet for George and Deborah. He had me there for that. Nonetheless, those were for specific reasons. He didn't want people coming to his sessions.

GEORGE STRAIT, *STRAIT COUNTRY* (1981, MCA)

BLAKE MEVIS

One of the songs on the charts was Bill Anderson's "Still the One (Country Disco)." We did go ninety degrees to that, but it's a crapshoot. When a million people drive down and buy the record, you're right. If they don't, you're wrong. That's the way that works. You can't take it personally.

The way it came down was Erv Woolsey, head of promotion at MCA, knew George. George had sung at a club that Erv owned down in Texas. Erv approached me. At the time I worked at ABC, which was bought out by MCA. In fact Erv worked for ABC Records. I worked for ABC Publishing. We'd gotten to know each other. He approached me about cutting some sides on George. That's how I got involved initially.

We went to Texas to see him work, and at that point in time George did mostly Texas swing stuff, which was what that audience was look-ing for. I came back and said, "Texas is another country altogether." I love Texas. If I wasn't living here, I'd move to Texas. I love Texas. But I wasn't familiar with all of the Texas swing music, so it was an education for me as well.

MERLE TRAVIS, *TRAVIS PICKIN'* (1981) (CMH)

THOM BRESH

He called me and asked me if I'd do it. He was recording for CMH in Albu-querque at John Wagner Studio. [Label owner] Martin Haerle kind of let him do what he wanted to do. They did one album, the album prior to the one we did. I don't even know what it was called, but Travis didn't like the mix. I'd been producing Lane Brody and different things. He asked me if I'd come in and help remix it.

He said, "Everything's on top of everything."

So I went in and remixed it, and then he calls and says, "I want to do an album, just guitar. Will you come and produce it?"

"Sure." So I went to Albuquerque and, basically, you don't produce Travis. He knows pretty much what he wants to do. It's generally a mat-ter of getting in and ramrodding things. What I found interesting about the way he tried to work was he'd get in the hotel room at night and say what he was going to play the next day.

He'd play you a whole bunch of stuff. There's where I wish I'd had a recorder. If they had DAT [digital-audio tape] machines in those days, it would've been the record there, in the hotel room. There were no pres-sures. Him and his ice tea. Sitting on the side of the bed, he would play these incredible things. He had all these arrangements worked out, and they were just wonderful.

Then the next day we'd get in the studio, and because he was Merle Travis, the studio would start filling up with onlookers. Travis started getting nervous because there were people in there staring. I'd say, "You want me to get rid of the people?"

He'd say, "No, no, I've known this one for twenty years. You can't say anything to him. Just leave them alone." He'd go in there and he would play, and all of a sudden, knowing what he was going to do, he would all of a sudden get out in left field somewhere. He'd hit a note, and he'd wind up changing keys and off he'd go somewhere.

John Wagner, who was engineering, he and I would just look at each other, and it was like, "Uh-oh, here we go. What do we do?" We cut a number of things, and John and I, at the time, we were not happy. We couldn't get Travis to play what he was playing like in the hotel room. We'd get in the studio, and he'd kind of fall apart. This was his older days, keep in mind.

When the session was done, we said, "We can live with it." We cut, I don't know, fourteen or fifteen songs. We said, "We'll pick our favorite twelve out of these. Let's let it sit for a month or six weeks, and then we'll get back in here and try to edit things."

We got the tape, and I have to be honest: we felt somewhat disappointed, both of us—but especially me. I thought, "Gosh, I wish we'd gotten him to do what he did in the hotel room—flawless performances." So a month or six weeks after we cut it and listened to it the first time, they'd sent me out a tape, and I'm sitting there with a guitar saying, "How the hell did he do that?" I'm sitting there figuring stuff out.

All of a sudden, it became apparent to me that what I was waiting for and what we were all waiting for at the time didn't work—[when] if he got off somewhere, he'd just take off in another direction. We thought, "Oh yeah, he stumbled around through something." But things that we thought were train wrecks, six weeks later [they] turned out to be brilliant, and here it is now, when you hear people play them, they're playing exactly these things that were, at the time, "mistakes," and have now become arrangements—and very brilliant ones at that. That was quite a lesson. All of a sudden, John and I had a rough time deciding which songs to put on the album. It was one of those situations. And then it wound up getting nominated for a Grammy.

Travis called and said, "You know we're not going to win a Grammy, 'cause Chet's up for something. Whenever Chet's up for something in the country instrumental field, he gets it." But we were one of the five nominees.

REBA McENTIRE, *UNLIMITED* (1982, POLYGRAM)

JERRY KENNEDY

We just stood back and let it happen. She was a pro when she stepped into the thing. She knew what she was doing. But I was leaving [Mercury Records]. I'd set as a target that year to go independent. They didn't really know where to go; they didn't believe as much as I did in Reba. That's really all I know to say. If they'd really believed, I think she probably would still have been there. But the offer they came up with was not anything that would match . . . a lot of people don't know, but she was offered real good deals at several labels. Everybody in town believed in her except that bunch I was working with.

HANK WILLIAMS JR., "A COUNTRY BOY CAN SURVIVE" (1982), *THE PRESSURE IS ON* (CURB)

JIMMY BOWEN

When I got to Nashville, it was like, "Damn, I'm starting over again." It was financial. They weren't selling records. You can only spend X if you're selling X. Plus, that's why the music tended to get stale and to repeat itself way too much. You're in a hurry. Before I actually moved there, I used to go to Nashville to visit and look for songs. I'd go into the studio, sit in the back, and watch what was happening. One of the musicians would be a session leader. They'd use a number system so they didn't have a chord sheet—the gospel number system: the one-chord, three-chord, four-chord, whatever. He'd stand up and say, "Four bars of one, two bars of two, dada-dada; you take the fills in the first chorus; you take the fills in the second chorus; boom-boom-boom." They could nail those suckers. They could cut a song every forty-five minutes.

But where's the artist? Where's the music? Where's the hook? I came out of pop music. By the first four or five bars, you knew who it was. Every artist had an identifiable sound, even with big orchestras. With Dean [Martin], I used those thirty-second notes in the strings, and just wore them out. That's all in there on purpose. You were using a certain kind of sound. They weren't doing that [in Nashville]. On some of the sessions I saw, the musicians were totally in charge of what the music was going to be.

For me the recording process took a much longer period of time. It took thirty days to do an album. I don't mean a month. I mean thirty days. I never took off weekends. If I'd ever stopped on a Friday night at midnight or at two in the morning and hadn't gotten back until Monday, I wouldn't have known where in the hell I was. I wanted to do my own sound. So I just went straight through until we were finished.

REGGIE YOUNG

Before Bowen got here, producers would get, the majority of them, would get $250 per side. They tended to go in the studio and cut four sides. They could make $1,000, which in my opinion wasn't fair to the artist. They just wanted to get four songs cut. They could care less . . . I say care less, that's too strong to say. Anyway, they'd do four songs.

Bowen was from L.A. and already had big budgets. His theory was, he said, "You only need one record. You only need one song to get your career going." He didn't want to go in and cut four songs. Some aren't going to be up to snuff, unless you're really lucky and you got a really strong song that made it. He said, "We're going to cut just one song," and that's what he did. He did more sessions, which was good for me. I made more money, but it took him more sessions to do an album than cutting four songs per session. You used to be able to do three sessions and have an album finished. Bowen might take ten sessions to get the ten tracks he wanted—and even more to overdub and all that stuff.

He was very professional. If I went thirty minutes overtime, I got paid thirty minutes overtime. I was working so much. I remember, I guess it was 1979. I was talking to Joe Osborn, a bass player who moved here from California. I said, "Man, you could work three or four sessions a day, seven days a week, if you wanted to. I've got to have some home time."

"Go double scale," he said. I think he and [drummer] Hal Blaine did that in L.A. "So you lose half your accounts. You make the same money."

A light went off in me. Me and Larrie Londin, drummer, went double scale in 1979. It probably did cut my accounts almost in half. But then it built back up. It became a status symbol. "Oh, you're not double scale?" It became like, you're twice as good as everybody because you're double scale. Which wasn't the case with me. I even called my guitar-playing buddies here in town and said, "I'm thinking about going double scale. That don't mean I'm getting twice as good as anybody, because I'm not." I told them what Joe Osborn said: do half the work and still make the same amount of money.

Bowen loved it. He said, "I'll be getting fresh musicians all the time." He paid double scale every session I ever did with him.

We kept a rhythm section pretty much—me and Londin, Billy Joe Walker, John Jarvis played keyboard a lot. We had a basic rhythm section that Bowen used all the time, but we were requested by the artists that he cut. He'd always ask them, "Who do you want on this?" They'd always say, "The guys you use all the time."

JIMMY BOWEN

The way I did it with the guys, I didn't do your normal session. Everybody came two [o'clock] to five and six to nine—two sessions. But the drummer was really doing three sessions, because he had a session in front to get everything placed right, miked right, sounding right. But everybody came in early, before the actual tune. So they made some money for that. And then I fed them at five o'clock. I didn't want them, between five and six, going home, having a fight with their wife, and having a couple of drinks. When I got them together as a unit, I wanted them to stay that way all day. And I paid them double scale. I caught hell for that, but I asked, "If Reggie Young isn't worth double scale, why did they invent it? What's the deal here? Are we nuts?"

I started it in California and got in a lot of trouble for it. I was watching Hal Blaine do three sessions a day, and by the time he got to that eight-to-eleven session at night, he was exhausted. I got called in, because the guys—the money guy—at Reprise, the label, found out that I was paying double scale. He thought he was over me, which would've been true in the old hierarchy of record companies. But he wasn't the head guy; he was the money guy. He was quizzing me.

I asked him, "What did that album sell?"

"What does that have to do with it?"

"If I'm going to answer your questions, you're going to answer mine. What did that album sell?"

He picked up the intercom and called over. The album sold about eight hundred thousand.

"Okay," I said, "what if I told you I'll go back to single scale, and you sell four hundred thousand. You decide." I got up and walked out.

Of course, I told his boss, "You either hire him to make the fucking records or me. But I'm not ever going to meet with him again." Sometimes you have to make a stand. I knew what I was getting out of these people in California when they weren't tired. When I gave them double scale, they couldn't do a morning session. It was part of the deal. "Sorry, I want you this afternoon, at the start of the evening." They loved it.

People don't understand that every person a producer works with in the making of a record is an artist. I didn't hire sidemen. I hired artists. Reggie Young was an artistic guitar player. He was an artist. Billy Joe Walker Jr., I never heard a better acoustic guitar player—and he was damn good on electric. Larrie Londin on drums or Eddie Bayers on drums, Leland Sklar on bass, these people were artists. Now, the person paying for it all, of course, is the singer—the *artist*. But they're all artists. In some ways that viewpoint makes it easier, but for some people it makes it more difficult. Still, you're dealing with an artist with every piece of it, including the second engineer. You either have that ability [people skills] or you don't. I don't know where it came from, probably because I learned when I was twenty-six, twenty-seven, and twenty-eight from Sinatra, [Dean] Martin, Sammy Davis Jr., and those people.

GEORGE STRAIT, "AMARILLO BY MORNING" (1983), *STRAIT FROM THE HEART* (MCA NASHVILLE)

BLAKE MEVIS

George was already doing that song in his show. It was almost like the national anthem of Texas at the time. I believe a fellow by the name of Kelly Schoppa had that [record] out in Texas. [The song was originally recorded by Terry Stafford in 1973.] It was sort of a regional hit, not a national thing.

We put that on as the last song of the session. We had fifteen minutes left. We ran it down one time. We got ready to run it down the second time, to put it on tape, and everybody asked, "How are we going to end this thing?"

I said, "Just keep playing. I'll fade it, or I'll figure that out when we get finished—in the mix." So what happened is, we had enough time—because we just kept playing, playing, playing—we had enough time that I came up with the idea to start dropping instruments out and bathing the fiddle in reverb. The further we went, the more reverb. It would sound like it was fading off into the distance. It kind of symbolized what the song was all about. He was driving away. He's going to be there by morning. That's how that ending came on.

I'm proud to say I don't think I've ever heard a disc jockey interrupt it. They let it play till that last fiddle finally fades away. So that was one of those accidents that turned out good.

The musicians were isolated: some in booths, some had baffles and stuff. So we just cut the record. Of course, if you don't change anything, a little bleed-over is okay. You'll get a little of that sometimes, but it's okay as long as you're not changing that instrument later. As I recall, it had no overdubs whatsoever. It was a finished record when we got done—other than the vocal.

In regards to working with George, he's a relatively easy fellow to work with. Obviously, we parted company. I think the reason—and maybe that's why I'm so adamant about producers being less visible—is that George felt, at that point in time, that I might have been too visible in terms of trying to move him musically. To some degree, George has moved, but maybe not as quick as I wanted him to move. I'd be the last guy in the world to say that he was wrong about that. History has proven that he was right.

I'm proud of the work that we did together. I think he is too. We were growing at two different speeds and, maybe, in two different directions. But we've remained friends, and Erv Woolsey, his manager, and I are still friends. I'm proud of what we did, and I feel like we made a mark on music.

GEORGE STRAIT, *DOES FORT WORTH EVER CROSS YOUR MIND* (1984, MCA)

JIMMY BOWEN

One of the things I did, with some artists, I made them co-producer. I made them understand how important that part of the process was. I insisted that their part of preproduction was mainly songs. If you don't know what you want to sing, you're probably not going to last long. If you can't listen to forty songs and pick out the ones you like, which means you want to do them, you're not going to last long. With Martin and Sinatra I could walk in with twenty songs, and they would pick the ten they wanted, boom-boom-boom. Of course, they knew who they were. And they were in their second time around.

When I got with George Strait, it was the old Nashville: "Here are twelve songs. We'll cut next week, and use the best ten." I had a meeting with him, and I explained how that's terrible. It's not going to sell albums. I said, "I want you to be a co-producer, but you have to be the final say in songs. If there's a song I think is wonderful, and you don't feel it, then that's that. It's your record, your music." George grabbed it and loved it.

REBA McENTIRE, *MY KIND OF COUNTRY* (1984, MCA)

JIMMY BOWEN

With the process that I used, the first and most important piece of the puzzle was a song hunt, finding the songs. Unless you got lucky, like with Hank Williams Jr., who just writes about his life; that's great because you won't have to spend six months hunting songs. Tony Brown will tell you how long it takes to find songs for a George Strait album.

I had a man I grew up with, Don Lanier. His nickname was Dirt. All the musicians in Nashville know Dirt. Dirt's job was to take the artist to the song, when they had the time and would do it. That was his only job — songs, songs for every artist on the roster. Dirt's job was to hang out with publishers, hang out with songwriters, and to get the writers and publishers audiences with the artists. And then to try and make the artists understand the necessity of getting good songs. Almost all of them could participate, if they didn't have their own songs. For example, Reba would sit for hours in meeting after meeting to go through songs.

Usually, after three to six months, when that process was over, Dirt, the artist, and I would have a meeting. In the case of Reba, they'd play me what they'd found. Every once in a while, a song would come to me, and I'd give it to them to listen to; it would be in the pile. But mostly songs were from them. I'd listen to the song, and I'd rate the song from one to ten. I rated it in two categories: one was radio; the other category was POB, for "piece of business." When we got down to the final twelve songs, we needed to have three or four radio songs in there. You need to be on the radio. But the majority of music was what I called the pieces of business, which showed off the artist's talent. It could be a great song that you could relate to in your life, but it would probably never get on country radio. As we did that, how we got down to the last twelve songs, was to get a mixture of the radio songs and the pieces of business so that there was a thirty, thirty-five, forty-minute concert there. It would be interesting to listen to the whole thing. It was a lot more involved than just telling it, because there was tremendous give-and-take between the artist and me: "Would you open your stage show with this?" That was a huge part of the preproduction, which actually took the most time.

Reba took the songs once they were agreed upon. She had her own band. She'd go learn the songs. One or two of the musicians could work with her as she learned the songs. Sometimes — like with Steve Wariner — artists took their bands into the studio and made demos of songs. They took two or three people and made demos, figuring out how to make it theirs, instead of copying the demo. George [Strait] would take the songs, live with them, and learn them himself.

Rarely did we ever get to a session and, when we laid it out for the musicians, the artist was there but needed developing. I'd almost force the artist to go out and get with one of those guys — get with the rhythm section. Of course, in country that's most of the record. But get with the guys doing the basic track and have the artist to comment, "I like this. I don't like that. That feels good. That doesn't feel good." I wanted to make it a thing they all did together. Each artist did that to different degrees.

VERN GOSDIN, "I CAN TELL BY THE WAY YOU DANCE (YOU'RE GONNA LOVE ME TONIGHT)" (1984), *THE TRULY GREAT HITS OF VERN GOSDIN* **(MUSIC MILL)**

BLAKE MEVIS

I think my job is to find songs that fit the artist or, maybe, at least to expose that song to the artist—let him decide. It might be a stretch. I'm also a believer that the duty of artists, the record company, the producer, and radio is to look for the edge. Now, the edge becomes the middle real quick, though sometimes an artist doesn't feel comfortable going as close to the edge as, maybe, a producer might. Ultimately, that decision has to be the artist's.

They're the ones who get up in front of the audience and perform. If it doesn't work, they're the ones stuck up there for three minutes singing a song that doesn't work. So a producer has to be sensitive to that information. But at the same time, the artist has to be sensitive to the fact that the producer's intentions, hopefully, are to go out and sell as many records as possible.

Sometimes an artist will feel a little like, "That song is not me." My thought on that is if you feel uncomfortable, then don't even think about doing it. But if there's only a little bit of discomfort, maybe try it. Maybe stylize it. Vern Gosdin didn't really want to do "I Can Tell By the Way You Dance," but it was his first number-one record. He went out and sang it one time. He said, "It'll never be a single." It turned out to be what he needed at the time. But when we were recording it, he was thinking, "I don't know if this is me or not." So it's a compromise and a negotiation. It is a compromise between staying where you are and looking for the edge. Sometimes that's scary.

MEKONS, *FEAR AND WHISKEY* (1985, QUARTERSTICK)

JON LANGFORD

Making art about your immediate environment, that's what immediately connected me with punk rock when that happened, which we were doing instinctively, writing songs about that. When I got into country music, I realized that's exactly what country music is doing. It's addressing the real world, in even humorous or poetic ways. There's a real attempt to take the world head on, to explain it or at least have a conversation about the real world. It's not like moon-in-June Tin Pan Alley, or progressive rock, faux–*Lord of the Rings* shit. It's people's lives. That's why the best country music strikes a chord, and the best punk rock is like that. It strikes a chord, points the finger, points at some hypocrisy, explains the world to you a little bit.

The whole thing about punk for me was that there aren't any rules. We made a manifesto when we started in the band, saying we'd only do this, and we'd only do that. It was pretty funny to see how fast all those things got torn down. It's kind of funny to do that: to make some rules, to have parameters. But the people I hang around with, immediately once you do that, the parameters become where the action is: people pushing against them.

A lot of times my personal taste comes down to hearing things that actually sound like a band playing in a room. But we've made records that don't sound anything like that. At the moment, money is an interesting thing. I do think the record industry is kind of screwed. And for bands like us, we can't really afford to spend a lot of money making records.

I did a project with an aboriginal country-and-western singer [Roger Knox, *Stranger in My Land*, 2013], which involved going to Australia and coming back: "Okay, I'm going to make something that's artistically very good, or I'll think it's very good, but it will never make any money." You've got to realize you're making art. That's the way I always think of it. That would be the only ethic. If you're thinking, "How well is this going to do on radio?" you might as well shoot yourself in the head, because I have no idea. I wouldn't know a hit song if it bit me in the ass.

REBA McENTIRE, "WHOEVER'S IN NEW ENGLAND" (1986), *REBA McENTIRE'S GREATEST HITS* (MCA)

JIMMY BOWEN

There are times when something hits you, and you communicate it to a musician. Sometimes it was a feel thing in part of a piece of music, or in all of it. You'd feel real strongly, and you communicated that to the guys. They always tried it. Sometimes it worked; sometimes it didn't work. But the key for me, to generate ideas, was getting five or six guys — we're talking about Nashville now where you don't do the arrangements; the arrangement happens between the musicians for the most part — that's why I took all that time to get those phones so wonderful to where they could hear what each other was doing. They'd get involved, and the artist was so important for this. Many times I played for them — before the artist ever got there — I played pre-demos when the artist made them. But I played them some things by the artist that I really liked. Sometimes I didn't have that, but when I did, I'd play it for them. If I had any live tape on an artist, I always played that for them.

When you've got great talents in that room — the artist and five or six other artists on the instruments — you'd be amazed where the great stuff comes from. Because they're not doing what they did this morning with artist X. The way we did it, that earlier artist is clear out of their heads. They're concentrating on just this artist; they're working with this artist.

What happens, of course, is a sound develops for Reba McEntire. A sound develops for George Strait. The sound part of it is very subtle, but the arrangement and the musicianship and how it's done is very apparent. The sound is very important, too, but to the average listener, they don't go, "Wow man, the bottom end of that guitar sounded good." They're absorbing the overall. So it pretty well took care of itself, if you set it up so that it could. It's almost like you take a bunch of those cones you put out on the highway. You set it up, and you can make cars go anywhere you want. It's not that simple, but it's almost.

STEVE EARLE, *GUITAR TOWN* (1986, MCA)

TONY BROWN

Guitar Town was the beginning of my tenure as a producer at MCA. I call myself a spiritual advisor and joke about it. My strength is I know when I hear something that sounds right. I brought Emory [Gordy Jr.] in on Steve and on *Patty Loveless* specifically for his arranging abilities. [Gordy co-produced both albums.] He's hands down, to me, the best country bass player in the world. His sense of country music is like . . . he knows bluegrass inside and out. He knows traditional country inside and out. And he knows pop music.

I'm there for my ears and to be the objective person: Does it sound commercially viable? I'm there to let the artist know that I'm the artistic part of the music. I'm definitely compassionate too, and so, being a musician myself, I definitely love that. But I found out that Emory naturally thinks commercial anyway. Where I aspire to think that way a lot of times, Emory just thinks in terms of hooks and good arrangements.

Emory brought in Richard Bennett. That's where Emory's arranging skills were great. Richard's Danelectro guitar was the defining sound of Steve Earle's music. When Emory got with Steve Earle, I think he heard that in his mind. Emory and Richard Bennett went back; they'd played with Neil Diamond together. So that became an important call—that Emory brought Richard Bennett in.

I always thought commercial music meant it had a hook. It had a great chorus, instrumental hooks, and all that kind of stuff. With *Guitar Town* I found out that not everybody at that time was quite ready for a voice like Steve Earle's, which was more, in their minds, more of a rock voice, like Tom Petty or Bob Dylan. To me, I thought he sounded like a Waylon [Jennings], but to them he was more like a Springsteen, that sort of rock-attitude voice. That was the thing that made it noncommercial in their minds. The songs, lyricwise and musicwise, were very commercial, I thought. Plus, Steve, his whole persona, was a bit edgy for commercial music at the time.

The sound of that album came from Emory working with Steve, from Steve hearing those lines, and then Emory bringing in Richard Bennett. He gets those sounds. He owns all those vintage guitars and those vintage amps. He's studied Duane Eddy. That lead line on "Guitar Town"? That's Richard Bennett. That's his forte. In other words, to me the two things that good producers have is the ability to cast the right people, as far as musicians and engineers, not only for their musicianship but for personalities so they don't conflict with the artist. The other thing is the psychology of how to make those musicians perform for the artist.

LYLE LOVETT, *LYLE LOVETT* (1986, MCA), *PONTIAC* (1987, CURB), AND *LYLE LOVETT AND HIS LARGE BAND* (1989, CURB)

TONY BROWN

I got involved with Lyle Lovett when MCA Curb signed him. I was the A&R person in charge of that project. Lyle brought in that first album, which was more acoustic than it was big-band stuff. But on that first album were a couple of tunes with horns. Those were his demos.

Lyle came in, and they had me set him up with some different producers for interviews. Everybody that was anybody back in 1985, whenever we signed him, I put him with those people. I could tell—if these were his demos—I could tell the guy was very knowledgeable about music. So I thought, "He needs to at least talk to Emory [Gordy Jr.]," who's a great musician and who writes. He can orchestrate. He's very knowledgeable. And to Barry Beckett.

Lyle came back to me. "Everybody wants to recut these tracks, but I just want to mix them."

I said, "Man, I don't blame you. They sound great to me, too."

So he said, "Will you help me mix them?"

"Sure," I said. "Let's just go through them and make sure." The tapes had been laying around for a while out in Arizona. We replaced a couple of acoustic guitars that had some leakage on them. It was my idea to put fiddle on "Cowboy Man." I had Roseanne Cash sing with him on one song, "You Can't Resist It." That was really all we did, and then we mixed it. I really had nothing more to do with the making of that album except for that.

The second album, which was *Pontiac*, had more horn stuff than the first album. By the time I got to *The Large Band* [1989], it was really skewed that way. But a lot of that stuff was laying around when the first album was made. That's what I found out later.

And so we went out to Arizona and re-demoed or demoed everything that was on *Pontiac*, and as opposed to mixing that, we came back to Nashville and recut it. That way we could cut it digital. Then on *The Large Band* we did the same thing.

But I found out all this stuff was in Lyle's brain. Plus, along with him came this guy named Billy Williams. He was a third producer on those records. Billy was a horn arranger. A lot of those ideas were his ideas. I started noticing how people play key roles in certain artists' music. Billy was a big part of that. In fact Billy is still involved with Lyle Lovett today.

Someone says, "Why haven't you found another Lyle Lovett or Steve Earle?" Well, those kinds of people don't come down the street every day. Back in that period, when [Jimmy] Bowen had first taken over MCA, the way he ran the company and the way he thought about A&R was let the artist run free. You help the artist do their music. That was his whole theory.

So when I heard Lyle, I wouldn't have known what to tell him to do different. What I heard just blew me away. I kept going, "Man, how'd you . . . ? You did that yourself?" When he asked, "Will you help me finish it?" my first thought was, "Hell, yeah, man, I'd love to have my name attached to this project."

Then I was really curious, and so when it came time for the next record, I wanted to know how he did it. I got to go to Arizona and watch how he put those demos down out there in that little studio. There was one horn player playing all the horn parts. They weren't written out. It was like they were head arrangements. It made me learn that all that stuff was in Lyle and Billy's head.

The label at the time, [Jimmy] Bowen, wasn't asking me anything like, "You need to take this and work this and pull horns off of this." See, Bowen was such a maverick. I'm afraid we won't have those times again.

Bowen just said, "Sounds cool." Like me, he said, "Incredible, amazing. This is nice and fresh." Now, I think if Lyle were to come into town today, somebody would be asking me to take the horns off of it. Or the first album had "The Wedding Song" [aka "An Acceptable Level of Ecstasy"]. It had a line that used the word "niggers." We pressed the record before we realized. And Lyle has always had black people in his band. The way the song was written, it wasn't a put-down to black people, but we asked Lyle to change it. We removed it. But there were a few copies that actually got out.

That was a big eye-opener for me to work around people like Lyle and Steve who really were free spirits. I didn't know any better than to have some blind faith back in those days. Now I've learned just enough to be dangerous, to question somebody.

NANCI GRIFFITH, "LOVE AT THE FIVE AND DIME" AND "GOIN' GONE" (1986), *THE LAST OF THE TRUE BELIEVERS* (NEW ROUNDER/PHILO); KATHY MATTEA, "LOVE AT THE FIVE AND DIME" (1986) AND "GOIN' GONE" (1987), *WALK THE WAY THE WIND BLOWS* AND *UNTASTED HONEY* (BOTH UNIVERSAL/ MERCURY)

JIM ROONEY

I did two albums with Nanci Griffith. The second one, *The Last of the True Believers*, we all felt when we were doing that record that we were doing something very good. I mixed the album at Jack's Tracks [Recording Studio], which Allen [Reynolds] had bought from Jack Clement, with its real echo-chamber and everything.

Allen heard us mixing the songs quite a bit. He really liked "Love at the Five and Dime" and "Goin' Gone." He had started working with Kathy Mattea, and in the course of time she recorded both of those songs.

I was at a point with Nanci—we were on Rounder Records—where she wanted to move to a major label, if possible. MCA was interested in her, but that was a closed shop. Jimmy Bowen was running the label. If she went with them, I wasn't going to be able to go with her to produce the records. I was trying to find some alternative, and I met with this very wonderful man, Jim Foglesong, who had run several labels. At the time he was at Capitol. I asked him if I could have an appointment, and I played him those two songs of Nanci's. He was very complimentary. He thought it was very good material—good songs, good singing, and good production—but he didn't think it was going to succeed in country radio the way things were, with people like Barbara Mandrell and Lee Greenwood having great success. He was very honest with me, and I appreciated his honesty. The upshot of it was Nanci went to MCA, and Tony Brown started producing her.

Meanwhile, Allen took those two songs and recorded them with Kathy Mattea. "Love at the Five and Dime" became her first top-ten single. "Goin' Gone" became a number-one single. I listened to the difference between Kathy's record and the record I'd done with Nanci. I kind of preferred the record I'd done with Nanci, but I understood what the difference was. It was all in the bottom—heavier drums, an electric bass, heavier bass, and a little more aggressive approach to the songs.

DWIGHT YOAKAM, *GUITARS, CADILLACS, ETC., ETC.* (1986, REPRISE)

PETE ANDERSON

Editing in the broad sense: Dwight and I talk conceptually when he's writing a song or we're doing a song. A lot of times we'll do it over the telephone. He'll call me up. He'll grab a guitar, and I'll grab a guitar.

He'll say, "I'm doing this" or "Check this lyric out."

He'll use me as a sounding board. I'm not a co-writer, but I'm able to go, "Oh man, that's great, but that second line?"

"Yeah, yeah, I'll fix that."

"What if you went this way?" That happens. Getting through making *Guitars, Cadillacs Etc., Etc.*, there was a lot of editing involved. He's a quick learner. He's like, "I won't do that again." But it wasn't like every time he wrote a song we had to go, "The intro's too long. Your bridge is here, and this goes there." No, he's flawless. He brings you songs that are jewels. They are finished, and they are done. Very much like Michelle Shocked, who's a great songwriter. She brings you finished little jewels. There's nothing to say, "Oh man, this lick should be here." They're done when you see them.

With an artist of Dwight's stature, I have to afford him every opportunity to make a record that is competitive with everything else. Technology has afforded me the ability to keep exciting, live-feeling performances that may have some flaws in them that, up till now, I couldn't fix, or that I couldn't fix without damaging them in some way. Actually, my records now feel more live, more exciting. If I get what I like and one word is out of tune, or one word doesn't work right, I can move it around. I can fix it. I don't have to ask the artist to sing it again, sing it again, sing it again, punch, punch, punch, punch. But you have to know what you're doing and how you do it. These things are tools; they are not the rules. It's not, "Okay, everybody get on your computer suits. Everybody get rigid in line, and do what you do." In fact, you can be more relaxed: "Oh, I can fix this. Oh, I can fix that." So everybody's a lot looser.

We're fortunate that we're all old-school musicians who had to do it the old way. Maybe we're not as old school as the guys in the '50s and early '60s who had to do it perfect. You talk about amazing. Listen to Buddy Holly or Elvis Presley or any number of records recorded in the mid-to-late '50s and early '60s. They're perfect. They're flawless. And that was live! Everybody had to be great.

Living in Los Angeles, we work with technical people who don't have preconceived ideas of what's supposed to be "country" music. They may work on Rob Zombie one day or Mötley Crüe. When they work on Dwight, I specifically preface, "Don't go out, start listening to country records, and come in here and start working on this shit. I want you to do what you do." We work in studios that are wide-ranging. In Nashville they make great records, but they've pretty much got a little factory down there. There're five or ten or twelve studios that you're going to make a great sounding record, but there are going to be similarities with other records.

KEITH WHITLEY, "MIAMI, MY AMY" (1986), *THE ESSENTIAL KEITH WHITLEY* (RCA)

BLAKE MEVIS

He'd done a little album with Norro Wilson on RCA, and then they asked me if I'd come in and cut the next album. The first thing we cut was a mini-album. It had six sides on it. At that time RCA was experimenting with six-sided albums with some of their brand-new artists. Then the "Miami, My Amy" thing came out, and they asked us to go back in and cut four more sides and make it a full album.

Keith had that magical quality. First off, he was an incredibly wonderful human being. You could not work with Keith Whitley without being his friend and truly caring about him. He was an incredibly talented singer. He had an incredible range. Unfortunately, as we all know, he had the disease of alcoholism. It seemed like when things were going the best, Keith had the toughest time. In his defense, Keith hated the disease as much as anybody. But it was a disease, and he couldn't control it. He fought it really hard, but for some reason, it won—sad to say.

RESTLESS HEART, *WHEELS* (1986, RCA), AND ALAN JACKSON, *HERE IN THE REAL WORLD* (1989, ARISTA)

SCOTT HENDRICKS

You just know, when some things get there, you say, "Whew, we may be crossing boundaries." I can remember a specific example of this. I remember a certain feeling that I've had many times in my career when recording something before anybody else had ever heard it. The first time was the first Restless Heart record. I remember when we recorded that, it was like, "Man, this is really . . . this is not at all what we're hearing on radio. I don't know if this will work or not, but I sure do love it."

The same feeling happened on Alan Jackson, total opposite end of the spectrum, when we were recording the *Here in the Real World* album. It was like, "Man, I don't know if country radio . . . even though this is country, it may be too country for radio, but I love it." It was a feeling like you're sneaking out of the house and getting away with something. Those feelings have turned out to be pretty good in the end because I guess that was the feeling that it was truly different.

MERLE TRAVIS, *ROUGH, ROWDY AND BLUE* (1986, CMH)

THOM BRESH

He did an album that we started at my house in about '82, I guess. He was in Tahlequah [Oklahoma], and he came out [to California]. Matter of fact, he came out because Merlene was getting married at the time. So Travis came out. He was going to be at the wedding. And he was in really great shape. He was in love. He was crazy about life again. It was quite a nice time for him.

He got out there, and he said that he had an idea for an album. We had a twelve-string guitar in there. He said, "Let's go in the studio and lay these things down for me. I want to do an album called *Black and Blues*." He said, "I want to do the old, black blues songs that I learned as a kid, when I'd sit around and listen down around the coal mines. You'd get around black people; they'd all be sitting around with guitars. They had these wonderful songs that they used to do."

He wanted to do them in the dialect and use licks on a twelve-string. He purposely made sure that the guitar was a little out of tune. We cut about a half-dozen songs, because he wanted to show them to Martin Haerle [head of CMH Records]. So he asked me to record that—which we did.

He took them to Martin, and of course Martin said, "You can't put 'black and blues' on an album cover." They went in and redid it, and the final album [*Rough, Rowdy and Blue*, 1981] was one of the last albums he did. But he did all these dialects. Again, we were at my place very calm, very happy, and he did them. Then when he got into Albuquerque and borrowed a twelve-string guitar, and everybody stared through the window, there was something that didn't really work about it. Even Travis at the end said, "We just couldn't get that same thing we got there at your house. You should have put some of them out." But a lot of people thought, "What? Was he drunk? How come he . . . ?" They didn't understand the concept of him trying to do the dialect. He'd tell the story and then do it. But it sounded like his twelve-string was all out of tune, and he was blowing meter and everything. People asked, "What's a matter with him?" It was a concept. That part was taken away, the concept, in the deal, because "you can't do that, and you have to do this, and you have to do that."

LUCINDA WILLIAMS, *LUCINDA WILLIAMS* (1988, CHAMELEON)

GURF MORLIX

I had been playing [lead guitar] with Lucinda in front of fifteen people in Hollywood, doing these stupid little gigs for a few years—kind of wasn't going anywhere. She'd given a copy of a demo tape that she had done in New York to this guy Robin Hurley at Rough Trade Records. He played it all the time because he liked it. He played it walking to work in his headphones. He decided that he'd sign her. So it just fell into our laps. All of a sudden: "Here's a record contract."

"Who's going to produce?"

"Why don't you guys do it?"

"Okay, great! That's no problem." It was the songs that she had and that we'd been playing for years. We pretty much had them all arranged. It was really easy. The record took about two weeks to make. We did it on a shoestring with a deadline.

Production to me is just common sense. It's like figuring out if something is not working, don't do that. We did a little bit of tailoring in the studio, but not very much. When I go into preproduction rehearsals— like three or four days of going over the songs—the arrangements fall together. That's common sense too. I can tell when it's not working and change it so that it is.

 **MICHELLE SHOCKED, *SHORT SHARP SHOCKED* (1988, MERCURY)**

PETE ANDERSON

That's my favorite record. If I have to grade myself . . . it's hard to say that grade yourself is what you do with a record. I know the state of projects when I get my hands on them, and when they are done. Sometimes I don't do anything, and, sometimes, I do everything. You can't always tell until you witness the whole process. That was a magical record. It just came together. It was fast. The spirit was great. It was a really great project. The whole record was done in, like, twelve days. It was so fast.

You close out the album with a bang—the punk rave-up.

"Fogtown," the track that's not listed? Michelle is a bit of an anarchist. She's politically active without a political policy, agenda, or country. And it's fun, and she was fun, and she was young. We had a great time working together, and this was her first real record.

She said, "I've got my friends. They're in a punk band called MDC."

MDC would change what that meant: Millions of Dead Cops, Millions of Dead Christians. They just made up their name as they went along. But they were called MDC.

"I want them to play on this record," she said. She played me something. It was really trash. I had worked with her long enough on this project to know that she was into shock value. "My friends are in town," she said, "and I want them to be on the record because they're my buddies."

Everything is wrong with doing this. You don't let the bass player play on your record because he's your cousin and you owe him a hundred bucks. [You don't] jeopardize your career. "He's my uncle. He should fly the plane. I told him he could."

"Can he fly a plane?"

"I don't know."

He's going to kill all of us.

She said, "My friends are in town, and I want to do a song. We went last night, and we rehearsed up the song 'Fogtown.'"

"I'll tell you what," I said. "You really want to shock people? I'll tell you what. We're going to set up. Bring your band in here right now." We were in the middle of recording . . . whatever we were doing. "Bring 'em in here right now. You get two takes—*live*. And one of those two is going on the record. You pick."

She was like, "Really?"

I went, "Yeah." And then she was kind of scared. I wasn't going to go into a long production thing on this track because these guys couldn't play. So she brought her buddies in, and they're all nice guys.

They go, "Wow."

"Yeah, set up man. Get your stuff. Okay. Got good sounds on everything? You guys ready? Run it down. Okay, let's go. Rolling tape."

We did two takes. She picked the one she liked. I said, "You like that one?"

She said, "Yeah."

I looked at my engineer, who was not my mixing engineer, and I said, "We're going to lunch. Mix it." We walked out of the studio, and three hours later it was done. "Put it on the record."

CLINT BLACK, *KILLIN' TIME* (1989, RCA)

JAMES STROUD

Clint Black's first album, that's a very rough-played album. It's not an amazingly well-played album, but it's a real album.

I was actually trying to take myself out of playing so much here in Nashville and start producing. But I couldn't get anybody to work with me because everybody thought I was a player, a drummer. So I started taking my own money and making my own demos with artists that I'd sign.

I worked with three guys—Tom Schuyler, Fred Knobloch, and Paul Overstreet—who are great writers, by the way. I signed them and put together a group called S-K-O. We had a number-one record called "Baby's Got a New Baby." That was a demo that turned into a master record that I produced.

Clint heard about it and liked the song. Clint met a friend of mine, and so he came to see me. He sat down and played me some songs. I flipped out. I told him absolutely I wanted to be involved. I met with his management company. That's sort of how it went. I did tell him, though, that I had an idea. I wanted not to use studio players here in Nashville. I wanted to use his band.

We went to a little town outside of Houston, Texas, to a little club. For about ten days, during the day when the club was closed, we set up on the bandstand, and we worked his album up. We tried different arrangements; we tried different tempos and stuff. Then at night we played the album to the people. Whatever stuck—when they got up and danced or when they applauded—we kept that song. If something didn't work, we threw it away. We picked our songs by doing that, and we went into the studio and cut those very same arrangements. We cut it as a band. It was like a territory band. The licks and stuff used on that record were very Texas.

We were ready to go. We went into the studio in Houston and set the band up just like we did when we'd been rehearsing. We got it as band-y sounding as we could sonically and then let them play. That's how we cut the record. It was a magical record. It used a process that had not been used in a long time. As a drummer, a session drummer, I'd always thought, "If I have a chance to make a country record, I want to make it with the band that went out on the road with the artist." That's where we went with it.

KATHY MATTEA, "WHERE'VE YOU BEEN" (1989), *WILLOW IN THE WIND* (POLYGRAM/MERCURY)

ALLEN REYNOLDS

Kathy came out of a more folky, even bluegrass, side of things. That was a factor when I was looking for material for her, to some extent. You're always asking and wanting to be sure that you're seeing the artist the way they see themselves. In some way, I guess you help them see themselves. But as much as possible I'm going with the songs that appeal to this person and also sound good to my ear, and sound like they would play well out there to a lot of people who make up that imaginary audience in my mind. I feel like I'm a part of that audience. Songs say things about the artist who presents them. I'm trying to measure how attractive any given piece of material is. I think everything flows from that.

On a lot of the most successful records I've been involved with, the vocal went down largely the day that it was recorded. Maybe you do a few fixes. But that was true of [Crystal Gayle's] "Don't It Make My Brown Eyes Blue." It was true of "Where Have You Been?" with Kathy Mattea. It was true of a great many Garth Brooks records.

I tell the artist before we go to work, "Don't be in there trying to give me a tracking vocal. I want the vocal. I want you out there flying like everybody else is." If you can get that moment, to me it's a discernible difference, and it's the thing that's most precious.

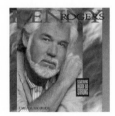

KENNY ROGERS, *SOMETHING INSIDE SO STRONG* (1989, REPRISE)

JIM ED NORMAN

There was a song that Kenny felt real strongly about, its potential, a song called "Planet Texas." He had this extraordinarily strong feeling about what it could be. Its images, he thought, were very striking, and he thought it would appeal to and connect with people. Right away, the business side of me got concerned: "Okay, I've got to support Kenny to the best of my ability, work with him in every way that I can to make his vision for this thing come alive. At the same time, I need to bring to it characteristics that I'm confident will be appreciated or accommodated by country radio." Ultimately, that's where we've got to go with this—country radio and to the consumer who would typically buy a Kenny Rogers record.

Why would they be compelled to buy this song from a guy who they've grown to know and, maybe, even love as a purveyor of story songs on the one hand, but who has more recently, on the other hand, trended to "Lady" and more pop-oriented material? In my mind, I'd seen him coming back more to the mainstream.

We ended up doing a song called "The Vows Go Unbroken," a piece of material that, to me, was going to work right down the pike for country radio, and be believable for Kenny as well. It was something that I felt people could accept from him. When you get an artist of Kenny Rogers's stature, it's almost as if there's a certain kind of song he can't do anymore. People know too much about the artist. There's material—things he could do—that would prove to be unbelievable coming from the artist: for example, if Kenny were to try a blues song about being down and out. It would fly in the face of your sensibilities about him. So in this case "Planet Texas" was a song Kenny felt really strongly about. It became the lead track on the album [*Something Inside So Strong*].

In the end your job as producer is to accept that you're working for the artist. Your responsibility is to the artist, number one. But you're always trying somehow to complement the aspirations of the artist with the record company. They've signed the artist and put up the money. They have expectations about what's going on in the studio and what's going to be accomplished with this music. Marry those two responsibilities together with your own sensibilities and aspirations. Realize, though, that your responsibility is first to the artist and then to the company. The phrase we use is "We live at the corner of Art and Commerce Streets." We try to do as good a job with that as we can, all the time.

I talked with Kenny, essentially about this notion: "Now that you've done all these songs, you've had a couple of records that haven't done well. Again, if you would find it appealing, try to go make some music that would be more geared, really, to country. We wouldn't try to come up with a record that can be all things to all people, a crossover thing, so it can get played on country and pop, but something that would be clearly geared soundwise, in an exclusive way, just to country radio."

He said, "Yes, I'd find that appealing. Let's go do that together."

In an effort to come up with material and a sound and a style that would leave no doubt that this was not a vain attempt to come up with a crossover kind of record, we ended up with "The Vows Go Unbroken." Its character—and having Ricky Skaggs doing background vocals on it—meant that we'd done all we could to erase any sense that Kenny was trying to make a record that was designed—once it had explored what it could do in country—to cross over into pop. On the very first record that we did together, we did a reasonably good job of that.

GARTH BROOKS, *GARTH BROOKS* (1989, PEARL)

ALLEN REYNOLDS

Garth had a good sense of who he was. That's one of the things I look for in an artist. He already had been gathering a lot of songs and writing a lot of songs. So with one exception, all of those songs that were in that first album came from material that was already gathered or written by Garth. That includes "The Dance." He didn't write that, but he had heard it sung at a writers' night and was blown away. He'd asked the writer for a copy. Then, when he passed it on to me, he didn't say, "Here's a song. I think it's great." He just gave me a boxtop lid that was kind mounded up with a bunch of cassettes.

I had said to him, "If you've got things squirreled away, I'd love to listen through them." In that batch of tapes was a song called "The Dance." It knocked me over.

With Garth a lot of songs were available. It was a matter of working through those songs and exploring them and getting to know him— 'cause this guy was different from anyone I had worked with. He was more western. The rodeo culture was a real part of his life. And at that time that was real uncommon in country music. They used to call it country and western, but they quit that a long time ago. I think a lot of the western aspect had kind of gone out of it.

Garth and I spent a lot of time together. It's my job to zero in on who the artist is and, as best I can, understand them and what they want to project and help them examine and refine that—see how we make that presentation. So the persona that was Garth was me trying to help present what I perceived to be the real, essential Garth, by working with material that seemed to describe this.

What I always do is this. It's a very simple device, and I've done it from way, way back. It is probably the most helpful single thing I've done. When we gather a group of songs that the artist and I feel is good and have promise, then we go into the studio with just a guitar player or just a keyboard player, whatever we decide on. And we make work tapes.

We don't try to refine them or spend a long time nitpicking. We try to find a good key and make a casual recording of the artist singing that song. It's astonishing how much you can tell about how that song fits the artist. Plus, you also get a key that's a good working key for the song to be in.

And then, when we go to the studio, I like to play those tapes for the band—rather than the demos. A lot of times the demos will set them off in directions that you'd like to improve on. I'd rather present them with just the song—with the singer and one instrument. Then we start from there building our arrangement.

In Nashville the musicians that you call, arrangements are really their gift. It's their skill. So I'm trying to be a catalyst and achieve some kind of unafraid atmosphere down there so that people toss out ideas. The arrangements—I may have a fallback position in my head—but the arrangements are really conjured up on the floor. A great deal of that comes from the musicians and their interaction with the artist. I may be throwing ideas in, or I may be over at the side just being real quiet at times, allowing things to happen. Ultimately, I have to be the guy that makes sure something happens, but it's easier if I'm there with the right ingredients and everybody is prepared and I know the right few words to say. Then these guys, the musicians, go to work, and wonderful things start to happen, if you don't get in the way of it.

GARTH BROOKS, *NO FENCES* (1990, CAPITOL NASHVILLE/LIBERTY)

ALLEN REYNOLDS

Fortunately, we didn't have any constraints. I'll tell you why. Jimmy Bowen was running the label, and Jimmy's a controversial music industry figure — was then. But I'll tell you one good thing he did. He went to see Garth perform, not too far away from Nashville. It was in Cookeville, a hundred miles or so away, at a college. And it just knocked him sideways. He was so impressed.

After that, he talked to me. He asked me about the album and what we were doing as we were beginning to get to work on it. He said, "Look, whatever you do, just bring me as much of that guy I saw on stage as you can get on the record. Just give me as much of that guy and that energy as you can get."

So this was wonderful. That's not the kind of mandate you get from record labels as a rule. They're usually more conservative. I can say that was one thing that was very helpful that Jimmy Bowen did. At that moment in time, he said, "Let it out. Let it rip."

I knew by then what this guy was doing out there on stage, and then we had these great songs to work with. We had things that were so rangy, like from "The Thunder Rolls" to "Friends in Low Places." Fun things like "Two of a Kind, Workin' on a Full House." It was just a delight because we had material that came from a place, but it was real expansive — pushing the walls. And it was fresh.

And I had a record label saying, "Don't be conservative for us. Don't worry about country radio. Pull out the stops and do what you want to do. Bring me as much of that guy I saw on stage as you can get on record." It was never pressurized.

I think an album ought to be like a show. Though you may never do it, it ought to be a piece of work you could take the stage with and do it from cut one to the last cut, in that sequence, and hold your audience's attention. I don't believe in album cuts. I think every song is important. Every song is a single, though you can't put them all out as singles. But every moment that happens is a part of the dynamic of that show. That's just how I look at an album.

I positively hate albums that have two or three hit singles that got you to buy the album, and when you buy it, the rest of the stuff in there sounds like they were trying to cut the singles. When they got through, they just dumped all that in the album. I think an album should be paced—different tempos, different subject matter, different keys, different musical feels—so that it's a real show. So you start at cut one, and you don't want to stop listening till it's over. And then you want to start it over again. Whether I achieve that or not, that's always my goal.

Do you spend much time on postproduction fixes?

I don't mind overdubbing. But I don't go in thinking that's what I'm going to do. We added the thunder, for one thing, in postproduction. Garth asked, "Could we do that?"

I said, "Sure." As it happened, Mark [Miller, engineer] and I had done, for our own enjoyment, an instrumental album about a year before and had put thunder on one of the cuts. It was a real nice mood thing. So we found some great storms and added that to the track, and it really deepened the mood a whole lot on that cut. But yeah, you're always doing "post" work. And of course in my case, and I guess it's the way most people work, you're doing overdubs to enhance the track or to flesh them out.

But I never, ever have an artist come in and sing a song eight times and then do what they call comping. That's gotten to be common practice around town. The artist pops into town and hears the track. They sing it eight times on eight different tracks, and then someone says, "Don't worry your pretty little head. We'll comp it." Then they start taking pieces of words and putting it together, and I never, ever, ever, ever do that—ever, ever.

You always try to do no more than necessary. I'm one of these people who doesn't want entertainers to yell at me and cram me. I'm that way about music or movies or anything else. I like for them to have a little respect and have a little dynamic range, instead of just yelling because they're afraid I'm going to tune out. If they do that, I will tune out. So in making records, I'm always trying to not get in a hurry to fill up all the nice holes.

I keep it real simple. I have real simple qualifications that I'm trying to live up to, time after time. It's a thrill if things go out there and sell like that, but the next time has nothing to do with the time before. I'm just trying to make the same good swing every time.

SUZY BOGGUSS, *ACES*
(1991, LIBERTY)

JIMMY BOWEN

Any time I first worked with an artist—well, the first thing was to see them in person—but in the studio you go in with just the artist, maybe with one of their musicians or with one of yours, and try all the microphones that you can find. Different voices came across better on different microphones. With Waylon Jennings . . . You ever hear that big old baritone voice—big and huge? If you stood next to him, he was singing soft. The microphone enhanced what he had.

But I found with women [that] many of the microphones that worked great for the male artists didn't complement the female voice: could not stand the dynamics, sometimes, when it was way high and smaller and more piercing. You had to work and work until you found the best microphone that did the best job. It's like being in an operating room. Over time, you keep breaking everything down so that it goes quicker and better. That's one of the things I ran into early. In California I didn't do many female artists, but I did enough to realize, "Uh-oh, there's got to be a better sound for her than that."

If you got too close to some microphones with some voices, it started turning into a negative. There was a spot where it was right. But since the artist is wearing the earphones, they hear when it's right and they hear when it's wrong. They move themselves forward and backward 90 percent of the time. When they didn't do that—maybe they couldn't tell or maybe they had their phones set wrong—you'd record a song and have them change their position with the mike all during the song. Then, bring them into the booth and play it for them.

They'd go, "That's the one I want."

"That's when you were six inches away."

I was a fanatic for getting the best sound I could get from every instrument. The better you make the musician sound, the better he or she will play for you. That's just human nature. That's one thing. Plus, I wanted the best sound I could get on the drums. I always had the drums come in one hour or an hour and a half ahead of the session. We'd work on the drum sound, each piece of the drum—the bass, the kick, the hi-hat, all of the cymbals, all the toms. You would use different mikes on different parts of the drum.

Some of the people in Nashville thought we were absolutely nuts. When I first got there, hell, they didn't even use drums on some stuff. For years they wouldn't let drums on the Grand Ole Opry. We played there in 1957 [as the Buddy Knox Trio], and they wouldn't let our drummer bring his drums into the building. When I moved to Nashville, they had an isolation booth for the drummer. The singer might be out in the room singing. I said, "Wait a minute! This is backwards. I want the drums out here so they can breathe. You can't stifle them. Let's put the singer in a room, isolated for obvious reasons."

Each instrument should be that way. I worked in the earphones. I put the earphone mix together in the earphones. Many engineers would knock themselves out on those big studio speakers while mixing the earphone mix. You can't relate the two; they're totally different.

Once I got the drummer sounding right, I had him mixed in the earphones perfect. Then I added the bass, got him sounding right, which is always easiest and quickest, usually. Then I put him in the mix in the earphones. Then the guitars and keyboards and whatever I was going to have. In the last few years of my career, each musician had an earphone box. One and two were stereo channels. The next six, everybody was on them individually, in case anyone wanted a little bit more of somebody. In our sessions you rarely saw those last six used at all; everyone was mixed into the earphone mix. It was almost like a perfect stage mix as we were doing it. I always thought that was terribly important when it came time to do the music.

Isolating musicians during the recording process allows a band to work together in the studio, and it enables the creation of separate tracks (i.e., tracks without bleed). But there's a problem. While recording, the musicians don't accurately hear each other. The solution that Bowen describes requires musicians to wear headphones (earphones) and to monitor the output of their bandmates via a mix.

MARTY BROWN, *HIGH AND DRY* (1991, MCA)

TONY BROWN

That's one of my favorite albums I ever did. When I met him, I went up to his house in Kentucky. That album was about capturing this guy on tape. That's what we did.

When I heard Marty, I brought him to the label to play. I said, "Check this out." I knew he was so hillbilly. Everybody loved him. I said, "Should we do a record on this guy or not?" Bruce [Hinton] said, "Sure, let's do it." We stuck Marty in that car and sent him around to all those Wal-Marts and stuff. I'm so glad I had the guts to do that. I don't think we lost money on the project. We probably didn't make any money. When I look back on some defining moments for me in the studio, one is cutting that record. 'Cause that guy, trust me man, he's a trip. He's from the holler. He really was singing wide open.

HAL KETCHUM, *PAST THE POINT OF RESCUE* (1991, CURB)

JIM ROONEY

I met Hal Ketchum through Jerry Jeff Walker. Jerry I've known for a long time, since he came to the Newport Folk Festival in 1969. "Mr. Bojangles" had just become a very big hit. Later, but before I went to Nashville, I became sort of an opening act for an agency that represented Jerry. So I opened shows for him. We're very good friends.

I did a couple of albums with Jerry. First, he was re-cutting a lot of his songs on his own label. He'd done some stuff down in Austin, and he asked me to do some things with him in Nashville. This was a record called *Gypsy Songman*. Then we did a live album at Gruene Hall, which is in Gruene, Texas. It's one of the great old dance halls. Jerry was telling me about this fellow, Hal Ketchum, who he'd heard on the Austin public station KUT, singing a couple of his songs. Jerry immediately recognized him as a really good songwriter and as a really good singer. He started to have Hal open shows for him. So I heard Hal, and he and Jerry were coming to Nashville to play at the Bluebird Café.

By this time I'd had the idea to start a publishing company, which was based—in my mind—on the kind of company Jack Clement had. We'd been in business for, I suppose, three or four years. I asked my partners to come and hear Hal. They were all impressed. I'd met Hal with Jerry two or three times before. He'd already made an album in Texas [*Threadbare Alibis*]. There was a guitar player and a producer in Austin named Brian Wood. He'd done a couple of albums with Nanci [Griffith], her earliest albums, and he also did an album with Hal. He makes good, nice acoustic-folk records.

I said to Hal, "If you ever want to make some demos, feel free to come up." We didn't tie him up to a contract or anything like that. I'm very leery about these business things. That was something I was very clear about with Iris [DeMent]. If I'm your producer, that doesn't mean I'm going to be your publisher, manager, or anything else. If something comes out of it organically, fine, but some people have these deals where, if I'm going to produce you, I'm also going to publish your songs and do a few other things. I don't like that approach.

Hal did take us up on our offer. A month or two went by. He came up. He had some songs, and I got three or four players together in Jack's Tracks Studio, and we recorded him. As soon as I heard his voice in an atmosphere I knew well, the studio there, I said, "Boy, he's a great singer, too!"

We liked his songs. We decided to sign him as a writer, but it had come into our heads that he could get a record deal in Nashville. (Eventually, that did happen.) So now, I was going to be working with Allen [Reynolds] on Hal's record [*Past the Point of Rescue*]. We used the same drummer that Allen had been using on Kathy Mattea's record, Milton Sledge. Milton was a good, solid, good-hitting drummer. And Bob Wray was the bass player. He gets a great big, fat-bottom sound. He's a lovely player. We also had Richard Bennett, who played really good rhythm guitar.

One of the first songs we recorded with Hal was "Small Town Saturday Night." It was a song we published, which Pat Alger had written with Hank DeVito. Pat had made the demo with a sort of Bo Diddley beat on it. We'd tried to get this song recorded for two or three years, and hadn't had any luck. Something was missing. We started out with Hal. He was doing it the same way he'd learned it on Pat's demo.

Richard got up out of his chair and walked over to Hal, and with his guitar went "voom-voom-voom-voom-voom-voom-voom." "What about that?" he asked. He straightened the song out. It was the difference between a song with a life or not. That taught me a lot as a publisher and as a producer. That's why I say I like the ideas to come out of the musicians as much as possible, because they are really good. I've been in sessions where producers are telling people when to play, what not to play, and what to play. It's no fun.

Hal was a great guy to work with. He didn't second-guess us in any way. He let us go. He trusted that we'd come up with something, maybe, that he could get played on the radio. That was my only experience with doing that kind of album. [Co-producer] Allen, of course, had a lot of experience.

BROOKS & DUNN, "BRAND NEW MAN" (1991), *BRAND NEW MAN* (ARISTA)

SCOTT HENDRICKS

When we [Hendricks and Don Cook] did Brooks & Dunn's first record, "Boot Scootin' Boogie," I thought, "Man, I don't know if this will ever get accepted, but it sure is good."

A year or two before, I'd recorded Ronnie Dunn after he won the Marlboro Talent Contest. Part of his winnings was forty hours of session time in Nashville to do a couple of songs. Barry Beckett produced that session, and I engineered it.

I fell in love with Ronnie's voice and his songs. So I maintained contact with Ronnie as he was living in Oklahoma. One of the songs that we cut was "Boot Scootin' Boogie." I've cut that song three times now. When we got through, I took the tape to Tim DuBois, who was at Arista. I was an independent producer.

I said, "Man, if you don't sign this guy, you're crazy."

Well, he didn't sign him, and about a year goes by or so, and Tim plays me a tape. He says, "I want a duo on my label, and Don Cook brought me this guy, Kix Brooks." Tim said, "I've got this other guy in mind to be his duet partner." He played me four of Kix's songs, and he played me about four of this other guy's—who I shouldn't mention.

He asked me, "What do you think?"

I said, "I'll be brutally honest with you. I don't hear the combination. I don't think it works."

I just happened to have Ronnie Dunn's tape with me at the time. I pulled it out and said, "Once again, I'm going to play you this and try to convince you into believing that this guy is an unbelievable singer. Maybe, he's the perfect guy for that match."

Tim listened to it and immediately said, "I think you're absolutely right."

Then he facilitated Kix and Ronnie getting together. That's how we got there. In the studio, I was more or less responsible for Ronnie, and Don was more or less responsible for Kix. But we both worked on everything together. They were fun albums to make. Nobody stepped on anybody's toes, and I think everybody contributed. The chemistry between us was, possibly, part of the reason why it worked, though our chemistry was definitely far shy of Kix and Ronnie's individual talents.

You know that tape I played Tim, when he was playing me that other artist? On that tape was "Boot Scootin' Boogie," "Neon Moon," "She Used to Be Mine," and one other song: three of the four songs on that tape were number-one songs. Without a doubt, it's easier for a producer when the artist is a writer of the caliber of Kix and Ronnie, or the caliber of Alan Jackson. Nobody's going to write much better songs than they are.

The hardest part of making a record is the songs and determining the direction. One of the easiest parts of making a record is recording it. That is largely due to the musicians that we have in this town. They're so unbelievable I can't even describe them. They seem to get taken for granted more than they should. It's just that with the musicians that we've got, it's relatively easy to make a record.

DON COOK

That was the first major-label project I ever produced. I was brought in because of my songwriting abilities and because Tim DuBois liked what he'd heard that I'd done in the studio. He wanted to have a songwriter that he'd known for a while be a part of the process and take a little bit of the pressure off the act finding songs, 'cause it's so hard to do on an ongoing basis. That's really why I was brought in.

That particular song ["Brand New Man"] was written by Kix and Ronnie and me after we'd already chosen all the songs for their first album. It was written right at the end of 1990, right before the holidays. We were all in kind of a good mood. We had our fifteen or sixteen songs picked out for the first recording, for the first album that we were going to do in February of '91.

That was just a bonus that we wrote. We were all sitting around at my house, and as we'd been doing for many, many days before, we were brainstorming and writing. Kix and Ronnie had this song that they'd run at several times. They'd never gotten it to come to life. They threw it out on the table at that meeting. We finished it and sang it in my music room around the little round table that I have there. We all knew instantly that it was a real marketable piece of material. We ran over to Arista and played it for Tim DuBois. He was very excited by it too. It ended up being the first single. But we were in a neat little zone where we really didn't need a song. We wrote it for the right reasons.

I was the one that added to the mix, figured out a way to make the chorus work, kind of came up with the chorus hook. That's what I brought to the song. At the point they brought it to me, it had one version. When we got through that day, it had two.

Our target, when we did that album, since none of us had really done what we were about to do, we decided to pick a sort-of workable target for that first B&D album. It was, "Let's make an album that the people from the places that we're from will like." That's Texas, Louisiana, and Oklahoma. That was our target. We weren't really concerned with demographics other than that.

Well, to make an album for Texas, you have to have dance music. There's just no way around it. You've got to have some. It just evolved that way. It was something we talked about once, and we never reminded ourselves of it again. It was sort of an operative guide, at least for me, in the creation of that album. It served us well. But coming up with something that would appeal to our target audience, we appealed to a lot more people in the process. It was a great way to start a production career.

PAM TILLIS, *PUT YOURSELF IN MY PLACE* (1991, ARISTA)

PAUL WORLEY

Except for one artist in my life, I've never worked with an artist that was already developed. I'm thinking of Collin Raye, who already had quite a good career going for himself. But Highway 101, the Desert Rose Band, Pam Tillis, and Martina McBride, they're artists that I got involved with from the beginning.

I signed Pam. I was working at Sony Tree Publishing at the time. So I signed her and was involved in shopping her deal to Arista. The pressure for me was that I really wanted to succeed. I wanted it for Pam. I wanted it for me. I wanted to show the world that I could do something like that. That never changes. I feel that way now about every artist that I work with.

But my belief is, the more you try to hold onto something, the more likely it's going to get away from you. People need to grow. I was really happy to do Pam's first two albums. That's some of the best music I've ever made. It just made sense for everybody to move on at that point in time. I would work with her again in a heartbeat because I think she's an amazing talent.

REBA McENTIRE, *FOR MY BROKEN HEART* (1991, MCA)

TONY BROWN

Reba has a lot of vocal licks that she does. There was a point where she and I talked about maybe straightening out some of those things if it didn't make her feel like she was being restrained. Like say, "Hey, maybe we can watch some of those things."

She might look at me out of the corner of her eye, but I've noticed that she started thinking about it. It wasn't that I was trying to make her stop doing anything. I brought it up because I'd always thought about . . . I just know no better than to do that.

I never like to restrain an artist, but a lot of times artists don't even realize how many things they do, when they're in concert, are more show kinds of deals. A live performance is not a record performance. In fact, a lot of people say, "Well, I like 'em live better than on record."

But the thing about it is, a lot of times I find myself telling artists . . . they say, "The tempo's too fast." I say, "When you get on stage, you'll speed it up anyway, but for the record, this is the right tempo." There's show tempo. There's record tempo. And there are certain attitudes that in concert you do 'cause you have to be bigger than life in concert. But on record if you go over the top, it almost always becomes abrasive in some way. I watch those kinds of things, but if I see for one second that I'm interfering with the psyche of the artist, then I back off, big time. That's the one thing that you don't want to do.

JIMMIE DALE GILMORE, *AFTER AWHILE* (1991, NONESUCH/ELEKTRA)

STEPHEN BRUTON

He knew me in Austin. He said, "I get a good feeling off you, man. I think I want you to produce my album."

I was, "What? Yeah, I'd love to. Sure, but are you sure?" Primarily, I was just a player. I was in New York. I did a very, very brief tenure with Bob Dylan. I was up there rehearsing, and I went to see Jimmie at the Bottom Line, just walked in: "Hey, surprise! Good to see you."

"Good to see you too. Want to produce my record?"

In all honesty, it was a pretty logical extension of what I'd done. I grew up in a record store. My parents owned one. My brother and my mother run it now. In other words, when I hear music—I've heard so many different styles of music and been involved in so many different styles of music in my career playing—a lot of things don't throw me for a loop. Also, I can draw on stuff that I've heard that a lot of people didn't hear, didn't have the chance to hear. When you're living in a record store, you hear very obscure stuff, and you hear stuff that's not the norm. You say, "Well, this reminds me of McKinney's Cotton Pickers. We should have that kind of track." Nobody knows it. That was the other orchestra, besides Duke Ellington, that was killing everybody up in New York in the '20s and '30s. There're little things like that where you can draw, that you don't think about while growing up.

Jimmie pretty much had all his songs picked. We had the luxury— really a great luxury on that particular album—because it was on a major label, to have some representative things. He didn't want to go back.

I said, "Well, look. As long as we're doing this and it's kind of a fresh start, why don't we pick out a couple of songs that you've done before, but let's do them differently?" A lot of times people do records, and they do them stylistically. They do all of the songs a certain way. One way I produce is I try to find where the song wants to go. I don't suddenly take a song that has one feel and then put straight eighth notes in it and call it a new-wave song. But songs, if they're good songs, can be interpreted lots of different ways.

There was a song here and there that he'd done, "Tonight I Think I'm Gonna Go Downtown." We did it completely different than it had been represented before. We did another song—"Treat Me like a Saturday Night"—using a completely different approach. And then there was the song that ended the album ["Story of You"]. We did it with piano. That's the way I heard them. Jimmie let me go with it.

A couple of times he thought, "No, that's not right."

"Let's just try it. Can't we try it this way?" I kind of put my producer's foot down. But I always try to do it where it's collaborative. In other words, I don't try to iron-fist it in any way and say, "We're going to do it this way, goddammit." I say, "Just try it this way, and tell me if it doesn't work for you. Live with it." A producer should have some vantage point that the artist trusts, admires, and respects. He should bring that to bear on songs.

An artist might have a song that's basically just the way it is. But maybe the producer can come in with different versions. You know, "This sounds great. Let's see how the song sounds real fast. Why don't we slow it down—cut it in half? Let's hear it in another context." People who write songs, including myself, will write a song and that's the way it goes in our heads. Well, that's the way it goes in *your* head, but everybody else might be hearing something else.

Unlearn is a good word for it. Another word is to discover the song again. Say it's a song you've been playing for a couple of years. Every time you play it, it's reinforced in your head: "This is the way it's going to happen on the record." I walk in and go, "That's a cool song. I really like that. I don't think it should go that way." Then, that's the first thing that makes you think, "Uh-oh, we're going to have a problem here." Better, get everybody together and say, "This isn't etched in stone. I'm not going to stomp my feet and make you do it this way. Just try it and see what happens." A lot of times, the song becomes a new song to them again. If the songs are there, they're going to reveal themselves. That's why a lot of times producers don't want people to record with their bands: they get stuck in a certain arrangement, stuck in an approach that's hard to get out of because that's the only way they hear something.

A lot of times, when you're producing, the real art is being able to tell somebody what you want them to play and then actually getting them to play it—pretty much make them think that they thought of it so they discover it again. They really are playing it, but you're getting your point across, not your vision, but just the way you hear the song.

14. Jerry Wexler and Willie Nelson at Muscle Shoals Sound Studio.
Photo by Dick Cooper. Courtesy of Paul Wexler

15. Waylon Jennings and Tompall Glaser at Hillbilly Central, Nashville. *Photo by Leonard Kamsler*

16. Steve Cropper. *Courtesy of Steve Cropper*

17. Allen Reynolds. *Courtesy of Allen Reynolds*

18. Jim Rooney.
Photo by Jim McGuire.
Courtesy of Jim Rooney

19. Tony Brown.
Photo by Gregg Roth.
Courtesy of Tony Brown

20. Pete Anderson. *Photo by Nelson Blanton. Courtesy of Pete Anderson*

22. (*above*) Stephen Bruton.
Courtesy of Dos Records

21. (*left*) Jim Ed Norman.
Courtesy of Jim Ed Norman

23. Blake Chancey.
*Courtesy of Blake
Chancey*

24. Gurf Morlix.
*Photo by Lynne
Hawrelko. Courtesy
of Gurf Morlix*

25. Paul Worley.
Photo by Vanderbilt Photo/
Daniel DuBois.
Courtesy of Paul Worley

26. Eric "Roscoe" Ambel.
© *Jim Marchese*

27. Jon Langford. *Photo by Barry Phipps. Courtesy of Jon Langford*

28. Jack Clement and Sam Phillips in Sun Studio, Memphis, 1990s

29. Ken Nelson and Cliffie Stone. *Photo by Joan Carol Stone*

INTERLUDE

THE WRITER AS PRODUCER

AN INTERVIEW WITH BOBBY BRADDOCK

Best known as a legendary songwriter, Braddock has seen at least one of his songs top Billboard's country chart every decade for the last fifty years. Among his compositions are "He Stopped Loving Her Today" (George Jones),"D-I-V-O-R-C-E" (Tammy Wynette), "Time Marches On" (Tracy Lawrence), and "I Wanna Talk about Me" (Toby Keith). He worked as producer on Blake Shelton's first five albums.

• • •

Basically, I am a writer who wanted to prove that he could produce, and my background as a writer helped me in a couple of ways. I often hear an arrangement when I write a song. So I got a reputation for doing demos that sounded like records, and often the records (such as "Time Marches On" and "I Wanna Talk about Me") sounded like my demos. When I started producing, I just used those producer/arranger skills that I had honed as a songwriter, the big difference being that you spend much more time making real records than you do demos; therefore, it becomes hard work and not as much fun. Also helpful to me as a producer were my likes and dislikes of how the producers had treated me as a songwriter over the years. For example, I made it my policy to get in touch with every writer or publisher who had pitched me a song for Blake Shelton, even if we were passing on the song (which 95 percent of the time we did), because I wanted them to know that the material had been listened to and that the pitch was appreciated. They weren't used to that, and they loved it. My motive was partly ulterior: I think this resulted in more good songs coming our way.

*In your autobiography [*Down in Orbundale: A Songwriter's Youth in Old Florida*], I notice you enjoying the way people talk—pronunciation but also the rhythms and melodies of speech. Tell me how this ear for the everyday has served your life in music.*

My literary mentor, [prominent journalist] John Egerton, tells me I have a good ear for the vernacular. I used to be able to guess where people were from, back before people started sounding the same. But speech is still an individual trait, like a fingerprint—you mentioned the rhythms and melodies of speech. So I suppose that a musician or creative person might be more keenly aware of that.

As a result of your career as a writer and also as a recording artist, you occupied a unique position where you were able to observe a number of producers at work. What different styles did you witness?

My perch of course is Nashville. There is the hands-on production style, which is pretty much how I did it. Billy Sherrill did that, and so did Owen Bradley. Both of them were musicians. Billy Sherrill was also an engineer and a songwriter. *Billboard* has a way of scoring writers in points, and he's right up there at the top. Practically all of Billy's songs are songs that he produced himself, but they wouldn't have been hits if they weren't hits. He came at it well armed from all of the different origins of producers: writer, musician, or engineer—he was all those things.

I would be reluctant to say much about producers from this era because, still being a songwriter-whore, I don't want to offend any present-day producers. I'm at their mercy. But from that era, I think Billy Sherrill and Owen Bradley towered way over everybody else. They were the kings. And oh yes, there was Allen Reynolds. He was a great one too.

It is said that Chet Atkins had a tendency to let the musicians work things out for themselves, even though he was a great musician himself. And you know what? That works too. There have been some producers who don't know jack shit and, somehow, that seems to work for some of them.

How did you come to learn what a producer does?

My tenure as a producer was just a few years. Basically it was with one artist. It was pretty successful, but there was just that one artist. He had the biggest debut single in ten years ["Austin"]. So there's not a lot of quantity there.

I swore I would never do it again; it's equal parts love and hate. Working with Blake Shelton was a delight. Going into the studio and record-

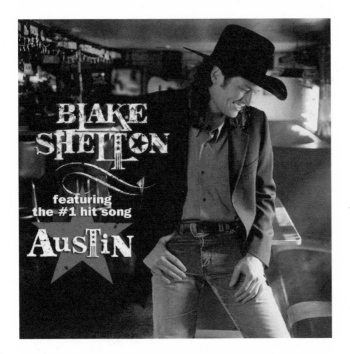

ing, I absolutely loved that—the creative process and coming up with arrangements. But a lot of the bullshit that goes with the political trappings, I didn't like that at all.

Having to listen to a lot of songs can be pretty grueling. The really great songs are a pleasure, the really bad ones are fun, the in-betweens are so boring. To me, the comping was just awful. I hated that. The engineer, Ed Seay, and I had to create ways to make it fun. Blake was a part of the comping process too, until he got so hot that he was out on the road all the time. Then he left it to us.

Did you come to produce Blake Shelton because you already knew him or because Warner Brothers approached you?

They wouldn't have approached me because I was an old songwriter. They wouldn't have even thought about me. I have a friend, [author and songwriter] Michael Kosser, who was running a small mom-and-pop publishing company called Gosnell Music. He was a good friend of mine. He told me about this kid. "You ought to be producing him," he said. I had a lot of people tell me, "You should be producing because your demos sound like records." I knew they did, and I knew I would love to produce. But I never really had that avenue to go down.

He called me up one time and said, "I want you to hear this song." I didn't pay that much attention to the song, but I asked, "Who is that singing?"

"That's the kid I was telling you about—Blake Shelton. He's the guy I was saying you should be producing."

I said, "Well, I want to meet him." We met, I liked him, and he really liked my demos. He wanted me to produce him. So I went, and I cut a few sides on him.

I peddled him up and down Music Row. I went to the first-choice label all the way down to the last choice. The last one I went to was Giant Records—not that it wasn't a good label, but I had heard that they were about to fold. I went there last, and that's where he landed. Everybody else had passed on him.

Giant did indeed fold. They folded a week or two after Blake's record came out. It came out only because there was a guy named Fritz Kuhlman—he was a promotion man—who committed mutiny. He knew the label was going to fold, and he sent Blake's record out to radio. It raced up the charts as they folded. Blake had a hit record and no label. The short version of the story is Warner Brothers picked it up.

But back to the beginning: when I took it to Giant Records, Doug Johnson, a man of few words, said, "I like it."

I said, "I've got him up in the mix more than most artists are. He's kind of in-your-face."

He said, "I like it." So that was it.

Did Giant, and then Warner Brothers, give you the freedom to do the job you felt should be done?

The record label had never told me how to do my job. Warner's Nashville president, Jim Ed Norman, though he was a notable producer himself, never told me how to produce or how to mix. When Warner fired Jim Ed, super-producer Paul Worley temporarily filled his position. Paul told me, "You guys are cutting great hit records. I think the best thing I can do is stay out of your way," which he did.

Then along came the new team. First was Tracy Gershon in the A&R department, who from the beginning started telling me how to do my job. Soon a permanent replacement for label head came along, Tracy's fellow L.A. friend, Bill Bennett. When I turned in Blake's fourth album—which I had told Blake would be my final one because I wanted to focus more on songwriting and authoring—Bennett and Gershon told Blake that he had to bring in a new producer to cut several sides. This happened right after one of Blake's biggest hits, "Some Beach."

People all over Music Row, including some of the leading producers, were asking, "Why did they fire you? You guys were making great records together." Bill Bennett said, "I don't understand what all the fuss is about. People in the music business get fired all the time." I had known Tracy for years, and she had always been friendly to me and continued to be after my departure, so I got no special pleasure out of her losing her job at Warner Brothers a few months later. But when Bill Bennett lost *his* job, I must say that a little smile did cross my lips.

Is it true that you wrote "I Wanna Talk about Me" for Blake Shelton?

I did indeed. I wrote it about a female friend of mine, and I wrote it in that style because I wanted to write a rap song for Blake. He was going around doing this very dirty, very funny thing that he had made up. It was very funny—this Oklahoma white boy doing this rap thing. He did it really good. I thought, "He would be a good rapper. I'm going to write this thing for him."

We recorded it. Giant liked it, but they did research on it. This was before they knew they were going to fold. Research came back bad: "Not only would this not be a good single, it should not even be on his album. Nobody likes it."

So I took it to James Stroud for Toby Keith. He and Toby loved it, and of course it was a big hit. Blake never got over that. He still hasn't stopped talking about it. He said he's still scratching his head over that research. He always says, "Research—whatever that is."

I think they do it with a Ouija board.

I'll tell you what they do. They play portions of it over the phone for people. Which is pretty stupid, I think. It has nothing to do with the song in its entirety.

It's not especially surprising that James Stroud would be interested in "I Wanna Talk about Me." He was a drummer.

And a good drummer. The head of A&R for his label: my publisher pitched the song to her. She said, "Not only am I passing on this song. I hate the song." And James didn't listen to songs. He produced so many people that he didn't have time. I cornered him in a market and said, "Give me about three or four minutes." I had him in a corner. He called his assistant and said, "Give me five minutes with Bobby Braddock." He loved the song.

At the number-one party, his head of A&R sidled up next to the song plugger. She said, "I still hate it." That's okay.

I'm guessing that there was plenty of preparation
for recording Blake Shelton's debut.

I came up with arrangements, and Blake would come over to my house. We did pre-session rehearsals with the musicians, but Blake would come over to my house the night before. I ran everything by him, made sure he was on board with my arrangements. I felt the time for us to disagree was in private, not in front of the musicians. Being a musician myself, I always had a lot of respect for the musicians. I never used the Nashville-cute term "pickers." I always called them players or musicians. In fact I went to battle with Warner Brothers when they wanted to pay the musicians single instead of double scale—and I won. They knew I stood up for them. I always had a good rapport with the musicians, and Blake being so funny, they got a kick out of working with him. We had a good thing going with the musicians and with our engineer, Ed Seay. With any of those elements missing, the one you could do without the most is the producer. No matter how good it is, if you have a bad engineer, it's going to sound terrible. And we had a great engineer.

I might mention one little trick I employed during my tenure as Blake's producer. In those days, the labels would cater lunch for the crew; it was figured into the budget. Whenever I called the caterer about the menu, I always made certain that the lunches would be low in carbohydrates so the musicians wouldn't get sleepy or sluggish on the afternoon session.

I certainly had my weak spots as a producer. One was harmony. Though I usually had a basic idea for what I wanted background vocals to be doing, I'm not really great about picking out harmony parts. I really have to work at it. And I'm not great at modern technology, not really good at taking files from my little studio to transfer at the big studio.

As I've said, my strongest production attribute is probably as an arranger, but there's another one: mixing. While producing Blake, Ed Seay—a meticulous, award-winning engineer—sometimes took a full day to mix a song. Then I usually spent two or three hours closing down the mix with him. There can be magic that doesn't come to the surface until the mix. It's that important. I might have spent my "closing down" time having Ed make this instrument louder, give that instrument more bottom end, a little more delay on Blake's vocal, et cetera, et cetera. A trick I learned long ago was if you want a female choir to reach out and bite a little harder, remove all reverb and echo, leaving them totally "dry." I would overnight the mixes to Blake when he was on the road, and he would call me to give his opinion. Usually he was totally happy with everything, but sometimes he would want changes, especially regarding the vocal level. It was after all his record, and my job was to give him something that suited him and not me.

Could you walk me through the process by which a song moves from composition to recording?

I do that in my book with a song recorded by Mark Chesnutt: "Old Flames Have New Names." I don't know why I picked that song. I just did. It's certainly not one of my biggest things, but it was big.

To start, I was at Rafe Van Hoy's house. He was then married to Deborah Allen. We were all very close. I said, "I'd like to write a song sometime like 'All My Ex's Live in Texas.'"

Rafe said something like, "How about this guy who had all these women? He went away and came back, and they all had new names."

I said, "Like 'All My Flames Have New Names'?"

"Yeah. That's it!"

I went home, started it. I called him up. We finished writing it on the phone.

My publisher was not wild about it, but he said, "If you feel strongly about it, go ahead and demo it." So I did. Two of the song pluggers had a meeting with Mark Wright, who was producing Mark Chesnutt. One of the song pluggers, named Walter Campbell, liked the song and took it along to the meeting. Mark [Wright] liked it, put it on hold—that hold being a producer's hold, which meant it was on hold until the artist heard it. Mark Chesnutt liked it, so then it was an artist's hold. That was a good, solid hold; nobody else was going to get to hear it.

The record label went through a process, saying they really liked it; it was going to be the first single. Then they said it would not be the first single. I was upset about that. They went in and cut the song. I remember going by the session right after it was cut. Mark Wright played it for me, and I really liked it a lot.

Okay, so they recorded it. That meant my publisher, Donna Hilley, was going to issue them a license. You can't put something out until the publisher gives you a license. The publisher has total control over the first person to put a song out. After that, anybody in the world can do it. Then my publisher told me, "Mark Wright called me. They want to change the title from 'Old Flames with New Names' to 'Old Flames Have New Names.'" Rafe and I had called it "Old Flames with New Names."

I said, "I don't like it as well. Let me ask Rafe about it."

"I already told him he could do it," she said. Which I really did not like at all.

My whole career has been feast and famine—one right after the other. I was coming out of a famine, wanting a feast, so I didn't say anything about it. I liked the record.

They changed their mind from it not being the single to it being the single again. It came out, and there you have it.

Give me a really good example about you being a hands-on guy with
Blake Shelton with those three albums you did with him.

I generally have parts that I want to hear—the different instruments playing, a groove that I want it to be in. The one exception to that is Brent Rowan, who I've been working with since he was in his early twenties. We know each other so well, it's almost like we can read each other's minds. With all the things I want the instruments to play, I got to the point where I would leave sort of a blank spot for Brent, knowing that he would come up with something great—like the intro to "Time Marches On." Even though he didn't play on the record—the other Brent, Brent Mason, did—what he did was such an important part of that song that you ended up with Brent Mason playing Brent Rowan's licks. He probably didn't like doing that, but he executed it beautifully. "I Wanna Talk about Me," the guitar intro on that is pure Brent [Rowan].

All of the other stuff is mine. For instance, we did a song called "Some Beach" with Blake. It was number one for four weeks. The guy in the song gets exasperated and says "some beach!" like he's saying "son of

a bitch." It goes, "Some beach, somewhere." There's this dreamy chorus where he's talking about being on an island, on a beach. It's a very clever song. Paul Overstreet and Rory Feek wrote it.

We cut it, and it had sort of an island sound. I thought, "Wait a minute. With these Kenny Chesney things and with Jimmy Buffett out there, this [track] is going to end up sounding like one of their records." I said, "Why don't we start over, and break this down? Let's take some of what we've got and turn this into a garage-band thing."

We went to Ed Seay's studio, Cool Tools, and we broke it down. All we had left from the original was the kick drum. I got Brent to come in there. He's a great stacker. That record, the majority of it, is Brent Rowan. It's like a one-man band.

I said, "Let's do it [the song] at the same tempo, but play something twice as fast as that, almost like you're playing double time to that tempo." He came up with an intro. I said, "That sounds kind of like 'Third Rate Romance.'"

He said, "I'll do something else."

"Nah, let's do that," I said.

He did, and it was mostly Brent stacking stuff. Ed Seay got some drums sounds from the computer. I say in my [forthcoming] book that "Paul Franklin is arguably the best steel guitar player in the world, and Dan Dugmore is arguably the best steel guitar player in the world." I use Dan a lot, but with Blake we weren't able to get Dan for a session. We ended up using Paul Franklin, and continued to. He seemed to work really well on Blake's stuff.

I would sit down with Paul, because I'm sort of a steel guitar aficionado. I love steel guitar. I know steel guitar players. I play pretty decent piano; I wish I played pretty decent steel. I love the instrument. I would sit down with Paul Franklin and tell him exactly the licks I wanted. I would hum them to him. He told me, "You're the only person that does that. I look forward to these sessions because . . . I would not want to do this all the time, but it works out so well between us; I love doing this because it's so totally different."

So Paul came in and played steel on what Brent had stacked. We had a percussion guy come in and put in something. Tim Lauer overdubbed some organ. But we built the song from scratch — hands-on. We totally tore one down, and built another one up. It was a big hit. I told Paul, "Let's leave, maybe, two island or Caribbean-sounding things on there. On the rest let's put standard country steel guitar licks."

That certainly illustrates why album tracks are so much more labor-intensive than demos.

The stacking thing: I don't know how many records have been recorded that way. Not many. We did two, but "Some Beach" was the only single we ever did that way from the ground up — stacking it. When you do that, you can really get hands-on, because you're not missing anything. You're there for every element.

I've read that Buddy Killen at Tree Publishing hired you as a writer to fill Roger Miller's chair. Is that accurate?

Buddy Killen seemed to think that. He thought I was going to be the next Roger Miller. Obviously I wasn't. I was not as successful an artist, even though I was on five major labels. I tell people that shows how easy it used to be to get a record deal. I'm not nearly as good an artist as Roger was. But I think Buddy thought of it as the Roger Miller chair. That's one of the reasons, I think, that led me there. They had just become the number-one company in town. But they didn't tower over the other companies, Cedarwood and Acuff-Rose, and Roger had moved to the West Coast. To be honest with you, a Ouija board told me to go there.

4

ENCODING TRACKS
COMPOSITING THE PERFORMANCE,
1992-PRESENT

The most interesting feature of the digital-recording paradigm—
announced by the 1992 introduction of ADAT ("Alesis Digital Audio
Tape") and by the subsequent adoption of DAWs ("digital audio work-
stations")—is music-industry resistance to any implication of the technology deemed radical. For example, available technology (my lap-
top DAW) suggests that folders full of tracks/files used to construct
our favorite songs ought to be commercially available—as a matter of
course. Why can't consumers mix and mangle tracks with ease and at
will? Instead, creative explorations of digital audio have—for a long
time now—focused on creative ways to composite tracks in the studio,
which is to say, on realizing fully dreams prompted by the older paradigm of multitrack tape.

**BROOKS & DUNN, "BOOT SCOOTIN'
BOOGIE (DANCE MIX)" (1992),
HARD WORKIN' MAN (ARISTA)**

SCOTT HENDRICKS
Before Brooks & Dunn, I had for some reason, and I don't even know
what made me think this, but I wanted to experiment with taking a
country song and putting a real heavy dance groove underneath it. My
thought at the time was really more, I won't say bluegrass, but more
acoustic instruments. You know, put a real jammin' groove underneath.

I actually went to one of my friends, Keith Thomas, who's an incredible producer in this town. Keith produced Barbra Streisand, all of the Vanessa Williams stuff, Whitney Houston. He's really talented. That is what he does: R&B, that real low-end rhythmic stuff. He wrote "Baby Baby" for Amy Grant. He's extremely talented. I've known him for twenty years. I went to him, and I told him about this idea. I said, "You know how to do the other stuff, but I know how to do the country stuff. Would you be interested in doing this?"

He said, "I'd love to do this."

"There's only one problem," I said. "I don't have the song to do it with yet."

Well, in the middle of recording "Boot Scootin' Boogie," it hit me. "You know what? This could be the song!"

I called up Tim [DuBois, president of Arista Records] and explained my concept to him, what I wanted to try. He was brave enough or stupid enough—however you want to put it—to allow me.

He said, "Go experiment with it."

I called Keith Thomas back, but he was so booked he couldn't get to it. He recommended another programmer by the name of Brian Tankersly. So I called Brian and told him the concept I had—told him that I finally had a song. Even though it wasn't the acoustic thing that I'd originally envisioned, I felt like it could work.

I said, "Meet me in the parking lot of the Shell station in Brentwood." He did. I played him the song. "Here's kind of what I'm hearing," I said. "I want you to expand on that with what you do best."

He took the tape, and about a week later he called me back. He said, "I've got about a minute and twenty seconds. I've done up through the first chorus. I just want to see if you think we're going in the right direction."

He came by my office and played it for me, and at the time it was radically different than anything I'd ever heard. So what I did, instead of playing it for Tim first, I surreptitiously got his staff to come over to my office in groups of three to six people at a time. I played it for each group and asked, "What do y'all think about this?"

They were dancing around like "What is that! That's really, really different." And so, when I got through, I'd played it for pretty much everybody on Tim's staff. I then went over to Tim's office, and before I ever played it for him, I said, "Hey, can I invite the staff in just to see what they think about this?" They all showed up in there, and they were all dancing around for that minute and twenty seconds.

Tim had this "I think I've been buffaloed" reaction on his face. He said, "What can I say? Go finish it."

There were some skeptics in that group. There were some of those—I won't name names—that said, "We'll never sell any of these. This is just a gimmick. It would be a good promotion." You'd have to check with the sales department, but I think they cut the single's sales off at around 400,000—something like that.

It wasn't at all an intention to change country music. Creative experimentation, that's what it was. I told Tim right then and there, "You know what? This is the very first 'dance mix' that's different." A lot of people in country music, for a little time before that, had been doing what they called "dance mixes." It was really pathetic. All they did was raise the level of the kick drum. It was no more of a dance mix than nothing. It wasn't a different mix.

I told him, "This could be either the greatest thing in the world, or we could have just created a disco movement that we will forever regret in years to come." But I also said, "I don't know, and I don't care. At least it's different. We'll just try it."

I always give Kix and Ronnie a lot of credit because none of this would have happened had they not had the guts to allow me to try it. You think about it from an artist's perspective. That's a real tough thing to do. It's their career. They've only got—usually—one of them. To allow someone to alter what they do that much, and to take a chance at it, it took a lot of guts on their part.

I have to give it to them. It wouldn't have surprised me a bit had they said, "Man, I think your idea's cool, but don't let me be the guinea pig." I think it worked out all for the good. Slowly but surely—probably thankfully so—the dance-mix thing really wound up, but Brian Tankersly found a whole new career for several years there doing nothing but dance mixes. He was really good at it. Finally, it cooled off.

WYNONNA JUDD, *WYNONNA* (1992, CURB/MCA)

TONY BROWN

She and I talked. I was just one of the people she interviewed to do the album. Finally, she said she wanted me to produce it.

I'd known her a long time so I was thrilled to do that record, but I must tell you I was scared. I was going, "Man, I hope that I don't screw this up." We talked about what we wanted to do; maybe we could make it a little more electric. We didn't want to keep doing the Judds. They wouldn't use electric guitars. Their whole sound was kind of skewed around acoustic instruments. So we said, "Let's take it a little more electric, use electric keyboards here or there, some electric guitar."

Basically I said, "Let's just let people play you songs, and see what they play you. Then, let's see if you and I agree on songs together." "No One Else on Earth" and other tunes on that first album—"She Is His Only Need"—Wynonna and I both kept gravitating toward the same kind of material. I could tell that it was pretty radically different than the Judds.

I remember when we were cutting. People would walk in, and I think, when we cut "No One Else on Earth," they thought we'd lost our minds. It was pretty funky. People would leave, and they'd say, "Which way are you guys going?" Those kinds of questions. But instead of scaring me, I thought it was incredible. I just basically dismissed them as being unaware. I was going home every night and saying, "This is killing me!"

Wynonna was into it big time. I said, "Are you cool with this?" She had started to get some feedback. Some of the family was going, "Wow, this is sounding pretty pop or pretty contemporary." Of course, Wynonna being the maverick, they should never have said that. She dug in her heels, and thank God she did because I followed her lead. That first album, no doubt about it, was Wynonna's defining moment. I think we kept trying to repeat that, but we never quite got back to it.

We cut that album while she was finishing that last tour [with the Judds]. I produced Wynonna when she was emotionally at a place she'd never be again. The only thing she looked forward to when she got off tour was going to the studio and doing her new record.

"My Strongest Weakness"—when she did that song, it was magic. That was like one take. There were moments during that record that we all looked at the each other. She was just singing from her gut. And also having an electric guitar with her and some electric keyboards, it wrapped more stuff around her voice. I don't think she'd ever heard that in the phones before. I think she discovered new parts of herself.

JOY LYNN WHITE, *BETWEEN MIDNIGHT & HINDSIGHT* (1992, COLUMBIA) AND *WILD LOVE* (1994, SONY)

BLAKE CHANCEY

We did a couple of albums on her here at Columbia. I used to do a lot of demos, and I used to work with a guy named Mike Henderson. We did demos just to pitch around to get songs cut. Mike said, "I really need a really country female singer."

My best friend at the time—we'd gone to junior high and high school together—was dating Joy. He's a great bass player in town. He said, "I'm dating this girl who's a great country singer. You should try her out."

She came over and sang four or five demos, and all of those songs got cut. Everybody started calling, "Who is this girl?"

When she got her deal at Columbia, they asked her, "Who would you like to produce your record?" And she said me.

I was like, "Well, thank you." That's how that all happened. She drug me in.

We had a style that we were doing with Henderson's songs. It was real Appalachian, very dry, very country, and very much in-your-face. As a matter of fact, a couple of songs that I cut for Joy's albums I've recut on the Dixie Chicks. They're huge fans. Natalie loves the way Joy sings. I do too.

JOHN ANDERSON, *SEMINOLE WIND* (1992, RCA)

JAMES STROUD

There are things that you have to do with certain artists to set that artist up for the creative process. Some artists write their own material, for instance, and have a handle on their direction before you go in and make the record. All you have to do is keep them in between the ditches. You don't want them to crash and burn with something that they shouldn't be doing. But there are other situations where you have an artist that may not be a writer, and he or she needs focus on the direction of the music, the type of lyrics, the emotion of the songs. You need to be more involved with song selection and focus on lyric and musical direction. You have that balance there, and you have to be able to determine when to be a little more forceful with what you need to do with ideas. And you also have to be able to back out and let the artist follow through with what you start.

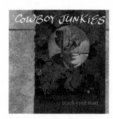

COWBOY JUNKIES, *BLACK EYED MAN* (1992, RCA)

MICHAEL TIMMINS

There are certain songwriters I've admired. I don't think I've ever tried to copy anybody, but they've inspired me. I can listen to their songs and think, "Well, can I even get close to that?" People like Townes Van Zandt and Lou Reed and Neil Young, to a certain extent. Bruce Springsteen, as well. I'm a huge fan. And then a lot from literature: the way story writers and modern-day fiction writers can develop a character, not necessarily stating the emotion, but putting the person or the character in a place, in a setting, in a situation and bringing the reader into that situation with that character, and bringing them through the situation, and then hoping that by doing that, the reader then begins to understand the emotions that the character is going through without really describing the emotions. It brings you into the story. People like Richard Ford, Raymond Carver, Tim O'Brien, and Michael Ondaatje—that type of writer, that sort of modern-day fiction. And I guess in some ways film. I've always really loved film, just the way a good filmmaker can set a scene or set the emotional content of a scene by an image as opposed to, again, having the actor portray the image. They can set a scene by showing you something, whether it's something physical or how something is being lit or the way the camera moves. That suggests emotion. Although you can't do that specifically in a song, it gives you something to aim for, another way of showing emotion, rather than just stating it. Those are my three, that's what I draw on really.

IRIS DEMENT, *INFAMOUS ANGEL* (1992, WARNER BROS.) AND *MY LIFE* (1993, WARNER BROS.)

JIM ROONEY

I didn't know her. I'd never heard her. She invited me to a night at the Bluebird Café, featuring songwriters living in Nashville who'd come from Kansas City. I went, and the place was very full. I couldn't get a seat. There's a mirror set up so that if you stand in one area, you can see the stage reflected in the mirror. I heard three or four people. It wasn't engaging me, so I didn't stick around.

I was at Renee Bell's office. She's an A&R person. I was looking for songs. She asked me, "Have you heard Iris DeMent?" I said, "I was supposed to, but didn't." So she played me Iris singing "Our Town" off the [mixing] board of that night—a tape they'd made of that night. "Well, I really missed that boat," I said. This was maybe a month or two later, after that night. I also heard that Emmylou Harris's steel player, Steve Fischel, was going to be working with Iris as her producer. I figured, "I missed that one." A month or two later, Ken Irwin from Rounder Records called me and asked if I'd be interested in working with her. The arrangement with Steve hadn't worked out. I jumped at it. So then we got together.

Iris is one of the most affecting artists that I've ever worked with. For a lot of people she's too deep or too strange, but I was pleasantly surprised at how many people got Iris and at how powerful she is at reaching people. Everything we've ever done together has been really, really moving for me.

The first album we did very quickly, before she even had time to think about it. Which I think can sometimes be a good thing. It has some unforgettable performances. To get that kind of energy in a recording studio is pretty rare. She could really do it to it.

Another function of the producer is to pick musicians and the place you're going to record. Jack [Clement] had a big house on Belmont Boulevard, with a big attic that he turned into his studio. He built many studios in his career, starting down in Beaumont, Texas. Every studio he ever built was a really wonderful place to play music, and they're all different. This one was just a big attic—a great space. It had a peaked roof. So you didn't have to do a lot of baffling and isolation because the sound has a place to go, and it doesn't come back. You can get beautiful blends of instruments in the room. A bit of leakage is not a bad thing.

Iris was not used to playing with other musicians at all. I eased her into things. I got her together with a lovely guitarist, Mark Howard, and a wonderful upright bass player, Roy Husky. Just the two of them and her, they'd rehearse the songs. Then I added Stuart Duncan [fiddle, mandolin]. I'd always heard a piano in her music, and I had Pete Wasner— a songwriter and a piano player I was working with in our publishing company. Pete isn't a flashy piano player, but he's a wonderful groove piano player. He has a great relaxed feel to his playing. On dobro, for one session I had Jerry Douglas; for the rest I had Al Perkins. He's also a very simple and clear player. He plays dobro and steel, though this was all dobro.

In these musicians I wanted people who wouldn't be showing off in any way and interrupting Iris's focus. When you listen to those recordings, everybody is so supportive and clear in what they're doing, when they're doing it. I didn't have to tell them anything. To me, that's the beauty of working with musicians at this level. For my money, the best musicians are the people who you hardly ever have to say anything to. They know when not to play. They're not trying to show off every lick they've ever known. You can really count on them to work with an artist and keep the focus on her. Those are all live recordings, and that's really the way that I like to work.

The second album: Iris had time to think about it. She also was growing. Before we recorded that album, she sent me a very detailed, long letter outlining each song and what she was thinking about. She called some of the songs "departure songs." One of the departure songs was "Easy's Gettin' Harder Every Day."

It kind of goes against my grain to plan everything that carefully in advance. I like it to come out of the relationship between the artist, the song, and the musicians. That's where I want things to come from, rather than telling people what to play, and when to play. I want it to come out of them as much as possible.

So we started recording, and I was pretty much—I was sort of ignoring her wishes. The first day was okay. We were recording songs more similar to the first album. The second day she basically ground to a halt. She came into the control room, and she was clearly upset. We took a long walk. I had all the musicians sitting there. We took a good long walk, and I had to admit that I needed to listen to her. We basically started again. All those musicians went home.

I had had it in mind that the guitarist Richard Bennett would suit some of the newer songs. I got him and Roy Husky, just the two of them, in with Iris. We got going that way. For some of the other things with the group, I added Jack Clement and Charles Cochran. They were a little bit more, not aggressive, but a little beefier. That seemed to work. It's always a good lesson—which you need to remind yourself—that the artist is in charge. I try my best to honor that.

On the first album, virtually all we did was mix it. On the second album, Joy White sang some harmony, and also Robin and Linda Williams. So there was a little bit of postproduction. We also mixed it in Jack's Tracks where there's a real echo-chamber, a live echo-chamber. Rich Adler was the engineer I used on most sessions. He did a lot of work with John Hartford. He was excellent for those two albums with Iris. Her voice isn't the easiest voice in the world to record. It's very powerful. You'd be tempted to limit it. If you sit next to her and she starts singing, you are literally blown over. She has a huge voice. You could be tempted to squash it a bit, but you'd be losing this other thing.

EDDY ARNOLD, *HAND-HOLDIN' SONGS* (1990, RCA), *YOU DON'T MISS A THING* (1991, RCA), AND *LAST OF THE LOVE SONG SINGERS: THEN AND NOW* (1993, RCA)

HAROLD BRADLEY

Eddy called me and asked me to produce a record with him. He was sitting at home, he told me, one Sunday morning watching television. He saw some big crowd scene. He turned to his wife and said, "All those people there, they don't know who Eddy Arnold is. Maybe I should do something."

"Yeah, why don't you record something?"

"I'm going to call Harold Bradley," he said.

We did three albums together which I'm very proud of. One album really captured what he wanted to do—pop songs. It's a beautiful album, but were I to do it again, I would insist on using strings instead of synthesizers. I think it's still tasty, and Eddie is a star. He has a beautiful baritone voice. When we started, he was a little bugged that he couldn't sing as high as he used to. I told him there was no law that he had to sing up high, and besides, he sounded so good in that low range. It took us three albums, the third album, to get what he really wanted. He was a lifelong friend, a wonderful guy to me.

NANCI GRIFFITH, *OTHER VOICES, OTHER ROOMS* (1993, ELEKTRA)

JIM ROONEY

That's another nice thing about Nashville. You can call someone up, and they can come right over. I did that on the Nanci Griffith album *Other Voices, Other Rooms*. It occurred to us that we had no Woody Guthrie song. Nanci said, "I know 'Do-Re-Mi.'" She remembered singing it with Guy Clark. We called up Guy, and he was up to do it. I called Roy Husky;

he came over. Pat Flynn was there to do something else, to put a guitar on something, and Pat McInerney was there. We thought about it at about nine o'clock, and by eleven o'clock we had it all done.

That album was conceived as Nanci's tribute to the people who really influenced her. It shows you how much of a listener she was. Emmylou Harris is the same way. They listen voraciously to other artists and find songs that suit them. I think that's really good; especially for a songwriter, it's always good not to do just your own songs.

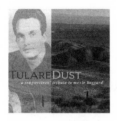

VARIOUS, *TULARE DUST:*
A SONGWRITERS' TRIBUTE TO
MERLE HAGGARD (1994, HIGHTONE)

DAVE ALVIN

Tom Russell and I came up with the idea. I was making a record of mine called *King of California* [1994]. We were sitting around discussing California songwriters one day in the studio. Tom said, "You know what would be great? Do a concept album of all of Merle Haggard's semi-autobiographical songs. You could do some of the prison songs. You could do 'Mama Tried.' You could do 'Tulare Dust.' You could do 'Kern River.' Do them in an acoustic format, and then make it somehow sequential—make it tell a story."

It changed from that original idea into approaching songwriters that we knew, who were influenced by Merle Haggard. It wasn't like, "Who can we get?"—but rather, using people whose writing was actually affected by Merle's writing. Get them to do it their own way. Too many people, when they do Merle, try to ape Merle. And understandably so. But songwriters—when you're talking with people like Iris DeMent or Lucinda Williams or Billy Joe Shaver—they don't sound like anybody but themselves. They bring a certain different perspective than, say, if you have a singer who's grown up imitating Merle Haggard doing a song.

There's so much baggage around Merle Haggard. That's all good and fine, but let's just boil it down to the songwriter. I didn't think that, at that point, he'd really been given enough credit as a songwriter. There're very few people who've consistently written good songs for as long as he has. There's Bob Dylan, Harlan Howard, Curtis Mayfield. There aren't many others. The idea was, people could put this on, listen to it, and think it was an album of all new songs by some new songwriter.

THE MAVERICKS, *WHAT A CRYING SHAME* (1994, MCA)

DON COOK

Tony Brown got together with me and asked if I'd be interested in working on their album. It wasn't their first album. I started with them on their second. He asked me if I wanted to be involved.

I said, "It seems to me, based on what I heard on their first album, that they're into a real artistic kind of trip that I'm not sure I can connect with. Compared to them, I'm kind of a mercenary."

He said, "You really ought to—in fairness to them—you ought to meet with them before you make a decision."

So I did meet with them. I came away from that first meeting realizing that they were a little more commercially driven in their expectations for their music than I'd ever imagined. I was all the time worried about interfering with artists' growth by my obvious need and preference to make "commercial" music. Of course, in every sense, the first album that we did together was very commercial, although it didn't have much radio success. We sold a lot of records, and that is commercial to me. I was very careful not to undo what I loved about them in the process of trying to help them become a great piece of business for MCA. I say that in the sense that a great piece of business is one that allows us to stay in the business.

I'm from the Harlan Howard school. We're all hacks, and occasionally, despite our best abilities to screw it up, we do something that's fairly artistic. Most of the time, we're just hacks. And I say that in the fondest sense. Some of my heroes, including Harlan, fall into that category. Really, I think my definition of "hack," not to get too far off the track, is somebody that does a lot of average work in order to get to the really good stuff. That's what the "artistic" music process is all about.

JOHN MICHAEL MONTGOMERY, "I SWEAR" (1994), *KICKIN' IT UP* (ATLANTIC)

SCOTT HENDRICKS

With one of the bigger songs I've ever had the opportunity to produce, I heard the demo. I pulled it out of the cassette deck in my truck. I put it on the dash, and I thought, "That's a really cool song. I don't know if it's right for the artist. It may be too pop, but I love this song." About every two or three days, I'd put that thing back in the cassette deck to see if I still liked it. This went on for about a month. It lived on my dashboard for a month. Every few days I'd put it back in, and every few days I'd still go, "I love this song, but I don't know if it'll get past anybody." This was when I was an independent producer.

I took the demo to a song meeting at the label, where the artist was present. I said, "This may be a really stupid pitch, but I've been hearing this song. I don't know if it's right for you as an artist, but I love it." I played it, and everybody in the room went, "It's a pretty good song. We might ought to cut that and see how it turns out."

We cut it, got the vocal on it, and only at that point—it took that long—only at that point did I realize that I had a very big fish on the end of the line. The song was "I Swear." It just goes to show you that it's not always obvious. "I Could Love You Like That" on John Michael's next album was obvious. I was like, "Duh." That was the song of the year, too, for ASCAP. But that song was much more obvious only because we'd had success with "I Swear."

LYLE LOVETT, *I LOVE EVERYBODY* (1994, MCA NASHVILLE)

TONY BROWN

Let's face it: Lyle is never going to be, he didn't want to be, as commercial and mainstream as [George] Strait. That's just not what he's about. But he wants his music to get out there to more people. In the beginning, with the first album, we had some radio success. "Cowboy Man" and "Farther Down the Line," some of those tunes were more accessible at radio, at a radio level than, say, some of the stuff he writes now, about penguins and stuff like that. But you know Lyle wasn't thinking about radio back then. He didn't write that way—whereas a writer like a Vince [Gill] or a writer like Alan Jackson or a Clint Black, they write at radio. Not so intensely that it's contrived. That's just the way they think.

ALEJANDRO ESCOVEDO, *THIRTEEN YEARS* (1994, WATERMELON)

STEPHEN BRUTON

I can consider everything I've ever done very collaborative with the artist. In other words, I don't think that there are too many songs or too many records that the artist and I would have done anything differently. I was with Alejandro Escovedo. We were talking about things. We might have taken something off. We would not have added anything.

Number one, they're going to have to go out on the road and represent it. What if you have a bad arrangement? You want people to be happy about playing the stuff. Like I said, it's collaborative.

We knew what we wanted to do when we went into the studio. He wanted to use a string section. We wanted to use it very innovatively. We also had this idea where, "Why don't we string these songs together?"

Every once in a while we have a theme that goes through the record. I said, "Let's try this. Let's write little insert pieces, themes. And then we'll play them."

There's a beautiful one at the end of the album by [pianist] Tom Canning. It's just fantastic. Then there's another one; I think it's on guitar. We wove that album together around a kind of theme. We really took our time. The first album [*Gravity*, 1992] was a nine-day wonder, from downbeat to final mix. *Thirteen Years* was probably about two weeks, but we did a lot of work which I insisted on.

BIG SANDY AND HIS FLY-RITE BOYS, *JUMPING FROM 6 TO 6* (1994, HIGHTONE/SHOUT!) AND *SWINGIN' WEST* (1995, HIGHTONE/SHOUT!); THE DERAILERS, *REVERB DELUXE* (1997, SONY)

DAVE ALVIN

My attitude is "whatever it takes." Probably my favorite producer is Sam Phillips. You could make a case for him as a "stay out of the way" producer, but that's not really the case. He created an environment for people to be their best. But on the other hand, I'm also a huge fan of Billy Sherrill. I really am. A lot of people are very negative towards the style of production that he did, say, in the early-to-mid-'70s. To me those are just incredible records. They manage to keep the soul of country music, and yet they had a quality that was like a Phil Spector kind of production. So between those two—that's one extreme to another.

My attitude with Big Sandy and the Fly-Rite Boys was more of a Sam Phillips kind of production. When I worked with them, it was from that sort of philosophy and approach, and really just down to waiting for the right take and deciding which one is the right take: the producer being the one to say "yes" or "no."

With the Derailers, it's a whole different approach. It's more a get-your-hands-dirty production, where you go in and, in some cases, construct songs. Like on their second album [*Reverb Deluxe*], there's a song called "Can't Stop a Train" that I'm really proud of as a producer. When they brought the song into the rehearsal, it was sort of a Johnny Cash, um-boom-chicka-boom song. I thought, "That's cool, but it needs more than that." Brian [Hofeldt] would play one little guitar lick, and I really liked that lick. It was something he twirled off at the rehearsal.

I said, "Play that again." He played it again. I said, "Now play it again and again and again. Keep repeating it." So he did, and it started turning into a James Burton or a Glen Campbell kind of riff, or something off one of the early Merle Haggard records. Then we completely reconstructed the song around that guitar riff repeated constantly, creating a hypnotic effect.

VINCE GILL, "GO REST HIGH ON THAT MOUNTAIN" (1995), *WHEN LOVE FINDS YOU* (MCA NASHVILLE)

BOBBY BRADDOCK

If I had to pick my favorite best-produced country record, it would be a contest between "He Stopped Loving Her Today" and Vince Gill's "Go Rest High on That Mountain." That is an absolutely great record. Tony Brown produced it. I'm sure Vince had input too. I'll tell you what's so great about it. It breaks all the rules. It's too long to be a single to start with. I think, if I were producing it, I probably would have said, "No, we certainly can't have an instrumental turnaround here. It will be way too long." They had the good sense to go ahead, even though it was long, and put a fiddle solo on it, and then after that, here comes Vince playing a guitar solo. It's almost like they were thumbing their nose at convention. "We'll see how long we can make this." It didn't get to number one—maybe to nine or ten on the charts. But it's an eternal song. It's a song that keeps on giving. "He Stopped Loving Her Today" has been that too.

When "Time Marches On" [Braddock's song for Tracy Lawrence] was nominated for song of the year, Vince told me, "If my song doesn't get it, I hope yours does, because it's a great song." He won. I didn't mind. I knew that his song—which he wrote about Keith Whitley and about his brother—meant more to him than mine meant to me. Anyway, the production on that recording was just stellar. It doesn't get any better than that. They had Ricky Skaggs and Patty Loveless singing harmony. And Tony [Brown] is a very emotional guy. He'd been known to cry after hearing playback. I like that; that's a good thing. I think the fact that he is an emotional man came through in such an emotional record. And like I say, I think Vince Gill is sort of the genius himself.

THE BOTTLE ROCKETS, *THE BROOKLYN SIDE* (1995, EAST SIDE DIGITAL)

ERIC "ROSCOE" AMBEL

I really like bands. I like the dynamic of bands. I like what bands can bring to a songwriter's songs. Most of the groups that I work with, they're either real bands with four guys that are members of the band, or it's a singer/songwriter that wants to have a real band feel, where the singer/songwriter wants to be put in the middle of a band.

Their first record [*Bottle Rockets*, 1992] was done with John Keane. The guy from the label, Steve Daily (who is now out of the business, but I'd have to say he's one of the few true A&R people that I've dealt with), before they even made their first record, Steve Daily sent me a solo demo of [the Bottle Rockets' frontman] Brian Henneman. Here's what he told me: "This is this guy's demo. They're making a record with John Keane. If you like this, I think you're going to want to do their second record." I was just knocked out by that band. I liked their record. I liked the songs on the record. The band, to me, was capable of a lot more. Their first record was a start. You have to start someplace. It had great songs, but it didn't catch the fire of the band. The big difference between first record and the one I produced is that I really tried to . . .

To me, the vocal is like the salesman on a record. On *The Brooklyn Side* on "Sunday Sports" and the vocal on "Pot of Gold," those are two completely different songs, and the vocals are completely different. "Pot of Gold" is what I would call a "bedroom vocal." "Sunday Sports" is a screaming rock vocal that goes with that song.

There's no way you could get those kinds of performances out of a rock guy by overdubbing the vocal two weeks later. Whitney Houston could do it because she's an actress. She could put herself in a place that she's supposed to be in. But for a rock guy, you may not have to use the vocal from the basic track, but say we got "Sunday Sports," and then you have the guy sing it a few more times—right then. I know from my own experience playing in bands that it's really hard to ever get yourself that deep into the song later on.

Saying that the vocal is the key thing, I think the next thing after that—and it all takes backseat to having the right song—but it probably would go song, vocal performance, arrangement. A lot of people get bogged down in the technical aspects of recording. There's no substitute for a great arrangement. If you don't have those things . . . everybody's heard people talk about turd polishing, but that's what you're doing if you don't have those things.

Usually, if I've decided to work with a band, I've seen them live, and I know that they can do really great things. I'll get a guy to make me what I refer to as the "Nebraska Tape," sit down with a boombox and just record all the songs. Me and Brian, we had a tape. I don't remember exactly how many songs. I would assume that it was about twenty-five songs. And then we listened for favorites. The A&R guy helped a little with the song selection with *The Brooklyn Side*. The other good thing about the solo tape is the band may already be playing that song and have their own band arrangement for the song. If I listen to a solo tape that's essentially no arrangement, it frees me up to . . . I might come up with a whole different idea. I'm not like pre-influenced on the thing. There's stuff on that record that was pretty different from how they were doing it or thought about doing it.

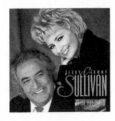

JERRY AND TAMMY SULLIVAN,
AT THE FEET OF GOD **(1995, SONOTEC)**

MARTY STUART

I'd been touring real hard for a whole year. I was pretty frazzled, fighting off some demons. I asked Jerry to come by the Astrodome and pick me up. I'd played a show there, and I walked out while the audience was still screaming and yelling, got on his bus, and we disappeared into the country. We parked the bus behind some people's house down in Louisiana and basically didn't come out of the bus for two or three days, other than to eat and just get some air.

We wrote songs. I was so frazzled and burned. We started writing the song "At the Feet of God." That's where we both wound up. I said, "I need some rest. Where do we get that? At the feet of God." For anything you need, you plow up to the feet of God, and there you are.

With Jerry and Tammy Sullivan, there's a bit of a sound built in. The first gig I ever had was with the old Sullivan Family Gospel Singers. That was when I was twelve. The Stanley Brothers had a sound, and Bill Monroe had a sound; Flatt and Scruggs had a sound; the Sullivan Family had a definite sound about it—their voices. It was this lonesome, Southern sound is what I called it. That's a good starting point, and there are certain kinds of songs that I know Tammy Sullivan sounds good singing. And then straight, traditional bluegrass songs always work for them. Once you start there, you can usually poke around in the air and find a melody.

The main thing is staying true to what they are. It got a little touchier on this particular record. The one we did for the Country Music Foundation [A Joyful Noise], I knew that we could play it just as hardcore as we wanted to. But with this one, they were trying to figure in a little more popularity with it, inside of mainstream gospel music. I knew that I had to have a little commercial conscience about it to some degree. The balance was keeping it pure, without staining it too much with anything that went out with hooks on it. Once again, I know their sound, and I've heard them with electric pianos. I've heard them with electric guitars. And it works when you leave it to the message and to the pure clarity of his and her voices. Decorate around that. The smaller you record, the bigger they sound.

HERB JEFFRIES, *THE BRONZE BUCKAROO (RIDES AGAIN)* (1995, WARNER WESTERN)

JIM ED NORMAN

I happened to see a tribute to the singing cowboy at the Autry National Center in Los Angeles. There was a parade of silver-screen, singing cowboys. People in their sixties, seventies, and eighties came out and sang.

All of a sudden this guy bounded out on stage. I said, "Man, this guy can still really sing. He's great." Then they showed a film clip, and I had a conversion where things all came together.

For our label, Warner Western, I'd been trying to recognize the full breadth of music of the West. When I looked at the development of what had gone on in the West musically, I realized that African Americans had certainly played a role in its development. There were black cowboys.

Now, in front of me, was a black cowboy singer. On the film clip that they showed, Herb was not only the star of the film, he led a background group — a "Sons of the Pioneers," if you will. They had this great almost doo-wop kind of thing.

So it all came together. I was already looking for someone to musically portray the African-American aspect of Western music, and then as fate would have it, I heard someone who was still an exquisite performer with a fabulous voice. You go looking for something long enough, you'll find it. I figured the guy was sixty, and when I finally called him up and had a meeting with him, out at his place in Woodland Hills in California, I found out that he was eighty-two! It was just extraordinary that this guy could sing like that at that age — that he could still render those kinds of performances.

BLUE MOUNTAIN, *DOG DAYS* (1995, ROADRUNNER)

ERIC "ROSCOE" AMBEL

My recording approach varies, but in the case of Blue Mountain, that's a three-piece band. I'll baffle stuff off, though sometimes I don't. I have a lot of specialized equipment that'll work, but I think that recording the band is the same thing as [recording] the vocal. If there's going to be an organ on a song by a guy in a rock band, it's much better if someone is playing organ on the basic track. So then those guys, dynamically, will hear that organ, and they'll listen for it, and they'll leave space for it, rather than overdubbing it later. Usually, I play a lot of stuff myself. So a lot of times I become fifth man. Or I have a lot of friends who play too. If we know there's going to be some extra stuff, I'm much more into having it go down on the basic track so everybody knows the record. You don't have to imagine the record. You know, "Imagine an extra guitar part under the solo." Why do that? Why don't we just play an extra guitar part under the solo?

FAITH HILL, *IT MATTERS TO ME* (1995, WARNER BROS.)

SCOTT HENDRICKS

Personally, I really like to work with artists who have a very clear sense of who they are versus an artist who pretty much will let anybody determine who they are. Most of my career, if you look at the discography of it, was spent on brand new artists—from scratch. I really enjoy that. I love to see it go from zero to whatever it can go to. That's a really gratifying process.

    The hardest thing in the world about a new artist, who isn't a writer, is finding that direction and finding the songs. If you put yourself in a writer's shoes, and you write what everyone thinks is a really great song, who do you want to record it? Somebody that's selling a million records already or somebody that no one's ever heard of yet? That's why new artist albums are tough. It's hard to get those great songs. That's why you see a lot of new artists come and go.

DWIGHT YOAKAM,
GONE (1995, REPRISE)

PETE ANDERSON

The record before *Gone* [1995] was a record called *This Time* [1993]. It was a huge record, triple platinum. I used computers, did a lot of editing, a lot of things that were new to the business at the time. I was trying to make a perfect record, perfect in that . . . I'll explain it like this. If I sat down to draw a picture for you, say I was an artist, *This Time* is an architectural rendering, whereas *Gone* is Grandma Moses. It's an impression. It's not hardline precise.

Coming off the earlier, perfect record, I wanted to make a record fast. We didn't use any computers. It was a lot of live playing. We weren't sloppy in any way, but we really jumped back, like two or three records in our concept, and made a watercolor: looser feeling, less rigid and strict, instead of the gigantic, pop-country record—whatever you want to call *This Time*. We used a different mixer. Judy Clapp mixed it instead of David Leonard. She brought a completely different concept to the project. I think, also, Dwight's voice had changed a little bit, but his vocal to me on that particular record is really rich and much more expressive and out front—glorious in its sonic shaping of material. I think the vocals sound really good on that record. They weren't as pushed and aggressive in the mix. I talk about things with Dwight, and he's like, "Hey, yeah, cool, okay."

DEANA CARTER, "STRAWBERRY WINE" (1996), *DID I SHAVE MY LEGS FOR THIS?* (CAPITOL NASHVILLE)

SCOTT HENDRICKS

When I got to Capitol, Deana Carter's record [*Did I Shave My Legs for This?*] had already been done by Jimmy Bowen, but I didn't feel it would be competitive. I urged her to find a producer, since Jimmy was retired, and to go back in and record more songs. I helped facilitate her connection to Chris Farren.

I suggested, "Find some more songs that will beat what we've got." She did. In that group of songs was "Strawberry Wine." We all—the A&R staff, Chris Farren, Deana Carter, her management, and I—really loved "Strawberry Wine," but none of us ever foresaw it as a single. I was the one who made the call to her, not to convince her, but to get her reaction and, hopefully, to support changing the first single to "Strawberry Wine."

We had another single pegged that we were all in agreement on. We'd actually gone and shot—I don't know—a sixty-five-thousand-dollar video. We actually had five thousand copies of the single laying in our office, already pressed up, artwork ready to go. We'd actually already put out several ads in trade papers—*Billboard, R&R [Radio & Records*], etc.— announcing that this single was coming on such-and-such date.

About two weeks before its release date, I called Deana and said, "Sit down. How would you react if I were to ask you if you would consider changing the single to 'Strawberry Wine'?" The long and short of it is Deana said, "Fine. Let's do it."

We did, and we scrapped the video. It was probably the more nervous two months in my life. I'd just pulled the trigger and thrown away all of that money. Luckily for all of us, it worked. There've been several songs like it, where it took radio a long time to get the song. For the first several weeks we were getting killed on the charts by Mila Mason over at Atlantic. Then, all of a sudden, the audience responded.

JIMMY BOWEN

It's always the artist's record. Some producers back then forgot that occasionally and some still do. If you see somebody with one hit with an artist, they haven't learned that yet. Still, there's always a freaky one-hit situation. That little girl I signed before I quit down there, Deana Carter, that had "Strawberry Wine," a huge record, and could not follow. It gives me cold chills if that's your line of work. I would've died if I couldn't have followed that—my ego. And what it does to that artist is awful. But obviously, there was no connection between producer and artist. It happened, but it wasn't the right way.

VARIOUS, *RIG ROCK DELUXE: A MUSICAL SALUTE TO THE AMERICAN TRUCK DRIVER* (1996, UPSTART/DIESEL ONLY)

JEREMY TEPPER

We really wanted to do something spectacular—to tie in some of the great truck-driving singers of the past with some of the exciting country artists of the present. When we're working within the truck-driving pantheon, we want to stay true to the roots but kind of extend and grow the tradition.

The two anchor tracks or the bookends are "Truck Driving Man" and "Six Days on the Road." They came out of a single session in Austin during South by Southwest. We figured, "Hey, we've got a lot of great tracks here, but probably the two most obvious classic truck-driving songs of all—'Truck Driving Man' and 'Six Days on the Road'—we don't have. If we're going to include those tracks, they have to be all-time versions for the ages."

So we booked an afternoon session in Austin. Rob Patterson helped us. It was really a timing thing. We put together a killer band with people like Casper Rawls, Will Rigby, Gurf Morlix, Scott Walls, Howard Kalish, Scott Hinkle—all great Austin guys, primarily. Don [Walser] agreed to sing "Truck Driving Man."

After we did that track, everybody we saw in Austin we invited down to the session; we figured whatever happens will happen. The guys from

Skeleton showed up. We put them in the studio, and we knocked out [the instrumental tracks to] "Six Days on the Road." I think it was done in two takes. And we came home with that.

That version of the song is so crazy. It's got all those vocals. They weren't all there [together]. We got a few of the vocal tracks while we were in Austin. Then we brought the tapes back to New York, and we added Dale Watson, Wayne Hancock, and Kim Richey. We did their vocals at our studio in Brooklyn. Next, we sent the tape out to Lou Whitney, and he did some more stuff. That tape made the rounds.

Every singer did a complete take of the song. Then, at our studio, we went through the song line by line and decided who was going to sing which line. We punched vocals in and out. It was fun. The mix was a bit of a challenge, but I think that version of "Six Days on the Road" is the icing on the cake.

When you're doing compilations, it's almost like doing a movie soundtrack. You're working with so many artists, different labels and different managers that it's almost like compiling, but there's producing involved because there's so much to sort through.

COWBOY JUNKIES, *LAY IT DOWN* (1996, GEFFEN)

JOHN KEANE

They're definitely the most close-knit band I've ever worked with, due to the fact that most of them are siblings. There's a different dynamic than a lot of bands have. Mike Timmins is pretty much the leader of the band. He writes most of the lyrics, and then he and Margo get together on melodies. They get that stuff hammered out and bring it to the rest of the band. Which is completely different from the way R.E.M. goes about it. When they're writing songs, the guitar, bass, and drummer tend to get together and put down tracks of just music, which they then give to Michael [Stipe]. He listens to them and writes lyrics and melodies over the top.

This was probably the most live record I've ever done in terms of not a lot of fixing, not a lot of overdubbing. It was very much like recording a jazz band because they all play off each other. If you separate them, they lose what it is that makes them such a great band. They all have to be in close contact with each other.

On this record, instead of doing it bit by bit, it was very much a live performance; then we'd fix small mistakes. So the music flows a lot more. It speeds up and slows down—and was also one of the most sparse records I've ever done in terms of overdubbing. They wanted to keep it very stripped down and basic, and capture the essence of the band without embellishing it too much. The overall sound quality of the record was something that I had a lot of control over since I did all the engineering and everything.

MICHAEL TIMMINS

We decided before we met John that we wanted to approach the record as the four of us again. We wanted to keep extra instrumentation as much as possible out of it. For the first time I was really happy with the recording of the instruments, and then the way John was able to find a space within the entire picture for every instrument. I thought he was able to shape a three-dimensional space where you can actually see the band playing as you listen to us. It's not flat. It's up and down. It's left and right. And it's forward and back. I can really hear that. It's a huge, huge job, and he was really able to do that. That, to me, was his biggest contribution. On the other side of it, he was very good at helping us hear good takes and bad takes, and pushing us a little bit more into trying a few more takes, as opposed to being satisfied with what we had. But to me his biggest contribution was shaping the actual sound. Once we decided on what we wanted, he was then able to capture it on tape, which is a really, really difficult thing to do.

TRACE ADKINS, "EVERY LIGHT IN THE HOUSE IS ON" (1996), *DREAMIN' OUT LOUD* (CAPITOL NASHVILLE)

SCOTT HENDRICKS

That song, like many—they're just pitched to us. A writer writes it; gives it to his publisher. The publisher plays it for me, or I go to the publisher and, somewhat, either by word describe what Trace is, or I play him something of Trace's. I go, "Here's the voice," and the best I can describe music in words—which is tough—I describe to him what I'm looking for. But they played me that song. Some songs, like that one, are no-brainers. That's why we picked it. I wish I could find another one like that.

JOY LYNN WHITE, *THE LUCKY FEW* (1997, LITTLE DOG/MERCURY)

PETE ANDERSON

We put the band together for Joy, and we worked really hard on the songs. She was doing things from the only way she knew how, which was a Nashville perspective: "I'm going to go around to the publishers, tell them I'm doing a record."

She was getting these songs from publishers. Then she's going, "I don't have a record deal. They're not giving me the good songs"—and this whole weird thing.

It was like, "Look, I've been doing this for I don't know how many years, and I've gotten a handful that I think are great. It's not them; they're just doing their job. It's not like there's a conspiracy." She had a pile of stuff that wasn't very good, that we didn't like anyway. We just went into our archives: [Jim] Lauderdale, Kostas, Lucinda [Williams], people we'd worked with in the past. We got a bunch of tunes together.

She's such a great singer. She's really gifted. She's a one-take, perfect singer—which is extremely rare. I work with k.d. lang, who can do that. A guy in Blue Rodeo, Jim Cuddy, he can do that. There's not a lot of people that go, "Okay, I'm ready to sing," walk out there, and sing it once, top to bottom—flawless. And she's one of them. She was the perfect songstress to wrap herself around these songs. I don't know many people that can sing a Lucinda Williams song and do it with the same energy and intensity that Lucinda brings to it. I was really impressed with her versions. And then Joy wrote two songs. "Too Big for This Town" she didn't want to put on the record. I'm like, "This is a great song!" So we got two of her songs on there. It was just a different way for her to work. The way we work is much more from a rock-'n'-roll, make-a-record perspective.

She'd made her records in Nashville. It's pretty much churn-it-out. The musicians are great. It's like "Why are you even talking to them? Get in the booth and sing. Here's your song."

K.D. LANG, *DRAG* (1997, SIRE/WARNER BROS.), AND CHRIS WHITLEY, *DIRT FLOOR* (1998, MESSENGER)

CRAIG STREET

When I sit down with somebody, I say, "Basically, I'm not opposed to anything." I don't have to go in and do something straight to two-track and have it unadulterated. Nor do I have to go in and do something to multitrack and do nothing but edits and worry it to death. To me, every project or every song has a different thing that it may want.

I've gone in and done things straight to tape with no reverb, no anything. Chris's record is like that. It's a guy in a room—stomping his foot and singing and playing guitar—and a microphone. That's it. There's nothing else, some cable in between. And I've gone in and done stuff like k.d.'s record where there's orchestration, there're loops, there're live musicians, there're layers and layers and layers of things. It's like going through and doing a painting or something where you pull things out, do little bits here and do little bits there, and let certain things exist. I love them both; the contrast is amazing. I look for people who are open to that.

There are certain things that I like to get, but it's not written in stone that I have to get them. I like to get live performances, essentially, as the foundation. If I go in with a group of musicians, I prefer to get everybody in the room playing a basic track. Maybe in the end I only use a portion of that, and I go back and overdub everything else. But I like to start from the idea, "Here's a great song. Let's let everybody play this in the room." I like it when things bleed on each other. I don't like perfect. That's probably part of why I don't really like recording studios. I prefer more nontraditional spaces. The spaces I tend to work in are more like barns or old warehouses or people's homes—places like that. They feel more conducive to making music.

Then we'll get a basic track that everybody in the room has a great feel about it. Everybody loves it. You know when music is good. You feel it. You don't have to analyze it.

If it's a multitrack thing, I'll go through and do fixes, but there's a difference between a wrong note and something that is simply alive. I believe that you should fix things that are wrong—somebody slipped off the chair, and there're four bars missing from the bass part. You go back in and you fix that. But you don't fix a note that's a quarter-tone off and then kind of resolves back into where it's supposed to go. Somebody might say, "Well, it's the wrong note." It's not the wrong note. It feels good. Why should you change it? So I like to keep as much as I can from both kinds of situations.

CLINT BLACK, *NOTHIN' BUT THE TAILLIGHTS* (1997, RCA)

JAMES STROUD
He's the kind of guy that you can talk to and do preproduction. He plays his songs to you. You give him your ideas, let him run with it. When we

get ready to make our record—and usually the label tells us when they need to deliver a piece of product—we back our time up from that delivery date.

For several months, we start listening to the songs and ideas that he's written or co-written. We go through a number of songs and pick out what we feel could be the direction and the focus of the album. If there are holes—if there's slack in the music—then we know at that time what he needs to write before we start recording. So if we're ballad heavy, let's say, then he'll know, after our preproduction meeting, "Okay, I need to write two or three of the up-tempo situations or mid-tempo situations." Or if a statement song needs to be written, or if a love song needs to be written or co-written. It's that type of meeting.

Then, after a period of time, we get together again, and we literally fill in the blanks of his album with what he's written. For instance, we knew that we wanted him to write with Skip Ewing. Skip is a great lyricist. But one of the things that Clint does well is Clint has a great knowledge of music with his guitar. He's a very good technician; he gets into some intricacies with his music. Well, Skip is that way too. He's a very good guitar player and a great lyricist and a melodic person. We figured that Skip and Clint writing together would be a good situation because they both have an intelligent lyric sense, and they also have a real intelligent music sense. On the album we cut the tracks in Los Angeles and Nashville, but we took it—the tracks—to his house. He has a real nice studio in Los Angeles. We'll sit there for days and work on guitars, vocals, background vocals. If we need a certain player or whatever, we'll bring that person in or go to that person. That's sort of a new way that Clint is able to create now because he has the time to go to his own studio, play with different solos and different rhythms, play with different songs, and make new demos. It just makes his music to me even better and more focused.

GEORGE STRAIT, *ONE STEP AT A TIME* (1998, MCA NASHVILLE)

TONY BROWN

Someone asked, "How do you work with Wynonna one week, work with George Strait the next week, and then work with Tracy Byrd?"

I said, "It's the same way when you're listening to the radio or listening to different CDs by different artists, pop artists and then country artists, or eating hamburger for lunch and then eating seafood for dinner. Let's face it, we're made to appreciate things that sound good or taste good. You just start knowing when something's good or not.

George is probably the easiest artist that I've ever worked with as far as not trying to push the envelope. He isn't trying to reinvent himself. He really likes doing the kind of music that he does. It doesn't bother him when the press says, "Another album of more of the same from George Strait." For instance, we did a song on the last album called "We Really Shouldn't Be Doing This." It sounded a little bit like Elvis. George and I thought that it might be pretty cool to do something like that—different. The first response from people at radio was no one knew who it was. They said, "George should do the stuff that people recognize." So he can't win if he tries to do something different. But bottom line, George doesn't worry about those kinds of things. I think some artists do. They've got to push the envelope because they're afraid that they've been to the well one too many times. Maybe some are right, but in the case of George, he does what he does so well, it's never ever not paid off for him.

EMMYLOU HARRIS, *SPYBOY* (1998, EMINENT)

BUDDY MILLER

It was a unique group, a real small band: just guitar, bass and drums, and Emmylou. The rhythm section was these two guys from Louisiana [Darryl Johnson and Brady Blade], who came at her music from a completely different place, rhythmically and vocally. I don't even know how familiar they were with her at all when they got on board.

I loved playing in that group so much I wanted to document it. I recorded some live dates. I wanted proof that I was actually in the band. It was really good. Emmy was thinking about maybe getting a live version of "The Maker," and then she got presented with the opportunity: somebody wanted to do a live record from it.

She asked me to work with her on it. We brought out a rack of mike pres [microphone preamplifiers] that I have and ADATs [digital audiotape recorders]. We used real good mike pres, and we tried to use good mikes here and there, but usually we just set up every night. We recorded twenty dates, I think. We had a lot of material.

Emmylou and I went through all of the dates. Actually, I was in Australia at the time, but we had a lot of long-distance phone calls. We'd talk about which performances were the best and why. Then we'd try and string them together the way a night would flow. Emmylou put together a set. She writes a different set [list] every night. She did that with these songs too. Then there were things we needed to fix. So we did those fixes. I dumped all of the songs into Pro Tools, and we did some slight fixing, but there really wasn't that much. Actually, I tried to listen to the overall picture. If something was obviously bad, we didn't use it. We went for the best overall performance.

With other people I've had times where I had to grind on a vocal. It's not a fun practice. So it was nice to get a performance as opposed to what they do in Nashville. A lot of times an artist will sing a song three or four times. They'll comp [composite] a vocal together and then tune it.

I record in Pro Tools. I have a pretty elaborate setup, but I really use it as a tape recorder. A lot of places in Nashville have complete Pro Tool systems just to tune vocals. To me, it can suck the soul right out of a vocal if you get it too right, and people get used to hearing things too in tune, in tempo, too quantized. Do you know that expression? It's with the drums playing too perfectly in time, even to where they line up drum parts to a click track within Pro Tools. They kind of get things too perfect, and I think people get too used to hearing things that way. Music isn't that way. I like a little grease in things—a little reality.

JIM LAUDERDALE, *WHISPER* (1998, BNA)

BLAKE CHANCEY

On every record I produce, I try to use a different band. I listen to each artist. I listen to their music. Part of my job as a producer is to help them put together a band for their album that, at the end of the day, sounds like them. If you listen to a Deryl Dodd album, it doesn't sound anything like Mary Chapin Carpenter's. Or it doesn't sound anything like the Dixie Chicks. Or it doesn't sound like the Jim Lauderdale album I did. Each album should sound like the artist; it shouldn't sound like me. I'm just like anybody else that listens to the radio. Sometimes you listen to it, and it all sounds the same. It's my job to try to change that.

Jim's from the Carolina area. He's a big bluegrass fan. He'd been working with Ralph Stanley for years. Jim wrote "I'll Lead You Home." He called me up and said, "Blake, I've got this song. I want to get Ralph Stanley to do it." We started looking at the logistics. Ralph was in town making this compilation album with all these huge guest artists.

They said, "While we're doing this, why don't you come over and cut with Ralph's band?" It was a cool moment for me. I'd never really worked in that type of music. Everything was cut live; everybody playing in a circle. They both sang at the same time, looking at each other. It was a really cool thing. Lauderdale put that together.

We walked in, and actually Jim had a real slow, kind of loping version of "I'll Lead You Home." Ralph goes, "Jim, check out the way we've worked it up." It was an up-tempo, trainy kind of beat thing. And that was pretty much the way we did it, because they worked it up that way.

LUCINDA WILLIAMS, *CAR WHEELS ON A GRAVEL ROAD* (1998, MERCURY)

GURF MORLIX

We actually did a version in Austin in, well, I don't remember what year it was, '95 maybe. Pretty much had the whole record cut. We were 85 to 90 percent done. Lucinda felt she was having some trouble singing— looking for reasons. She ended up bagging the whole album because she felt like she wasn't singing well, although most of the singing is, I think, better than what came out on her Mercury record. Her vocals were just really honest. I think some of the stuff on the new album sounds a little forced. Obviously, they were going for something, but I think the stuff we cut in Austin has a better feel to it. It's more relaxed. I would say that between the two versions of the record, the best record would have been about half and half, but it had progressed beyond that point. There was no turning back at that point for her.

She has no perspective, and artists aren't expected to have perspective. They write the songs. She gets in the studio, and there are too many decisions, and she's not a good decision maker. At some point, I was telling her what I thought, and she stopped hearing me somehow. Her thinking got clouded or something.

Morlix produced the original version of Car Wheels on a Gravel Road— *now a widely circulated bootleg. Williams dismissed Morlix as producer, however, and re-recorded the album with the production team of Steve Earle, Ray Kennedy, and Roy Bittan.*

ROBERT EARL KEEN JR.,
WALKING DISTANCE (1998, ARISTA)

GURF MORLIX

Robert is kind of unique. He writes all of his songs pretty much in about a week or so before we start rehearsals. I know that, and I trust him. I wouldn't do a record if I hadn't heard the songs. I wouldn't agree to do it, except that I know Robert works that way. He came through fine. I knew he would. He came in with the songs, and that was all he had.

If an artist comes to me and says, "I've got these great songs; I need a band," then I can put a band together, and it'll be professional session players, but they'll play passionately. It will sound like a band. Whereas in Nashville it really doesn't. It sounds like factory work. I think that that whole Nashville thing, it's gotten so diluted. I don't feel like it's important to those players to play like they're in a band. They're just doing a job.

JONBOY LANGFORD AND THE
PINE VALLEY COSMONAUTS,
SALUTE THE MAJESTY OF
BOB WILLS (1998, BLOODSHOT)

JON LANGFORD

When I was a kid, I thought of country music as quite right-wing music. I was misunderstanding it. Actually listen to it, and it comes from a weirder place. I don't think of Bob Wills as a redneck, a narrow-minded person. I think of him as someone who was incredibly open to all different influences. He was a kind of magician pulling together all these different things that I don't think anybody had pulled together before. It's almost avant-garde music, what people call postmodern now. He was doing that then: "Oh, we'll take some mariachi horns. We'll stick some jazz, blues, and steel guitars on it and some old-timey fiddles." Country music becomes—it is actually—really inclusive. There are a lot of simi-larities between country music and the blues. It's basically blues music for white people.

The idea for the album came from the paintings. I did a bunch of paintings of Bob Wills, and we did an art show. We put a little band together, and we learned a lot of the songs. It sounded fantastic. Blood-shot [Records] was probably there. We got talking: "Let's see if we can make an album of this." For me, it was no one's really playing this stuff; no one's playing it in a way that I really like.

I love the songs, and I wanted to record them. We had a bunch of musicians who understood them well enough, like Tom Ray and Steve Goulding, who were there as a rhythm section, and John Rice, who could play those twin-fiddle things. He knew the material. And we had people like Kelly Hogan and Jimmie Dale Gilmore who came and sang. I felt we could actually do the project justice. We could do something good.

It's a weird thing with country music. Whenever you do tribute al-bums—all these albums where you get a lot of people who are very fa-mous, and they all come together and make these albums, all recorded in different studios with different production styles—the one thing they tend to do is slow the songs down and push them into a more folky singer-songwriter direction. I notice this all the time, when people cover old honky-tonk stuff. It's like they haven't really listened to it, and they try to make it sound more precious and sweet. I like the kind of gnarly-ness of all that stuff.

I wanted to put a band together where we played it warts and all: made it more like those Tiffany Transcriptions [recordings Wills made for radio broadcast]. I've heard people that do Bob Wills covers make it somewhat soft rock with a bit of twang on top. I wanted to get some-thing that was a bit more earthy.

VINCE GILL, *THE KEY* (1998, MCA NASHVILLE)

TONY BROWN

Vince wanted to do something really country, and I wanted him to do something really country too. We'd always put a few country tunes on every album, like "When I Call Your Name" and "No Future in the Past." But we wanted to cut something really raw country. That's why we sort of strayed from using the normal session players and got [pianist] Pig Robbins and Randy Scruggs. We used the same band on every session; we actually scheduled sessions around those particular musicians. We could cut only when they were available. The only preproduction we did was talking amongst ourselves about how we wanted it to sound. Everything happened on the floor like in the old days.

Like when we cut "If You Ever Have Forever in Mind," we talked about doing a song that sounded like Ray Charles's *Modern Sounds in Country Music*. I had Bergen [White] listen to "Born to Lose" and copy that little string bend when he did the chart. When we got ready to cut the track, we talked about it sounding like that stuff. Before we rolled the tape, I looked at Pig, and I said, "Pig, give me a famous intro," just joking.

And then, when he played, I was going, "God, this sounds incredible. It sounds famous!" As soon as he did the intro—you could see it in the room—the rest of the band all clicked back into retro-time. They became Ray Charles's band. A lot of magic moments happened during that album. Plus, when Vince sings in the headphones—some singers don't really sing their songs like they're performing them—but he does. It's inspiring.

A lot of times you'll cut it, and you'll almost get it. Something will happen, and you'll bring everybody in and say, "Hey, there's a good sketch here. Listen to the intro. Do that again." You start telling everybody, "You did this on the second verse. Do it on the first verse instead of the second." You start telling them what to do.

But occasionally, you'll say something like what I said to Pig. They kick it off, and every guitar fill, all the solos, are live, and you keep going,

"This thing is going to fall apart any minute. This is not going to be a take." And then, it is a take. It sounds incredible.

You say, "Let's do it a couple of more times—see if we can beat it." And you do it two more times. They know that you liked what you heard because, you know, I'm in there screaming. They play it two more times, and it sounds really good, but then you go back and listen to the very first time they did it, and it's better than the next two times. They're such great musicians. They actually had something—that little whatever that thing is. You know what it is when you hear it.

RANDY TRAVIS, *YOU AND YOU ALONE* (1998, DREAMWORKS SKG)

JAMES STROUD

There are great singers out there that don't need a lot of tuning and comping and stuff. Clint [Black]'s one. He's a great example of somebody who just sings so well, you don't have to beat up his vocal. Lorrie Morgan is another one. She's a great singer. When I worked with her, there are songs on her album that are live vocals. Randy Travis is another one—an amazing singer.

He and I had weeks and weeks of talk about what we needed to do. If you listen to the album, you're going to hear some tradition in there, but you're also going to hear a new Randy. We tried to draw from my background to freshen up some of the things that he does. For instance, listen to "Out of My Bones." I told him, "We need to cut this thing like the Band, in that kind of style, where it's pretty loose and pretty piano-y, and it sort of grooves real lazily, but it has some force to it."

He was listening, and he said, "Okay, these are things that I might not necessarily know. I trust you."

That's the way we went after it. Of course, Byron Gallimore co-produced that with me, and he brought in his great ideas as far as guitar work and the things that he does with backgrounds. But with Randy, it's sort of a no-brainer. If you get great songs and you can put some unique-ness to the tracks, he will sing the fool out of it. It's amazing.

If you go back and listen to "Out of My Bones" and you listen to the bridge, it's a direct cop from what the Band would play. It's a good example of bringing my background, what I used to do, into today's music, and then updating Randy to where he's a mainstream artist again.

DIXIE CHICKS, *WIDE OPEN SPACES* (1998, MONUMENT) AND *FLY* (1999, MONUMENT)

PAUL WORLEY

The Dixie Chicks are a classic example of artist development from an A&R and a producer point of view. A lot of us in Nashville had been aware of the Dixie Chicks for a long time. They'd been performing for some seven or eight years down in Texas and around the Southwest and had quite a business of their own developed. They would send flyers and keep us all aware of what they were doing. Many in the Nashville community had seen the Dixie Chicks in their various stages of development.

Blake Chancey, who works with me here at Sony, contacted them. Actually, Scott Simon was here with me at Sony at the time. He encouraged Blake to get with them. He knew their manager. Blake went down to see them and found that there was something there. He was intrigued. He very slowly and methodically worked with them, fed them songs, talked to them about musical direction, for about a year. They would put down acoustic demos of songs.

At one point during that process, they even changed personnel. Their original lead singer left the group, and they found Natalie Maines. They knew Natalie's father, Lloyd Maines. Lloyd had helped them produce some sides on their own, and they met Natalie through him. They tried Natalie out, and she fit like a glove. They did some more demos of some songs. Blake brought them back up here from Texas, and he and I agreed that this was ready to take to the next level. We set about taking them into the studio and actually recording some masters. Blake and I have worked together for years. We enjoy working together. He wanted me to work with them on this project. Having heard the demos he'd cut, I was real interested. We discussed it. He felt that I could add an element to it that would be good. We agreed to do it. So basically, it was at his invitation that I got involved.

And then we brought the girls up [from Dallas to Nashville]. The song search was very long and drawn out. A lot of the community was really put off by the name, the Dixie Chicks. They were reluctant to give us songs that we needed to record. And so one approach we took was to bring the girls up to personally visit many of the publishing houses—dozens and dozens of publishing houses. The girls performed acoustically to give them an idea of what their sound was like. I would play along with Emily and Martie on the acoustic instruments, and Natalie would sing. We did that a bunch until we got the community a little bit aware of what their talent was.

Even so, it's hard to find great songs for new artists. The writers and publishers like to give their fresh new songs the best possible home. We worked for about another year on finding songs. The girls tried a lot of songs out, played them live with their band, made sure that they fit really well.

To do this project, Blake and I ended up using a lot of songs that we had recorded together on other projects in years past that had not, for whatever reasons, come to fruition, or the songs were not singles by other artists. We had to go to that well to find several of the songs that made it on the album. The girls brought in songs—like "Wide Open Spaces" from a friend of theirs down in Texas—and I think it was their idea to do the cover of "Loving Arms" and the Bonnie Raitt tune "Give It Up." The album ended up being a mixture of a lot of the elements that we'd all collected over the years.

We knew that the instrumentation would have to heavily include fiddle, mandolin and banjo, and acoustic guitar. That's what the girls do. We knew that their background was bluegrass, and yet they had a real rocking presentation in their shows. Those things were given. Blake has always been interested in a real honest sound, in trying to get country music to embrace a sound that's a little more raw and honest and less affected. That idea seemed to fit with the Dixie Chicks really well. So we went off in that direction. Things came out really nicely.

We always worked really hard to make sure that the musical performances and the vocal performances were really solid. We really wanted to show the fact that these girls are great musicians as well as great singers. We gave them a lot of time to work out their parts. Then we took a lot of care in putting their parts down. Natalie is a very emotional singer. It needs not to be too perfected for that to be allowed to happen.

I'm head of A&R here at the company [Sony Nashville], and Blake is second to me in A&R in the company. He's a vice-president. So once we decided what was the right thing to do, there wasn't any difficulty in having the budget that we needed. Given that the girls all lived out of town, there was a lot of travel involved. That was logistically a little bit difficult and expensive.

BLAKE CHANCEY

I was a publisher for a long time. My job was to find artists early on and to take two, sometimes three years developing them: helping them find a direction for themselves, helping them find the right music as a writer or as an artist cutting outside songs. We took our time until we had the total package done. Then, it was my job to go shop it to record labels. I did that for years.

When I came here to work, when I said, "Hey, let's start developing artists," it was not well received right off. If you've had an artist signed to a record label for three years, the label looks around and goes, "Who's that person on our roster for three years that I've never heard?" Most record labels want some type of turnaround in a year or year and a half. They want to put out an album.

The Dixie Chicks were my first experiment at a record label developing artists. I originally signed them in Austin, Texas. They had a different lead singer. We started working out of a house, just sitting around in a circle working on music. Then the band itself kind of evolved, getting Natalie to become the lead singer, changing musical directions, trying to record some stuff and going, "Uh, that's not really us. Let's try this." They developed as musicians, and they learned the process of recording.

When it came time for them to make their own album, they were ready. They knew what it was like to walk into a studio and record. They knew what it was like to listen for songs for their album. They were green, but they'd been through the development stages. It was not like throwing somebody a curve ball. It happens a lot that we go out, and we sign artists. We expect them to walk offstage from playing in a club or whatever. We throw them in a studio with a budget and all these producers and musicians and songs. And we expect that everybody knows what to do. They don't. So I'm glad that the Dixie Chicks process worked.

Paul [Worley] is very—what's the best way to put it?—spur of the moment, go for the moment, very creative, very much musician's side of the glass, that sort. We both have a very similar song sense. I'm more on the control-room side of the glass, more of the conservative: thinking everything out, meticulously making sure everything is right on that side. I'm more the, as you would say, the conservative. He's more the liberal, if there was a way to explain it in producing.

When we're tracking, Paul is always playing. He's playing acoustic guitar, and he's a musician. He's getting into it from a musician's standpoint. I'm sitting behind the console, where the speakers are, listening to it as a record—more as somebody listening to it at home.

I'm going, "Hey, you know, I think we need to change this part of the song, because it would make it more of a record."

Paul's on the other side going, "Hey, steel player"—Lloyd Maines or whoever—"I think you should play this lick here." It's like Paul's a band member really. He's like the session leader, guitar guy. And I'm sitting on the other side—from the more technical side—going, "We've got to make this . . . this is sounding more like a record," or "It's not sounding like a record."

MANDY BARNETT, *I'VE GOT A RIGHT TO CRY* (1999, SIRE)

HAROLD BRADLEY

When my brother passed away, I helped Mandy Barnett finish her album. Owen had done four sides with her; we did the other eight sides. It was really hard, because when he first asked me to do that, I didn't warm up to the idea. A month after my brother passed away, I had a mild heart attack, and so it took a while for me to get strong enough even to consider it.

It was really hard to go back in his big footprint. The four sides he'd done had strings on them. The budget didn't allow for them on the rest of the songs. Our challenge was to make it sound like Owen did the whole album. From what I hear, people think that he did that. It goes seamlessly from one part to the other.

The idea for the nostalgia came from the songs that Mandy Barnett wanted to do. That's the era she identifies with. She'd be a big star now, except that she refuses to do new country. She just loves the old songs, wanted to hang on to the old musicians. Owen did wonderful work with her. No telling where they would have gone if he had lived.

HAL KETCHUM,
AWAITING REDEMPTION (1999, CURB)

STEPHEN BRUTON

You could do it by the book and say, "I'm supposed to get the studio and the engineers. I'm supposed to get the players. I'm supposed to do the arrangements and pick out the songs and whatnot." That all falls into the job description.

Most people, however, have their songs together, or they have a pretty good idea what they want to do. I can put together a rhythm section, unless they have some people that they specifically want to use. At which point I have to find out if who they have are up-to-snuff players, and even if they are up-to-snuff players, whether they get red-light fever, which all of us have had in the past. (It's just part of the game.) That's if you do it by the book.

I probably do things a little bit different. I haven't hung around a lot to find out how different people produce, but I've been there enough to know that my approach is pretty different.

I'll tell you why. I was producing this album by Hal Ketchum. It was shelved but it's coming out now. I was in the studio with the engineer at the end of the first day—a musician-engineer. He was laughing. He goes, "Boy." He looked at me. "Do they know what you're doing out here?" That was his quote.

"Who's they?" I asked him.

"The record company."

"Well, what's different about it?"

"This is a completely different session than what we're used to out here [in Texas]."

I said, "Unless they call ahead, I run a closed session. So no one's going to be here, and I wouldn't know the record company if they walked in the door, unless they announced themselves." I really wouldn't have. I'd had no contact with them. They merely said, "Go ahead and do the album." They'd given me the go-ahead to management and the business people. We did it on that level. I never met with them. "Go ahead and do it."

This is funny. He said, "When you first got here, we thought you were the roadie because you were helping. You came here with your equipment. You showed up first, got your gear in here, and then everybody else who came in, you helped out with their gear." Then later on in the session, they said, 'We realized, hey, that guy's the producer!' You were using his band, which no one in Nashville uses."

I don't know if that's particularly all-the-way, 100 percent true, but I used Hal's band because it means a lot to have your band on the records. He has some very fine players. You know how it is in Nashville. I don't know if it's always true. It seemed to be the truth for a long time that there were road musicians, and then there were studio musicians.

I was one of those guys who was a road musician. I did it for years with Kristofferson. You'd come to Nashville. You might be included on the session, but more than likely you weren't. Gradually, I started getting included, but only because Kris insisted on it. The producer would normally say, "Leave them at home. We'll cut with our guys down here."

I think it's real important to have your guys from the road, when you have the quality of players that Hal has, guys who've been with him, guys who have given it their all every night; it was their life. It wasn't just a gig. It's tough on relationships. It's tough on everything. The artist gets to go home, and he stays the artist. The musician goes home and waits for the phone to ring. Man, that's a tough life, a very uncertain life. So anyway, I like using those guys. Also you get a different flavor. You listen to this album. I'm very, very proud of it. Those guys played their butts off. They gave more than a lot of studio players would give because it wouldn't be just the third session of the day.

Here's what happened. I got hired to do the album. They said, "Produce him like you hear him." I thought Hal was closer to Van Morrison than to Hank Williams. I did a much grittier album than what he's used to. Then, I get a phone call from this guy named Chuck Howard, who in fact informed me that he loved the album, thought it was really great, thought it was the best work Hal had ever done, but it needed two songs for radio. Radio dictates everything to those poor guys down there [in Nashville]. It's weird. It's like the tail wagging the dog.

To make a long story short, Chuck Howard got hold of the project. Next thing you know, they've cut twelve songs, and they've put my album on the shelf. The whole thing was just a sham. He came in there blowing smoke, telling me how great I was, when in fact he was just saying, "I don't think this record's going to fly in today's market." But I couldn't say anything because, hey, they let me have my chance. They didn't like it. So no big deal.

They put out their album [*I Saw the Light*, which included three tracks produced by Bruton], and it stiffs real bad. Now they're going to put out the album that I did [*Awaiting Redemption*]. I don't understand the logic, but I'm anxious to see what happens.

What's happened down in Nashville, for example, is everybody moved there, and you've got all these guys who are dying for something new—anything new. They want to cross over. But you wind up being neither fish nor fowl. You don't have real country music. I'm sorry. You've got all this cookie-cutter stuff. You've got songs that sound like Hallmark greeting cards. It's generated by the enormous amount of people buying records.

I'm trying to fit two thoughts together. You have people doing rock 'n' roll records, heavy metal, whatever. Their jobs are dwindling, they come to Nashville, they have a resurgence in their career. And so the country records that they're so-called "producing" suddenly come out rock 'n' roll. As a matter of fact, they bring the same production values into play.

I don't think you have to be super conservative. I just think those guys need to open their freaking ears and listen to the songs and listen to the artists. Everybody wants to sell a bajillion records, but more and more artists sell a bajillion records—once, and then they're done. The band breaks up, and you never hear from them again. Record companies support you only if you sell a bajillion records every time. That's what's happening with the record companies now. Maybe you can't sell a couple of million records every time out. It's unrealistic to put that expectation on somebody. So what do they do? They put them into these little cookie-cutter deals.

I just hope all these big shots that got their asses fired don't start showing up at independent labels, telling everybody how to run things—bullies out to be the avenging angels on the big boys. There again, they may walk in and make a liar out of me and say, "You know, I see where this is going. I think we can help." In the long term, this might be the exact thing that's meant to be happening. You have to look at it that way, because it was so bloated the other way.

It's gotten to where it's very easy to be a naysayer. It doesn't require any intellect to say, "Everything's over there." You have to hope that the guys who are supposed to be in the business will stay in the business, and the guys who should be selling sheetrock will ultimately find their way there. The only thing I distrust is corporations, and that's what we're dealing with here.

THE DERAILERS, *FULL WESTERN DRESS* (1999, SIRE)

DAVE ALVIN

That was the biggest budget we'd had yet. In fact it's the biggest budget for any record I've ever produced. I have to admit, I was a little afraid. Tony [Villanueva] and Brian [Hofeldt] were kind of scared this time, in a different way, but instantly it became obvious—this is fun. We had Floyd Domino in to play piano; Gene Elders, from George Strait and Lyle Lovett's bands, played fiddle; we had a lot of great musicians in there. And it was fun because of that.

We recorded up at Perdenales [Recording Studio], which is Willie Nelson's place out there in Texas—so really a great studio. We had Stuart Sullivan, one of my favorite engineers. He's done everything from Sublime to the Butthole Surfers to the Antone's blues records, but he was also Willie's personal engineer for like forty years. If I make a stylistic sound reference, he knows exactly what I'm talking about.

The biggest thing that I learned [about production from the Blasters and X] was I don't like to waste time in the studio. The Blasters, we wasted a lot of time arguing and a lot of time goofing off. Some of it was even fun. But it was all because of fear. As a singer, when you're playing roots music and you go into a state-of-the-art recording studio, there's a tendency to be afraid. How can this modern technology capture what we do?

It's almost like jazz. When you make a jazz record, what do you do? You have a great musician in a great studio with a great engineer with great microphones. And he just does what he does. Then you put the record on, and it's timeless because of that.

There's nothing to be afraid of in the studio. The technology is there to help you, not to hurt you. A lot of times it does boil down to finding the right engineer and finding a studio where people feel comfortable. But the actual technology can only help. It can hurt you only if you want it to. If you have an engineer whose only concept of music is Pink Floyd or Yes—that kind of production technique—then it could harm you. But if you've got the right engineer, you've got the right environment, it's work, but it's fun work.

THE BOTTLE ROCKETS, *BRAND NEW YEAR* (1999, DOOLITTLE/NEW WEST), AND SHANIA TWAIN, *COME ON OVER* (1997, MERCURY NASHVILLE)

ERIC "ROSCOE" AMBEL

A lot of times when people are working on albums in a studio, you have records that you listen to: that you kind of get going with, to sort of cop the vibe, or to check out the speakers in the studio. Over the last year, I heard a lot of people busting on Shania Twain.

But when I was riding around with my wife, and I listened to that song "Still the One," and I listened to that vocal, it blew my mind. It was such a great vocal. It had no histrionics, no tricks. That's one of the best pop vocals I've ever heard. A lot of times you're in the studio, and you're listening to a favorite record, like *Exile on Main Street*. It's definitely one of my top-ten favorites. Granted, we love it. So what's the point remaking it?

I got together with the Bottle Rockets, and it turned out that they had just started to go nuts over Shania too—just in a rebel way, after hearing all of these people put her down and call her the most expensive lapdancer in Nashville and all that stuff. I really believe that to be sour grapes. They went whole hog into this Shania thing: the Church of Twain. We had Shania stuff all over the studio. We'd listen to the record.

They had posters of her. Before we'd do a take, the whole band would walk over to the poster, and everybody would put their hands on her tummy for the inspiration, to feel the power. It was really helpful to have some inspiration like that. I'm lucky my wife likes it. Some women are threatened by Shania.

The first record that she made with Mutt [Lange] had some really great stuff on it, and this new one—there's still a couple of songs that I'm going to skip—but it's a benchmark of every trick in the book. The arrangements are interesting. The thing moves. And her vocal is so good, it really gave us something to shoot for.

I've heard some stories about how they make those records. The story that was related to me, and this makes sense, is that they write those songs. They've got their über–home studio [in Switzerland] with an SSL9000J [a ninety-six-channel mixer] or whatever. They do full-on home demos. Everything's programmed; they're playing everything themselves. Then they go to . . . they cut the last record at the big Masterfonics Tracking Room [in Nashville]. They get all the hot guys in there. They get everybody set up. They have her sing, and the band plays with the demo. The demo is in their headphones. They tell everybody to play their asses off, and they take it back [home]. There must be squadrons of Pro Tool guys working on it after that. There are songs on there where you hear, they're not guitar sounds, they're manipulated guitars, or there are little licks that they grab. It's a very interesting thing.

JOHN PRINE, *IN SPITE OF OURSELVES* (1999, OH BOY)

JIM ROONEY

When I made the first album [*Infamous Angel*] with Iris [DeMent], I gave John a cassette. I said, "Listen to this." He of course just loved it, and he wrote very quirky liner notes for it. He started having Iris open shows for him, and they began to sing a couple of songs together.

He said, "I just have to record something with Iris, some duets." That was the germ of an idea. The more we thought about it, the more duet partners we considered. We went to John's manager, Al Banetta, with the idea. He said, "People don't want to hear you singing other people's songs. They want to hear John Prine songs."

He said, "Well, John Prine doesn't have any songs right now." John is the head of his own company, so he got the final say.

He rented an apartment [in Nashville] for a month. He and I went there in the afternoons with all our records: our George Jones and our Melba Montgomery records, George and Tammy, Conway and Loretta, Porter and Dolly—all the duets. Everly Brothers. We sat there listening to our favorite records. We made a list—kept adding things to it and subtracting things from it. John made a list of the female singers he'd like to sing with. Eventually, everybody said, "Yes."

We started off with Iris. At this point, she'd actually fired me. It was a strange experience. It was a feeling she had that we shouldn't work together anymore. I said, "If that's what you feel, that's fine. Go ahead and feel that way. Break my heart." At any rate this was the occasion for us to get back together again.

It was just amazing. We cut three or four things with her, and then with Melba Montgomery. You should see my copy of that album of George and Melba. It's in tatters. I've had that album for so long. Of course, Melba is a great songwriter—"We Must've Been out of Our Minds." Then we had Connie Smith, who's also a great, great singer. She did "Loose Talk," which I'd heard with Buck Owens and Rose Maddox. Carl Smith had the original record. I used to sing it at the Club 47 with Betsy Siggins. So there were a lot of songs on there that I knew very early on in my musical life. "Back Street Affair"—that Patty Loveless did on the record—it was one of the very first songs I sang. I was playing it with the ukulele when I was thirteen or fourteen years old. "Let's Turn Back the Years" was one of the first songs I played on guitar because it only had two chords. When I was fifteen, Hank Williams was my real idol. Lucinda Williams did it and "Wedding Bells." That was John's idea, to put those two songs together. We had such a wonderful time.

After the first group of sessions, John was diagnosed with neck cancer. We didn't know if we'd finish that album. It was more than a year. He went through surgery and treatment. Eventually, he got his voice back.

He got involved in a movie Billy Bob Thornton was making called *Daddy and Them*. It was great for John in many ways. He had very few lines. He was like somebody's uncle who sits in the corner reading the paper and every so often says something. It was a great role. It kept his mind off his troubles, and his voice had a chance to come back slowly. He was getting paid, which was a help because cancer is so expensive.

Marty Stuart had become friends with Billy Bob Thornton. He was in charge of music for the film. They asked John if he could write something. He came up with the song "In Spite of Ourselves." Their idea was a duet. They'd hoped for some star person, female singer. I think they approached one or two people, but the lyrics—involving "sniffing panties" and stuff—no managers thought they were a smart career move for their artists. Then John said, "What about Iris DeMent?"

"Okay, sure. Try her," they said.

He sent the lyric to Iris. She called him back. "Do you really want me to sing this?"

He said, "I had you in mind all along." They did it.

I was spending a lot of time in Ireland at this point, and I came back from Ireland to Nashville just before Christmas. We were in John's car. He put this cassette in, and it was him and Iris singing "In Spite of Ourselves." I was alternately laughing and crying—laughing because the song is so funny and quirky, crying because he had his voice back. It was lower, but he had it back. That meant we were going to be able to finish that album. We also had the title song for the album. Everything was just perfect. We went ahead and finished the album the next two or three months. It's one of my favorite things I've ever done.

Bobby Braddock's song, "(We're Not) The Jet Set," was a perfect fit for John Prine.

John picked it, and I think it definitely suited him. Country music has always had the kind of wit, the word associations, that appealed to him and to me. John is a master of that. There was a songwriter exhibit over at the Hall of Fame, and Harlan Howard was talking about "Pick Me Up on Your Way Down." He used the phrase, "Now they've changed your attitude, made you haughty and so rude." He said, "I put that 'haughty' in there so those hillbillies would have something to think about."

MONTGOMERY GENTRY, *TATTOOS & SCARS* (1999, COLUMBIA)

BLAKE CHANCEY

I signed a group here [at Sony] called Montgomery Gentry, did the same process [as with the Dixie Chicks]. One of our people who works here, Anthony Martin, he was assigned the project. For right at a year and a half, all he did was guitar, vocals, find them songs—try and help them find their direction. Then we found them a producer, Joe Scaife, who went in and cut the album—after they had already learned what it was like to be in the studio, learned what it was like to find songs, and figured out who they were. They broke all *R&R* [*Radio & Records*] and *Billboard* records for the highest debut of a new artist ever. And people are kind of looking around going, "Where did these guys come from?" Well, they came from finding them way early on, heavy development, and making sure they were ready before we put them on the launching pad.

ALLISON MOORER, *THE HARDEST PART* (2000, MCA)

TONY BROWN

When people question me, I have to go to the artist: "You know, everybody's sort of saying maybe we're missing something really commercial on this record." If she goes, "Well, I love it," then I'll go back down the hall and say, "It's coming out the way it is." I still roll with an artist like that. But it's harder for an artist to make the impact that Steve [Earle] and Lyle [Lovett] did back in 1986 and 1987, because there's just so much music right now.

I'll actually give her the option. "Hey, do you think there's anything we can do to maybe sort of skew this a little bit toward the right—make it a little more mainstream?" Then, if she fights it, because she's a real artist (she's like Lyle — a singer, songwriter, artist; she's really deep into her music), if I see it really, really is going to upset her, the first thing I do is back off, because I already like it.

Mainstream music isn't going to like everything. So I support all kinds of music. The thing about it is, if you can help an artist, like Allison Moorer, have a bit of mainstream success, even if it's only one hit, like Tracy Chapman when she had a couple of hits — she's not a mainstream artist either, but she had a couple of songs that rang the bell — if you can just expose those artists to a bigger audience, to me that's success, too.

THE YAYHOOS, *FEAR NOT THE OBVIOUS* (2001, BLOODSHOT)

ERIC "ROSCOE" AMBEL

Working on a record is a very difficult thing. It's sort of like when you throw a party. If you clean up your house before you throw the party, it's a lot easier to clean up afterwards. If you do your homework on a recording project, if you do the preproduction — you really know the material, you really know the people — if you do all that work beforehand, then you can go crazy and let things fly.

You don't go into the studio to stroke each other's egos and say, "You're great." We all realized before we got there that everybody's great. This holds true for a lot of people. I think that most of us are more critical about the stuff that we really love. All that is a precursor to saying something like, "That wasn't the one. Let's do some more."

Have you ever seen those oblique strategy cards [created by producer Brian Eno as an aid to invention]? We drew one that read, "Do nothing for as long as possible." We emended it so it went: "Do nothing for as long as possible. Then, go eat."

TIM McGRAW, *SET THIS CIRCUS DOWN* (2001, CURB)

JAMES STROUD

It's like building a house. If you don't have a great foundation, you're going to have a shaky house. So I pride myself on making sure that the track, the basic track, is as solid as anything around. As a drummer and learning from that instrument, the one thing you do learn is that there has to be not only a consistent drum track but a musical drum track, so that it doesn't get in the way of the building process.

It helped me as a producer when I was playing drums—to understand the beginning of the track, getting through to the mix, and how the music fit on top of what I played. I apply what I learned as a drummer to the basic tracks. Once I know I have a solid basic track, then it's going to be pretty tough to screw up the rest of it. You're going to have a pretty good foundation, and you're not going to mess something up as long as it has that great basic track.

[Jean Knight's] "Mr. Big Stuff" and [King Floyd's] "Groove Me" and all that old stuff [tracks on which Stroud played drums]: that was just learning. I grew up playing R&B, and I apply a lot of those ideas to our country music today. I can give you an example of one of the things that I apply that background to on Tim McGraw's record. When Byron [Gallimore] and Tim and I make the records, I do a lot of the arranging for the basic tracks. That's my forte. Byron is great at doing vocals and overdubs. Of course, Tim has his ideas. It's a wonderful process that we use. But I utilize some of the ideas and techniques and processes that we used to do making the old R&B and rock-'n'-roll records. Tim's records, if you listen to them, they're really well-made records, but there are some real unique things going on within the records.

The other thing that I do is utilize some of the arrangements that we used back then, the real clean guitar, syncopations with the bass and drums that country now is starting to use—and that's starting to work in a real good way. Instead of things being real straight, there are a lot of syncopations in the tracks that I cut. It's a wealth of knowledge that

I've been real blessed to get, through my playing, to apply to country productions.

NORAH JONES, *COME AWAY WITH ME* (2002, BLUE NOTE)

CRAIG STREET

My understanding from her was that she knew a little bit about me. When we first started talking, it turned out that the second recording I did with Cassandra Wilson, *New Moon Daughter*, was apparently a majorly influential record to Norah. It was a touchstone for her.

I don't think we would've spoken if she hadn't wanted to sit down with me. But that's a really difficult record to talk about without it getting politicized in a certain way. And so it's one that I don't necessarily talk about. She did request me, and we did some things together that were based on what she asked for. We recorded about twenty songs. It was a lot of fun. It really was. But there were a lot of other things going on at the same time. A lot of people involved have had a lot to say about what I did in the context of that project. I've never publicly commented on any of it, and I won't. I'm not going to say that what anybody else said is inaccurate. It goes against my nature to talk negatively about anybody.

Norah was an absolute pleasure to work with: very, very open to trying lots of different things. It was clear that she had a lot going on that she was able to explore later on. She's one of the sweetest people that I've ever met in my life. It's always interesting to work with people who have not done a lot of stuff before. There's a huge difference. It's such a different thing, walking in with Bettye [LaVette] or with Jimmy Scott, where I feel, "Why are you willing to talk to me?"

You're dealing with a creative process that's also a card game. It potentially can lead to massive financial remuneration. Given that, you've got people who are in it for all kinds of reasons. You've got people in it just because they need to do it, and then you've got people who are in it because there's big money to be made—in particular at the corporate end, but also on the creative end. There's a lot of stuff that's all mixed in together. It's bound to get dodgy.

As the role of consumer has vanished or is vanishing, not only are the lines blurred between who's in there doing what, but in a certain sense the line is blurred between what is real and what is not. It's amazing watching all the trailers that run before movies nowadays. Stuff comes up, and you can't tell what it is. Is this an advertisement for the Army? A commercial for gum? Some new band I haven't heard of? Is it a movie? There's so much stuff that is, quite possibly, simply about what kind of money can be made and where. The flipside of that is, musically, we may be living in one of the most amazingly creative periods ever.

The focus is not: What do I get out of this? The focus is: What is worth doing and how should we do it? If something happens and we make money, beautiful. But if nothing happens, beautiful. It doesn't matter. If a record company can make the kind of money that it makes from somebody like Norah Jones, there's a blurred line there. They're kind of saying, "Yeah, we believe in art," but they're also kind of patting their billfolds. But popular music has always been like that. It may just be that some of those lines are more blurred now.

Hired by Blue Note to record Norah Jones's debut, Street was eventually removed from the project. Arif Mardin, who had found massive success with the Bee Gees, was brought in to produce. Ultimately, three Street-produced tracks made it to the completed album.

MONTGOMERY GENTRY, *YOU DO YOUR THING* (2004, COLUMBIA)

BLAKE CHANCEY

Usually, when I hear a song—a person playing their song acoustically for me, just singing it—I hear the record already in my head. I hear a lot of the instruments or where I think something's going to go. I can actually hear a record being made in my head, sometimes, before I make it. I don't know if that happens to other producers or not.

I was born and raised in this town. I laugh about it, but I grew up across the street from Maybelle Carter. She started country music. If it wasn't for her, none of us would have a job. Funny thing was, I didn't know. When I was little, I just knew that she cooked a mean chocolate pie. Everybody who lived around me was in country music. Bob Moore, who was part of the A-Team, lived behind me—and Lightnin' Chance. [Bashful] Brother Oswald's backyard touched ours; he was in Roy Acuff's band. All these people lived around us. Johnny Cash was courting June right across the street. And my mother listened to country music all the time. She listened to George Jones and Tammy Wynette; she was a huge Glenn Campbell fan. You get something hammered in your head enough, you learn where your roots are just by growing up. I didn't go to some library and learn about country music. I grew up in it.

My father was a producer. Growing up, I was always in the studio. I've watched a lot of producers work, and I've never seen two producers ever work the same—unless they were an engineer before or they used to work for somebody else. Then, you'll see them pulling out traits of the people they used to work for. But normally you don't see that. Everybody has their own completely different style.

GEORGE STRAIT, *IT JUST COMES NATURAL* (2006, MCA NASHVILLE)

TONY BROWN

Some people in town actually use the same studio and the same band for every record they do. A record, depending on the artist, calls for a core group of people, but still there are just some engineers I'd never use on certain artists, and some musicians I wouldn't use. Not that they couldn't do it. It's not something that I think would work, so I don't take a chance at it. I love it, then, when a musician I've always used on a certain artist can't make it at the last moment, and I have to slide somebody in. It gives me the chance to do something I didn't have the guts to do to start with, which is to try somebody new with, say, Strait. Or try somebody new with Vince [Gill].

I go to Vince or to Strait. "Hey, listen man. So-and-so couldn't make it, so this guy's coming in. Trust me, he's really good. He's going to blow you away." Their response is "I trust you, man. If you say he's good, I believe you." That's the best compliment you can have.

VARIOUS, *CRAZY HEART: ORIGINAL MOTION PICTURE SOUNDTRACK* (2010, NEW WEST)

STEPHEN BRUTON

There're lots of different ways of producing. T-Bone Burnett and I grew up together in Fort Worth. I love his productions, but the way he goes about it is completely different than me. He puts a lot of things on, and then he takes . . . he's like a painter. He goes in, and he gets certain things. He'll put more tracks on than you can believe, but he comes back in and strips them off in layers. It's like deconstruction. I'm sure that approach doesn't hold true on everything that he does. But I've been witness to it. It's just his style.

To the people I've produced, I say, "What's going to happen during this record is that at some point—it may be more than one time—we'll lock horns on something. I'll probably defer to you if you stand up and say, 'No, no, no—this way!' It's your record. But if that happens, there goes the sum being greater than the number of its parts. Suddenly, it becomes one person's record. If you'll listen and say what you want, then we'll try and get that. I assure you. I'll do everything I can to get it."

You've got to have one guy making decisions—and not just his decisions, but making decisions tempered with what the other people involved say. Believe me, there's a third party that you've got to listen to a lot. That's the engineer. He can tell you, "This is working; this isn't. These two parts are real cool, but they're canceling each other out." There's really a triumvirate in there. You want to have your little team together where everybody knows how to talk to each other.

INDEX

ABOUT THE AUTHOR

MICHAEL JARRETT is professor of English at Penn State University, York.
He is the author of *Drifting on a Read: Jazz as a Model for Writing* and
Sound Tracks: A Musical ABC.